EFFACING THE SELF

SUNY series in Theology and Continental Thought

Douglas L. Donkel, editor

EFFACING THE SELF
Mysticism and the Modern Subject

Marc De Kesel

SUNY
PRESS

Giovanni Lanfranco, *Mary Magdalen Raised by Angels*, 1616. National Museum of Capodimonte. Courtesy of Wikimedia Commons.

Published by State University of New York Press, Albany

For information, contact State University of New York Press, Albany, NY
www.sunypress.edu

Library of Congress Cataloging-in-Publication Data

Name: Kesel, Marc De, author.
Title: Effacing the self : mysticism and the modern subject / Marc De
   Kesel.
Description: Albany : State University of New York Press, 2023. | Series:
   SUNY series in theology and continental thought | Includes
   bibliographical references and index.
Identifiers: LCCN 2022053646 | ISBN 9781438494142 (hardcover : alk. paper) |
   ISBN 9781438494166 (ebook) | ISBN 9781438494159 (pbk. : alk. paper)
Subjects: LCSH: Self. | Selflessness (Psychology) | Mysticism.
Classification: LCC BF697 .K464 2023 | DDC 155.2—dc23/eng/20230316
LC record available at https://lccn.loc.gov/2022053646

10 9 8 7 6 5 4 3 2 1

To Janneke

Modern mysticism focuses on the ego.
We cannot break free from it.

—Hugo Ball

Contents

Illustrations

Introduction

Let us be the holocaust that, in the fire
of love, turns into ashes.

—François de Fénelon

Known for her hair so long that it covers her entire body, we now see her fully naked, her long locks blowing in the wind. She is floating high above the woods and lakes below, carried by three little angels. Her arms open wide and her eyes looking up, she is surrendering herself to what awaits her in heaven.

So we see in the painting by the Italian Baroque artist Giovanni Lanfranco, entitled *The Translation of the Magdalen* (1617) (Figure I.1).[1] And in the *Legenda aurea* we read that Saint Mary Magdalene makes this journey a few times a day.[2] Indeed, "every day at the seven canonical hours" (that is, at each of the hours of the day when monks gather to pray), angels take Mary Magdalene all the way to God's celestial places, where she is given the opportunity to feed herself, not with earthly but entirely with heavenly food.[3] As is known, in the past, she used to take all too earthly food, living the sinful life of a prostitute. But since, burdened by repentance, she washed Jesus's feet and received his blessing, her life has become that of a saint. After Jesus's death and ascension, so the *Golden Legend* continues, she played an important role in the settlement of the first Christians in the Rhone Valley in Gaul (France). There, after a life of charity, she suddenly "disappeared." Only thirty years later, she was rediscovered. During all those years she lived in the woods in absolute isolation. It is during this period that, seven times a day, she was carried to heaven to be fed by celestial food only.

1

Figure I.1. Giovanni Lanfranco, *The Translation of the Magdalen*, 1616–17.

It is in this sense that Mary Magdalene can be seen as an emblem-
atic example for monastic life and for mysticism in general.[4] To fully live
her love for the unique God, she has left behind the finite and sinful
way of life that she knows like no one else, in order to anticipate a life
that will be lived in the other world to come, in the divine realm that
God has brought us thanks to his Son Jesus. In her radical isolation,
she has stopped living off nature and, even in her most basic needs, is
directly nourished by the divine. It is the result of a life-long asceticism
in which she gradually eliminated all reflexes of natural self-interest.
The state in which she is now, is of course due to God's grace, but it is
also the consequence of a lifelong effort of fighting against her natural
selfishness, of effacing her own self. Effacing the self: this is the practice
of the Christian mystic: erasing my own I as the center of my life in
order to really live by God's grace only.

Effacing the self. Did Mary Magdalene succeed in it? Of course, she succeeded in effacing her human, all too human self. But did she indeed efface *the* self? In fact, by effacing her own finite self, she regained an infinite Self, the Self that is at the basis of everything that is, including her natural self. By effacing that false self of hers, she is absorbed by God's true Self. This is what Lanfranco's painting shows: she has lost everything and has given up even her "self," but precisely for this reason, angels carry her to heaven in order to regain her true origin, her true ground, which is in God, and which is God.

Effacing the self. Is it something that is limited to Christian mysticism only? Has such an intention become outdated since our modern, multicultural societies have ceased to be dominated by Christianity? Is "effacing the self" incompatible with a typically *modern* way to understand life?

Figure I.2. Rémy Zaugg, ICH/ ICH BIN/ NICHT/ ICH, 1999.

Of course, modernity is characterized first and foremost by a non-effaced, strongly self-assured self. And yet, the desire to get rid of this self and the effort to efface it are far from absent. To stick to the realm of visual art, one can easily find modern examples that express a message similar to the one of Lanfranco's seventeenth-century painting. Take, for instance, a work by the Basel conceptual artist Rémy Zaugg, entitled *ICH / ICH BIN / NICHT / ICH* (I / I AM / NOT / I, 1999) (figure I.2). The message cannot be misunderstood: If there is a "self" mentioned in this work of art, it is there to efface itself. "I am not I." Zaugg's work perfectly fitted the Frankfurt exhibition that it was part of, entitled ~~Ich~~: the German word for "I," *Ich*, struck out. The exhibition collected all kinds of "iconoclastic" self-portraits, each of them performing a particular way of effacing the self.[5]

The difference between the Lanfranco painting and Zaugg's work of art is that, in the latter, the effacing of the self is not linked to regaining another, true, divine Self. Is, then, the modern version of "effacing the self" more radical and sincere than the Christian version exemplified by Lanfranco's *Mary Magdalene*? Is the modern version *really* "effacing the self"?

Looks can be deceiving. Does it really suffice to strike out the self to eliminate it? Is this not also an excellent way to emphasize it? By claiming "I am not I," one is also able to perform a particularly strong I. Pablo Picasso became a great painter precisely by *not* painting the "Picassos" with which the public identified him over and over again. His "lack of self" made him the giant he became. Many modern artists are serious when they seek to leave their ego behind in an attempt to make, if this is at all possible, completely selfless art; yet the more explicitly they strive for it, the greater the risk of their ego coming even more to the fore.

The trick that the ego often succumbs to in its attempts to become selfless is not the exclusive privilege of modern art. This ruse is every-where. Almost every Hollywood movie presents an ego brimming with self-confidence, recklessly flirting with selflessness and repeatedly on the verge of drowning the self in a bath of evil and seduction. What we see, in fact, is an unstable, threatened ego. And precisely the threat of selflessness ensures that, at the end of the movie, the ego reemerges stronger than ever. It is with this strong ego that the spectators identify themselves—not without allowing themselves to give vent to a surrep-titious desire for selflessness.

This trick is typical of modernity in general. Being modern, we cannot do without a solid, self-assured ego, yet we are haunted by the dream of finally being liberated from our very self, leaving our problematic ego-condition behind and losing ourselves in mere selflessness. The latter is indeed never more than a dream, in the service of an ego that never fails in performing its sovereignty. So, the modern performance of a strong ego easily goes hand in hand with the inclination (hidden or not) to have that ego effaced.

What is at stake with an ego that is asked both to overestimate the power of its own self *and* to cherish the dream of getting lost in selflessness? How is it possible that the modern human promotes an exaggerated self on the one hand and on the other longs for selflessness?

Each from a different angle, all chapters in this volume deal with this question. However, to investigate the subtle-yet-complex battle between self and selflessness, I do not focus on contemporary art or Hollywood movies but on an altogether different area: Christian mysticism.

Rather than to the experience of being one with the divine, the term *mysticism* as used in this volume refers to the written tradition describing in detail the vicissitudes on the path toward that union. In this tradition, descriptions of the experience of the union with God are in fact rather rare, and most of the textual reports focus on the inner struggle to get there. The mystic tries to reach a God who is radically "other" and "beyond"—that is, beyond anything that has to do with the human "self." To become one with God implies overcoming the own self—to efface it—and becoming selfless, in the strongest sense of the word. This is not without paradox. For to follow the path to selflessness, the mystic needs a solid self. And yet, the strongest obstacle that has to be overcome on this path is nothing but that very "self." Only the strongest self is able to fight—to efface—that self and become selfless. This paradox, which I mentioned as being at play in both modern art and Hollywood movies, is clearly at the heart of mystical texts. Moreover, these texts often explicitly question and reflect on this paradox. Those searching for insight into the strange dialectics of self and selflessness will benefit greatly from a close reading of texts from the mystical tradition, and this is exactly what I intend to do in this volume.

The thesis I defend here is that our contemporary ego-mania, together with our penchant for selflessness, is rooted in the typically modern self-understanding that emerged in seventeenth-century Western Europe. At this time, the perspective from which we related to the world (including ourselves) shifted from God to our own free, independent ego. René Descartes's *cogito* is a significant and influential expression of this. The establishment of this self-assured Cartesian ego aroused all kinds of countermovements, however. One of the movements that profoundly questioned the Cartesian ego and analyzed it in a highly critical way was the mysticism that permeated seventeenth-century French spirituality.

This is why the first chapters deal directly with early modern Christian mysticism, and more specifically with the French *spiritualité* that became popular at that century, even far beyond the boundaries of the French kingdom. In the numerous texts that emerged from this *spiritualité* wave, the role played by a Cartesian kind of ego is often as hidden as it is decisive. Issues of a "spiritual" nature were not only dominant in discussions among mystical and theological authors but also in the important public debates of the time. The nature of "pure love" for God, for example, was hotly debated in France, not only among theologians at the Sorbonne, but also by people in the streets of Paris and, last but not least, at the courts of the Louvre and of Versailles.

Of course, these disputes in terms from centuries ago sound outdated to the contemporary ear. Yet, once one manages to overcome the historical threshold and fully enter into the variety of arguments of that time, it quickly becomes evident that the questions seventeenth-century *spiritualité* dealt with, in fact, remain surprisingly relevant today. To mention only one of them: What is love? What, within the act of love, are the precise parts played by the loving subject and the beloved? And how is the ego involved in the passion of love? Does it finally *find* itself, or does it *lose* itself there? Does the ego, in the act of loving, discover its ground or rather its abyss? More than three centuries ago, these kinds of questions were already addressed with unprecedented lucidity. As will be explained, such questions are ours still, persisting in texts by twentieth-century mystics (such as Simone Weil) and mystical theorists (such as Michel de Certeau).

Effacing the self: is it not what the first Christian communities tried to put into practice? Chapter 1, "Love's Intimate Violence," starts with a brief analysis of the Early Christian love ideal and shows how, contrary to popular opinion, it is not really free from violence. When, seventeen centuries later, the same kind of selfless love becomes the topic of heated public debate in early modern France, a hidden violence is once again at play. This chapter compares two interpretations of selfless love: one by François de Fénelon and one by Nicolas Malebranche. Their discussion not only establishes—and brings into focus—what is at stake in the act of "pure love" (*pur amour*, their term for selfless love), it also reveals the incapacity of both authors to answer the question of the violence haunting the core of selfless love. The role of this kind of love, including its violence, appears to be far from played out in the post-Christian age. It reemerges, for instance, in the "love for revolution" that totalitarian regimes require from their citizens. It is by referring to this kind of love that Maximilien Robespierre spread his infamous terror and, more than a century later, Nikolai Bukharin became the victim of one of the Moscow show trials.

In Chapter 2, entitled "Selfless," Meister Eckhart, the fourteenth-century mystic, and Fénelon, the seventeenth-century author on mysticism, are brought into discussion with one another. Both authors comment extensively on the link between love and the effacement of the self, and at first sight they seem to have quite similar opinions. However, where Eckhart still thinks within the framework of a medieval worldview, in Fénelon's thinking, despite his claims to the contrary, modernity has sneaked in. This modern perspective is crucial to shed the correct light on the unseen harshness of "pure love." A close reading of three of his *Lettres spirituelles* reveals the modern abyss that yawns beneath the pious ideal of *pur amour*.

Is *pur amour* a strictly individual matter? Does it only concern the intimate realm of the soul? Fénelon's *Lettres spirituelles* seem to move toward such a conclusion. And yet, there is also a strong political dimension in Fénelon's mystical thought. His novel *Les aventures de Télémaque* (*The Adventures of Telemachus*) is highly political, and his famous *Letter to Louis XIV* is one of the sharpest critiques addressed to the absolutistic monarch. The exploration of the political dimension of Fénelon's mystical thought is the object of chapter 3, "Love Thy Neighbor Purely."

What if the self has to efface itself in the very act that reports its effacement? This paradoxical procedure is a central issue in the oeuvre of Jeanne Guyon, the mystical lady who introduced Fénelon to the tradition of *spiritualité*. To Madame Guyon, the *unio mystica* is not so much located in the peak experience reached after having passed the several steps on the mystical path. It is, rather, the effacement of the self that takes place while going that path or, rather, while being lost on it. This is why she realizes that, while reporting on her mystical life, it is not she who has to write. Rather "no one" or "nothing" must do this. Only the complete absence of a human author can allow God to be the hand that writes her mystical texts. Referring to the French literary critic Maurice Blanchot, chapter 4, entitled "Nothing Writes," explains how this selfless condition of writing persists in the way in which a lot of modern twentieth-century literature understands itself.

Thus far the first section of the volume, entitled "Fénelonian Promenades." It focuses on seventeenth-century French *spiritualité*, with an emphasis on the works and influence of Fénelon. The second section, "The Mystical (of the) Self," deals with twentieth-century mysticism and mystical thought, and analyzes the way in which three different authors write about the mystical requirement of effacing the self.

The title of chapter 5, "The Power to Say I," is a quotation from *Gravity and Grace*, the first posthumously published collection of aphorisms by the French mystic Simone Weil. She only turned to Christianity (without ever being baptized) rather late in her short life (she died at the age of thirty-four) and within only a few years, she wrote a remarkable number of "cahiers" combining mystical thoughts with, among other things, reflections on antique literature, Vedic texts and, even, mathematics. The chapter analyses Weil's aphorisms on the ego and shows how, despite her attempts to annihilate it, the ego persists and ends up being the central problem in her "mystical theory."

Chapter 6, "Contra-Religious Religion," presents a close reading of an early work by Kornelis Heiko Miskotte, one of the most well-known Dutch Protestant theologians of the twentieth century. Notwithstanding his antimystical and antireligious Protestantism,[6] the work explored here offers a gripping account of an experience that cannot be characterized, despite Miskotte's own vehement protestations to the contrary, as anything but religious and mystical. So, what does it mean when a mystical experience does not even need the term *mystic* to be described correctly? Or when the account of a religious experience can omit the word *religious*? What if the terms *mystical* and *religious* could just as well be replaced by *philosophical*? What does this imply for "mysticism," "religion," and "philosophy"? A reflection on Miskotte's Protestantism—and, more precisely, on his rediscovery of the monotheist axiom ("Not who you think God is, is God: only God is God")—sheds some light on the core of his "experience" (and of the mystical, religious experience in general).

The title of chapter 7, "The Path of Mercy Means Simply that You Abandon Self," is a quote from *Silence*, a novel by the Japanese author Shūsaku Endō, published in 1966.[7] The novel brings us back into the seventeenth century, to Japan this time, where Christianity, after having flourished for a few decades, is now prohibited. Two Portuguese Jesuits illicitly enter the country in order to contact their old mentor, who is rumored to have renounced Christianity and converted to Buddhism, and now to live a quiet life in Osaka. Only one of the two Jesuits survives the journey past the few clandestine Christian communities, but is caught by the authorities. Confronted with his old mentor, he learns firsthand that the rumors are indeed true. The title of this chapter is taken from this moment in the story. If Christian love demands the effacement of the self, does this not mean that the confessional, religious "self" should also be renounced? Does the Jesuit missionary's love for the persecuted Japanese Christians not require him to cast aside his own Christian self so that their persecution can end? The entire novel revolves around this abysmal question, which in the end remains unanswered.

The title of chapter 8, "As a Drop in the Ocean," is a quote as well, this time taken from an essay by Michel de Certeau. This famous expert on the history of early modern Christian mysticism emphasizes the tendency toward effacing the self and toward selflessness within that tradition. The God for whom the mystic longs is preeminently the Other, which is why the mystic has to get rid of everything referring to him- or herself—including his or her very own "self"—in order to get to God. Certeau applies this argument to Christianity itself: confronted with a modern culture that opposes Christianity, the latter has to relate to the former as its "Other" and therefore abandon any fear to get lost in this Other. The chapter discusses the implications of Certeau's radical thesis.

The third and last section of the volume, "Mysticism in a Modern Word," covers the strange locus that mysticism as well as selflessness occupies in contemporary culture.

Chapter 9, "Down with Religion, Long Live Mysticism" approaches "mysticism" as a contemporary social and cultural phenomenon. Why is it that, from a social perspective, the idea of "mysticism"—or "spirituality," which is often used synonymously—is on the rise, while "religion," with which mysticism certainly has an affinity, has a negative connotation? Aiming to answer this question, the analysis focuses not on mysticism and spirituality as such but on the social, and more precisely on the way in which the social has become *modern*. Here, too, the insight into what modernity is about sheds light on what is, in fact, one of its symptoms: the success story of spirituality and the decline of religion.

Is there a link between mysticism and politics? Does the ideal of effacing the self play a role in theories about political power? The relation between mysticism and politics—or, which amounts to the same thing, between selflessness and power—is much closer than commonly thought. Indeed, those who want to understand the underlying paradigm of political power in the West must read Dionysius the Areopagite, the "founding father" of negative theology and a decisive point of reference for the entire mystical tradition. This, at least, is the thesis of the Italian philosopher Giorgio Agamben. Chapter 10, "Selflessly Powerful," discusses Agamben's analysis. Inspired by the French philosopher Claude Lefort, this chapter also reflects upon the persistence of negative theology in the way political power is legitimized within modern democracy.

Is the problematic of selflessness limited to the domain of mysticism? Chapter 11, "Selflessness and Science," discovers selflessness in a number of domains where it is least expected: the erotic libertine novels of the eighteenth century, and the materialism that inspired the paradigm for modern science and the human sciences to be put on the same footing during the nineteenth and twentieth centuries. Despite their diversity, these domains all share a formally similar selflessness with mysticism, yet draw different conclusions from it. Unlike in mysticism, selflessness does not emerge as a proper theme in any of the other domains, not even in the human sciences—except one: psychoanalysis, which can only do so by criticizing the paradigm of the ruling human sciences. The latter is why, notwithstanding its massive success in the twentieth century, psychoanalysis has lost most of its credibility in our age—mistakenly, as will be explained. For an understanding of selflessness and its inherent link with the modern self, psychoanalysis can broaden horizons.

Just to close the introduction, a few more words about mysticism, the theme of this volume.

When an age such as ours takes an interest in mysticism, it is not in the last instance because of the effacement of the self that it promotes. The selfish, ego-oriented age in which we live seems to find in this tradition a welcome counterbalance. But do we not, with mysticism, introduce first and foremost its paradox? Is our fascination with it not a way of giving the ego back its typical, modern, self-assured position at the very moment we think we are losing it?

Because who else but the ego walks the path of effacing the self and fulfils the deed in which the ego relinquishes, surrenders, gives way, or destroys itself? Does the selflessness to which we surrender in our fascination with mysticism not secretly prove how strong our ego is? Does it not lay bare that our ego remains the master over our existence, whatever may occur, even the loss of our own "self"? Do we really understand what happens when the mystic leaves the "self" behind? Or do we use mysticism precisely to avoid any confrontation with what is really at stake here?

The modern paradigm, as becomes clear in this volume, makes the mystical experience, where selflessness is at issue, harsher and more abysmal. Today's enthusiasm for mysticism can also serve to cover—or even deny—the harshness of this abyss. And it is precisely to this abyss that the modern ego must relate, as openly and clearly as possible. For this "mystical" abyss has everything to do with the ground on which modernity rests. If this volume turns to the mystical tradition, it is to discover in it reflections on the abyss that is at the base of ourselves. Mysticism's selflessness is not what the modern ego *lacks*, something that is forgotten or lost; it is, on the contrary, what constitutes the core, the "ground" of our modern ego.

Mysticism might have the reputation of being of all times, yet it definitely does not escape history. Taking position against the idea that mysticism is a universal phenomenon transcending all kinds of historical and cultural contingencies, the diversity of chapters in this book defends the thesis that it is a thoroughly contingent and historical phenomenon. The reason why we should be interested in mysticism today, is not to transcend the limits of our Western point of view but rather to better realize how we are characterized by these limits—and how typically Western and modern it is to intend to escape the limits of our own perspective and to embrace the universal.

I close this introduction with a few words of acknowledgment. First of all, to both the faculty of Philosophy, Theology, and Religious Studies and the Titus Brandsma Institute (TBI) at Radboud University, in Nijmegen, the Netherlands. The excellent TBI collection at the University Library was of great help for my study, as were the inspiring discussions with my colleagues of the faculty and the TBI.

Special thanks go to Joey Kok, who translated the original Dutch versions of chapters 1, 2, 6, 7, 9, 10, and 11, and to Ad Poirters who revised the English of the entire volume.

Fénelonian Promenades

1

Love's Intimate Violence

Selfless Love in Fénelon and Malebranche
(and Robespierre)

> In short, God's pleasure is the soul's highest goal. . . . If [the soul]
> knew that its damnation gave God a little more pleasure than its
> salvation, it would let its salvation go for what it is and rush to
> its damnation.
>
> —François de Sales, *Œuvres*

Despite the religious violence we encounter daily in the media, many
claim that religion is basically not a matter of fight but of love. "God is
love," they quote from the First Letter of Saint John. And, so they add,
this goes not only for Christianity but for Islam, Judaism, and Buddhism
as well, and in fact for all religions.[1] The claim of all religions is that it
is by love—including religious love—that we will be delivered from all
violence. Whoever God may be, He does not drive a wedge between
people but rather unites them. He tempers their egoism and shows how
to live together unselfishly. However beautiful this may sound, however
popular chapter 13 in Paul's First Letter to the Corinthians may be,[2] this
widespread perception needs to be adjusted.

 This chapter is on Christian love. First, I sketch the provenance of
this concept: how it replied to a deadlock the Jewish religious narrative
was stuck in, and how it provoked new impasses as well. Next, I discuss
the public debate on *pur amour*—pure, disinterested, "selfless" love—that

15

deeply touched France's (and Europe's) religious and intellectual life in the late seventeenth century. This debate clarifies a deadlock that has accompanied Christian love since the beginning of Christianity.

Moreover, this early modern theological debate about love, including the violence it encompasses, is also instructive about the condition of the modern subject—the Cartesian "self"—that emerges at the same time. The dimension of self and selflessness will play a crucial role in this. Is love basically about the lover, about the one who loves? Or is love rooted in the beloved, in one who is loved? The *pur amour* debate invites one to opt for the latter. This makes love a heroic act of selflessness, and yet, at the same time, turns it into something painful and even cruel. The fact that the beloved is God does not diminish that violent character. On the contrary. Despite the positive tone of the Christian narrative, a persistent, inherent rawness can be seen in the ideal of love it puts forward. Yet, whoever thinks that this only characterizes Christianity will have to conclude—so I will show—that love's uncanny cruelty affects post-Christian modernity as well.

Agape

"God is love." Love, indeed, but not *eros*. Precisely not. God knows no desire, no feeling of lack, no love pain. For He is perfect, not marked by any kind of lack. When the earliest Christian texts speak of "love," they refer to this state of perfection. Their term for it is *agape*, which indicates the state in which we find ourselves once we have come to live in the right connection with God—"in justice."

"To live in justice": this was the drive and purpose of the Jewish religion from which Christianity originated. By Adam's "original sin," humankind had lost its connection with God. God, however, had given one people a gift that promised reconnection to Him. The Jewish people had been given the Law, the Torah. Worship no other than the true God, and therefore do justice to the wicked, the widow, and the orphan: these two commandments made up the core of that Law.[3] To worship solely the Truth and, therefore, to establish and maintain a *just* society: this is what Yahweh God required from Abraham's descendants. This message Isaiah, Jeremiah, Hosea and the other prophets never stopped delivering to the Jewish people. Only two principles—worshiping the true God, and a just society—return us to a "just" relation with God.

These two principles gave Jewish monotheism its final shape during the sixth and fifth centuries BC and were reflected in the books that would eventually become the Bible.

Some writings that came to be included in the Bible express a certain frustration with this basic monotheistic regime. Consider, for example, the book of Job. Even though people take the Law to heart, it often seems not to lead to a more direct (more "just") relation with God, since the state of perfection—the "land of milk and honey" that God promised—does not come any closer. Job complains that his "unjust" neighbor, who does not care for God and His Law at all, can nevertheless indulge in all kinds of "milk and honey," while he himself, no matter how "just" he tries to live, is put in a dump.[4]

This frustration results in the creation of a new figure within the Jewish religious narrative. Because we are unable to fulfill the Law and have a direct connection to God, God himself is supposed to intervene once more. He will send a Messiah, who will redeem the entire creation of all lack and sin, of finitude and death (eschaton) and completely remove the blind spots that characterize our human knowledge of God (apocalypse).[5] Christianity is based on this messianic hope. More specifically, it defines itself as the fulfillment of that hope. Even though Jesus of Nazareth's actions culminated in His condemnation and death, He is recognized as the Messiah by those who, based on the messianic hope, call themselves "Christians." Christ rose from the dead and freed the world from the sin (and all other kinds of shortcomings) that kept us indebted to God.

One who has faith in Christ, therefore, finally lives in a "just" relation with God. It is for this state of being that Christians coined the term agape, love. "God is love." Here, love is the name for a state of perfection and not for one of (erotic) desire (for, for instance, perfection). When the first Christians claimed to live "in love," they were convinced they were living in a state that was no longer characterized by time, death, lack, and sin; it was a state in which a just society, as promised in the Law, had turned into reality.

At least, this was the Christians' conviction, in spite of reality, which painfully remained characterized as before by time, death, lack, and sin. The narrative of "ascension" brought relief here.[6] It was said that the Messiah had come and that the messianic kingdom was a fact. Yet, because the Messiah had "returned to the Father" for a while,[7] the definitive factuality of this kingdom was postponed for the time being.

Meanwhile, the Christians considered it their mission to bear witness to that "already come/yet to come" state of absolute perfection—in other words, to testify about the "Kingdom of God" realized here on Earth. Hence, their way of living together in a perfect social community where everyone "loved" everyone and nobody owned anything because everything was common property. What the Jewish tradition calls the "Promised Land" was turned into reality here: living in a "just" relation with God became directly visible in the way Christians lived in a "just" relation with each other.

So, had violence been overcome in this ideal "love community"? Not quite, it turns out. The "ideal" was in reality not without potential negative effects. After all, the ideal love community placed itself above the reality of sin and lack, and woe to reality if it did not fully behave according to this ideal. I quote a passage from Acts, where it becomes clear what happened to the one who left room for the gap between the ideal and reality.

> Now a man named Ananias, together with his wife Sapphira, also sold a piece of property. With his wife's full knowledge he kept back part of the money for himself, but brought the rest and put it at the apostles' feet. Then Peter said, "Ananias, how is it that Satan has so filled your heart that you have lied to the Holy Spirit and have kept for yourself some of the money you received for the land? Didn't it belong to you before it was sold? And after it was sold, wasn't the money at your disposal? What made you think of doing such a thing? You have not lied just to human beings but to God." When Ananias heard this, he fell down and died. And great fear seized all who heard what had happened. Then some young men came forward, wrapped up his body, and carried him out and buried him. About three hours later his wife came in, not knowing what had happened.[8] Peter asked her, "Tell me, is this the price you and Ananias got for the land?" "Yes," she said, "that is the price." Peter said to her, "How could you conspire to test the Spirit of the Lord? Listen! The feet of the men who buried your husband are at the door, and they will carry you out also." At that moment she fell down at his feet and died. Then the young men came in and, finding her dead, carried her out and buried her beside her husband.[11]

Great fear seized the whole church and all who heard about these events.[8]

To this day, commentators feel uncomfortable with this passage and seek explanation in historical context and the customs of the time among other things.[9] All this does not prevent the story from revealing a possible consequence embedded in the early Christian idea of "living in God's love," that is, in a state where death, lack, and sin are overcome. This state of being contradicts the reality of death, lack, and sin and therefore condemns all those who do not go along with that contradiction. Like Ananias and Sapphira, anyone who secretly refuses to pretend the ideal beyond death, sin, and lack has become reality is immediately confronted with what happens to those who disbelieve the ideal: the truth literally beats them to death. Ananias's and Sapphira's deaths reveal to those who still live in the world of death, lack, and sin that they are indeed still living *there*, and not in the ideal world of the love community, where personal property no longer makes sense.

Here, violence lies in the ideal or, more precisely, in the pretension this ideal upholds that we are far *beyond* the reality of everyday life. This pretension quickly leads to simply denying this reality, and that we are marked by death and finitude. And in no time, this denial becomes fatal for the genuine fellow human beings who do not fully accept this ideal as fact. Because still being marked by death, lack, and sin is then seen as the result of not accepting this ideal as fact. It is fully *their* fault that they bear the mark of lack and death. No wonder, then, that they fall dead on the spot when it appears that they do not embody the ideal. How can it be anything but their deserved punishment?

The finitude and death that one denies in oneself are thus transferred to the other and denied there once again in the sense that they (lack and death) are denied a right to exist; therefore, those who claim the opposite are beaten by death. According to this weird logic, the claim "death is no more" finds its proof in the fact that people die—more precisely those people who do not believe that death does not exist. Ananias has remained secretly attached to the world of death, deficiency, and sin, so no wonder that, when Peter's actions reveal that truth, Ananias is also judged, condemned, and executed by that very truth.

The violent aspect of the early Christian *agape* is that it comprehends itself as a state of perfection, and therefore must inevitably keep up the *appearance* of perfection. The *agape* community denies the reality of death and finitude by shifting it to others, to non- or "false" Christians. The reality of death is acknowledged *with the others*, but as something that in fact *is not*, and therefore *may not be*—which is why those others are deprived of their right to exist and, consequently, are allowed to be eliminated.[10]

What is cruel about early Christian love? That it is pure *agape* and not *eros*. That in the facticity of loving, it recognizes no shortage, no yearning, no desire, and therefore denies us the way we actually are: finite, yearning and longing, marked by lack.

Later Christianity, however, did not develop exclusively on the basis of *agape*. It is no coincidence that passages such as the one about Ananias and Sapphira were already difficult to digest for some early Christian authors.

These radical agapeic communities were most likely only very briefly the social reality of Christianity. As early as the second century, Christians had become "normal" citizens, with possessions, and, despite local persecutions, they were fairly well integrated into existing pagan society.[11] Their *agape* ideal had by this time already been internalized and spiritualized. Their loving community life was seen as evidence of another, perfect world, and this did not prevent them from conscientiously assuming their responsibility as citizens in the imperfect world of everyday life.[12] They already participated in the perfection revealed by Christ, but at the same time allowed themselves to yearn and desire—that is, to implicitly admit to be marked by imperfection, lack, and finitude.

In short, *eros* entered Christian agapeic love. Origen of Alexandria was the first to think it through theoretically, and with Augustine both terms became almost synonyms. He might have translated the Greek word *agape* with *caritas* (charity), but at the same time promoted *eros*—*amor* in Latin—as a hundred percent Christian term and smoothed out the original difference between both. It is God's perfect love, his *caritas*, that has planted in us our longing love, our *amor* for Him.

Despite what authors such as Anders Nygren may claim, the entanglement of *agape* and *eros* provides the richness of Christian culture.[13] The yearning for God, and therefore the notion of being imperfect—or, biblically speaking, of not being in line with God—produces a long, hybrid, and rich mystical tradition in this culture that is at times overtly erotic. It suffices to read medieval authors such as Bernard of Clairvaux (1090–1153) and William of Saint-Thierry (1085–1148), or the more recent John of the Cross (1524–1591), whose Christian mystical poetry can just as much be read as genuine erotic love poetry, without doing it any injustice. His poetry shows how, precisely because the object of religious desire is inaccessible perfection, the subject of this desire is above all confronted with its own finitude and deficiency.

Has this, however, neutralized the violence hidden in Christian love? That it no longer needs to deny the reality of finitude and deficiency indeed seems to point in this direction. But, the elimination of the underlying violence is not at all guaranteed. This Christian acknowledgment of the subject's deficiency and finitude is not without violence either. For who is the finite human being anymore, when the one being loved is a creative perfection? *Who* are *we* anymore, when we love God?

The question of the subject of God's love has always been at the center of Christian thought. The very first lines of Augustine's *Confessions* make it abundantly clear: when I love God, I love the person who has given me my own and his love, and myself.[14] In the course of Christian history, there have been numerous controversial disputes about the status of the human Ego in the love for God—disputes that often saw emotions running high. In what follows, I will elaborate on one of these disputes, the famous *Querelle du quiétisme*, a public debate about the *pur amour* that mesmerized French religious and intellectual life in the last years of the seventeenth century. I limit myself to just two voices: François de Fénelon (1651–1715) and Nicolas Malebranche (1638–1715).

Loving Is Willing

In the late eighties of the seventeenth century, a young prelate at the court of Louis XIV, François de Fénelon, came into contact with a group of devout noblemen, all fascinated by the ideal of a "spiritual life" (*vie intérieure*)—a devout, mystical form of Christian practice that had been introduced in France only a century earlier. The group was particularly enthusiastic about the teachings of the mystically inspired Jeanne Guyon (1648–1717), whose ideas and writings had an excellent reputation at the Versailles Court and in Paris. Her works were also among the first to expose Fénelon to mysticism and its tradition. Guyon's influence on Fénelon cannot be overestimated.

The success of Madame Guyon, however, drew so much public attention that it was considered necessary to submit her writings to a committee of authorities, chaired by Jacques Béninge Bossuet (1627–1706), bishop of

Maux (near Paris) and intellectual anchor for many of his contemporaries. Later, Fénelon also joined this committee. It took almost a year to reach a decision, which was negative. Guyon was placed under house arrest and explicitly prohibited from delivering sermons. Meanwhile, "spirituality," "mysticism," and "love" became some of the main topics of public debate, in Versailles, Paris, and the whole of France—a debate to which Guyon secretly kept contributing, despite her imposed limitations.

The central issue in this debate was the question of *pur amour*: *pure* love for God. All participants agreed that, rather than a matter of orthodox doctrine, our relationship with God is a matter of love. Only, they clarified, it is not self-love. Precisely not. Those who truly love God have purified themselves from every hint of *amour-propre*. Love for God must strive to become pure love—*pur amour*—"pure" because freed from any form of self-interest or self-love.

What the authorities distrusted about the proponents of *pur amour* had always been distrusted in every mystic. In mysticism, the relationship with God was so concentrated in the soul of the believer that any mediation between us and God seemed to be rendered superfluous. Sacraments, religious practices, the role of priests and of the Church in general: they all threatened to lose their *raison d'être*. In other words, the authorities were suspicious of mysticism because they considered it an inclination to Protestantism. Certainly in Catholic France at the time of Louis XIV, only a slight suspicion was enough to be condemned.

Not only Madame Guyon, but also Fénelon was under suspicion. Throughout his entire oeuvre (which was, not coincidentally therefore, largely published posthumously), he attempted to defend and support the mystical *vie intérieure* with references to the greatest doctrinal authorities of the Catholic tradition. But he had to abandon this attempt, certainly in the public domain. In March 1699, undoubtedly under pressure from the highest political powers in France, the Vatican condemned twenty-three statements from his *Maxims of the Saints*.[15] Already having been exiled to his archdiocese of Cambrai, Archbishop Fénelon was now prohibited from commenting on spirituality at all, in the whole of France. Louis XIV put an end to the public debate on the issue. It would take more than a century before the subjects of spirituality and mysticism could be openly discussed again.

In a way, the *Querelle* about *pur amour* resumes the old *agape-eros* debate. The love for God, it is said, is only pure if it is purified of all imperfections. And what makes love impure? The Ego, the self, or more specifically, the stake the Ego can have in its amorous activity, the "return" the Ego can get for it. *Pur amour* must be radically unselfish and 100 percent selfless.

The return one can get from loving God, however, is far from insignificant. Christian doctrine states that God loves us so much that, despite our sinful condition, God will grant us eternal bliss in the afterlife. Why, then, would one hesitate to love God for the eternal life He could offer? One could certainly love God for that reason, Fénelon replies, and that the majority of Christians think like that is not a problem. The only thing is, this is not the *spiritual* or *mystical* way to God, the way of a *vie intérieure*. This particular way is only reserved for a few. It is not a universal obligation at all. But those who feel called to this *vie intérieure* realize that loving God for the sake of the return one can get from it, is anything but perfect and "pure" love. It is at least not a way of loving that corresponds to God's perfection; it is not a love that adequately proves we are the image of God.

For what could God Himself get in "return" for the love He has for us? Absolutely nothing, if only because God, precisely because He is perfect, needs nothing; there is nothing we can give Him that does not already come from Him. God is perfect, also in His creative goodness, so there is no point in giving Him something or, more commonly, consorting with Him in a mutual gift-giving relationship. God only *gives*; He never needs to *receive* anything.

So, when His believers offer Him something, is this not a denial of—and, consequently, an insult to—his perfection? It is a testimony of how extraordinarily good God is that He nevertheless allows believers to bring their prayers, hymns, sacrifices, and the like, and that He is even receptive to the apologies the purest among them send with their inadequate gifts.

One who loves God perfectly realizes that one can only give Him the fact that one cannot give Him anything at all. Recognizing the inability to offer God, who has given one everything, even the smallest thing: this is the only genuine gift one can—and also *must*—offer to express one's gratitude to Him.

In light of the perfection of our creator, we are, in the most radical sense of the word, "nothing." But that need not prevent us from offering God the "nothing" that we are. This radically void and selfless sacrifice is the ultimate form of pure love, *pur amour*. One of Fénelon's *Lettres spirituelles*—letters of advice to those who have opted for a *vie intérieure*—makes it clear. I quote the beginning of the letter:

> Really be nothing, in everything and everywhere; but do not add anything to that pure nothing. It is on nothing that there is no grip at all. It can lose nothing. The real nothing never resists, and there is no I it takes care of. So, be nothing, and nothing more. Suffer in peace, abandon yourself; go, like Abraham, without knowing where to. Receive from the hands of men the comfort that God will give you through them. You must receive it not from them, but through them from Him. Mix your abandonment with nothing, and do not mix that nothing with anything else either. Such wine must be drunk pure, unmixed; even one drop of water destroys its worth. One loses infinitely by willing to keep the slightest part of oneself. No, restriction, I swear.
>
> Love the hand of God that beats and destroys us. The creature is only made to be destroyed as the one who has made it for Himself sees fit [*au bon plaisir*]. What a prosperous use of our substance! Our nothing glorifies the eternal Being and the entire God. May that which our *amour-propre* likes to preserve get lost. Let us be the holocaust that love's fire reduces to ashes. The trouble is always due to selfish love, divine love is but peace and abandon. The only thing to do is to suffer, to renounce, and to lose; do not hold on to anything; never at any time stop the hand that crucifies you. Nature detests this non-resistance; but God donates it.[16]

Have we ended up in a universe different from that in which we met Ananias when he died because he disobeyed the demands of Christian love? The Christian culture of the late seventeenth century might have changed almost unrecognizably compared to that of the first Christians, yet something of the former still persists in the latter. In a sense, we find an "Ananias" in Fénelon as well: not the Ananias who is executed immediately when Peter reveals his sin, but the Ananias who is, as it were, incorporated by Peter—the Ananias of whom Peter realizes that he himself is not that different from him. In the story in the Bible, Ananias has been reduced to nothing (i.e., to death) precisely because he held himself for someone, because he maintained his own property and individuality, denying that these belonged entirely to God. God's lethal intervention made him what he was (in the eyes of Christian teaching): nothing. The seventeenth-century universe of *pur amour* is one in which someone like Peter would realize that he is actually the same "nothing" as Ananias. The dead Ananias, reduced to nothing, is the true Ananias, the one who purely loves God. He offers himself to God as a "self" reduced to nothing. "Let us be the holocaust that love's fire reduces to ashes."

Here, the violence that is concealed in Christian love and that struck Ananias is internalized. It affects the very "self" of the Christian. He allows himself to be voluntarily crushed by the overwhelming gift of God, on which he realizes he is fully dependent, and he therefore gladly and lovingly offers that crushed "self" as an all-burning sacrifice (a "holocaust") to God. He proves the radicality of his sacrificial love by renouncing every possible reward or gift that he could receive from God.

In this context, *pur amour* finds one of its most extreme formulas in what Fénelon himself describes as a "supposition." Since that supposition challenges Christian orthodoxy, he stresses explicitly that it is only meant for those who have chosen to follow the "inner path." Suppose, so Fénelon writes in various versions throughout his oeuvre, that you know with absolute certainty that at the beginning of time God has predestined you for eternal damnation in hell.[17] Does it still make sense, then, for you to love God? The answer seems obvious. Why would one love someone knowing one gets nothing—or, even worse, eternal torture—in return? It is not Fénelon's conclusion. "What is my love worth when I get Eternal Life in return?" he asks. At least not as much as the love that loves without expecting any return. Only a radically disinterested love is truly love: *pur amour*. Even if God has condemned me, nothing prevents me from loving Him. On the contrary, only when I embrace the violence of God's damnation without hesitation, my love for Him is pure.

Is this true? Is this kind of love as pure as it pretends to be? Is it really freed from every self? If it is really devoid of any human "self," does it, then, find its ground entirely in God? Is it God to whom the loving believer leaves the final decision? It seems so, since the devoted believer agrees to be condemned by God forever. But is it God who gets to decide in this love? Is God the basis of this love that has given up any selfishness? Not at all. Here, it is the believer himself, and no one else, who has decided to love God, whatever He is up to. On closer analysis, God is no longer involved, and so the infernal punishments with which He can strike no longer matter. It depends solely on the believer whether or not he loves God. One who decides to love God says that he offers the self as a "holocaust" to God, but on closer inspection his love supposes a self that is stronger and more self-assured than ever. The ideal of *pur amour* presupposes, above all, a pure *self*, a self that is pure because nothing can dissuade it from its decisions, not even the certainty of eternal infernal torture.

In Fénelon's defense of *pur amour*, a Cartesian drama can, formally speaking, be identified that, just as with Descartes, culminates in the establishment of a strong, self-assured ego. Descartes had turned doubt into a hyperbolic duty, but it is precisely in the doubt itself that he discovers what escapes any doubt: the doubting "self," the ego, the subject, the "thing" that underlies that doubt. Likewise, Fénelonian mystics, out of love for God, cleanse themselves of any kind of self, but only by doing so do they really find their "self": whatever God intends for them, *they* decide to love God. Their love for God, therefore, is ultimately about the establishment of an ego that wants what it wants, regardless of whatever God intends to do with that ego.

The violence that, in *pur amour*, is lovingly embraced by the Ego betrays a violence with which the same Ego surreptitiously turns against God. That God condemns the world to hell does not bother the Ego. On the contrary, it appropriates that violence to free itself completely from God by loving Him regardless of whatever He is or does. For Fénelon, love is a matter of *willing*, of sovereign will. With Fénelon, the *cogito* becomes a *volo* (*amare Deum*): "The *pur amour* is exclusively in the will alone; so, it is not a love of sentiments, for imagination is in no way a part of it; it is a love that loves without feeling, as pure faith believes without seeing."[18]

Willing Is Loving

This criticism with respect to Fénelon's *pur amour* is not completely new. Some contemporaries already published critical responses, from a different conceptual angle. One of them is Nicolas Malebranche, author of one of the great philosophical systems of the seventeenth century. He too became involved in the *Querelle* around the *pur amour*, although most of his polemic was aimed not at Fénelon but at his own former soulmate François Lamy, who sided with Fénelon in this matter.[19] Malebranche, as devoted a Christian as Fénelon, saw in the apparently pious ideal of the Fénelonian *pur amour* a violence that in essence turned against God. Malebranche took it upon himself to defend God and give Him the honor he believed He deserves.

"God is love": this is the point of departure of the *Treatise on the Love of God* (*Traité sur l'amour de Dieu*, 1697), Malebranche's most direct attack on Fénelonian *pur amour*.[20] It is God who is love, the author emphasizes from the first page onward. This basic tenet of Christianity has already been overlooked by the adherents of the *pur amour*, Malebranche adds. For Lamy and Fénelon, it is primarily we, more specifically our human will, who are loving—even when God lets loose the very opposite of love, with eternal infernal torture and pernicious predestination. Hence the violence within the Fénelonian universe: both because of the cruel, predestinating God and because of the Ego that, in loving God, in fact shows radical disaffection toward Him.

It still remains to be seen, however, whether Malebranche's alternative reading of Christian love will be able to neutralize or eliminate the violence it conceals. He too will struggle with the evil implications of agapeic love; and that is precisely why, like Fénelon, he often dances on (and over) the edge of orthodoxy.

"God is love." It is first and foremost God, not we, who is love: this is Malebranche's starting point. And that is why love must be defined differently than Fénelon does. Love does not find its ultimate ground in the person who loves, in their will. After all, you cannot just love anything you want. You cannot love the abject, the destructive, the pain of torture and damnation. Love is only possible if you are affected by the intrinsic quality of what you love—if you are touched by it, if you like it, enjoy or want to enjoy it. Love has its basis in its object, in *whom* or *what* you love. Love loves its object as its cause, as what gives pleasure.[21]

"Pleasure," "*plaisir*": this is the principle of love, according to Malebranche. God has created pleasure in us, and this is why we long for Him and for the bliss He promises us. It is simply a sin to think that we should not long to share God's heavenly pleasure. We cannot but want to be happy; anyone who claims otherwise does so because they try to achieve the same goal in a devious way. Malebranche is referring to this when he writes: "It seems very much that those who suppose they really accept their condemnation try to do so only to ensure their

salvation, fearful of insulting God and thus of being condemned."[22] For
Malebranche, loving God is not a heroic act of willing, as Fénelon
suggests. Love has its ground in its object: in God. We were created by
God-who-is-love, and our existence—including our will—is grounded in
God and his love. I cannot *want* to love when the One I love has not
already aroused in me my love for Him.

Fénelon is wrong when he thinks that love is a matter of the will.
It is the other way around: *the will is a matter of love*, of being affected by
what makes me willing, in this case God, who has already laid his love
for Him in me even before I was aware of it—as, like already mentioned,
Augustine wrote in the first lines of his *Confessions*. That is why love,
for Malebranche, is primarily a matter of affection, of feeling, of pathos,
of being touched; it is a matter of pleasure and of desire for pleasure.
This is what God offers us. It is not always evident in our earthly vale
of tears, but in the hereafter, his offer of pleasure and enjoyment will
be felt as limitless and perfect. This immeasurable love, this *agape* as
the perfect fulfillment of human desire: that is what touches us when
we are touched by God. That is why it is not that hard to love God.
Perfection is hard to resist.

So much for the "realistic" side of Malebranche's understanding
of love: that God is love implies that the core of our being is to have
pleasure in God and to long for merging into the fullness of his love.

However beautiful this may sound, Malebranche does not shy away
from the dark, problematic aspects of this picture. Our love for God may
be more or less understandable, but the love of God for us is less so.
That God loves Himself is not problematic in Malebranche's perspective,
since God cannot resist the charms of His own perfection. But how, then,
to understand that He loves something or someone other than Himself,
something or someone in which perfection is absent? You cannot love
something that is less than yourself; you can only love what is more
than yourself or at least equivalent. How can the perfect, infinite God
love his finite creation and the imperfect human being in it? And if it
is indeed true that God is the creator of all that is and that He created
everything out of pure love, how should one think about that? If He
could not love that creation (because of its imperfection), how could
He (since loving is the essence of *willing* and wanting) have *wanted* it?

Here, Malebranche is forced to draw fully on Christian doctrine,
even though he does so in a way about which the guardians of that
doctrine are not entirely enthusiastic. How could God have wanted

to create His creation? How, in God's eyes, could that creation ever be lovable—and therefore worthy of creation? The answer could not be more Christian: through Christ! It is Christ, God's own Son, who, by incarnating within the finite creation, gave this creation a divine touch, the touch that was needed to awaken God's love and, at the same time, his will to proceed to his creative act. The crucifixion with which Christ delivered the world from deficiency, sin, and death is at the basis of creation as such, because that act of redemption provided a reason to ignite God's love.

As savior, Christ can hardly be moved forward in a more prominent way. But it is immediately clear that something is amiss. Christ is supposed to have redeemed creation *before* it was created. His act of redemption precedes the sin from which His intervention redeems the world. Even in the hypothetical case that Adam had not sinned, Christ would have had to redeem the world. His redemption was necessary, regardless of the reason for that redemption.

It did not escape the notice of critical contemporaries: Christ's entire performance, including his death on the cross, appears to lose any sense. It is hardly surprising that the infamous *Index librorum prohibitorum* (the list of books banned by the Catholic Church) was soon supplemented with a number of Malebranche's writings.[23]

A Violent "Self"

For Fénelon, love is a matter of free will that, if need be, can mean loving a God who will torture you forever. In contrast to what the Fénelonian ideal of love claims, that love installs a radical—and therefore modern—"self." The human "self," and not God, is the foundation of love. One could call it the realistic side of Fénelon's theory.

But that theory has a downside. The "self" underlying love appears to call up—and in a certain sense even need—a violent context in order to establish itself. Precisely where God does not grant me life—damning me forever—am I able to profile myself as a lover who is enough for himself to love their beloved. God's perfection, precisely where it threatens to crush me in untold ways, is the ideal context to keep my love for Him pure as well as to foreground my own pure, untouchable "self."

The "holocaust" and sacrificial pain in which the Fénelonian love is submerged offers an exquisite platform for installing a radically free and modern subject. As if this free modern subject, if it wants to position itself religiously, cannot do so without that violent platform. The various forms of "spiritual life" that flourished in the seventeenth, eighteenth, and nineteenth centuries make this abundantly clear. The cruelty with which mystical men and women treated themselves and their peers, the psychological terror with which they harassed themselves and others, the horror they committed to their own and other people's bodies (starving and self-flagellation are not just marginal examples): all of these show the violence hidden in Christian love. "Let us be the holocaust that is reduced to nothing by the fire of love." Fénelon's words probably cover more reality than we could imagine.

Is there less violence and cruelty in Malebranche's conception of love? For him, love is indeed not the act through which we secretly position a sovereign self, thus establishing a context of cruelty and violence. Love has its basis, not in the subject of its yearning, but in its object, in the perfection with which God loves Himself. The object that gives all human love its ultimate *raison d'être* is itself love, God's love, a perfect love that—as Malebranchian theory demands—necessarily loves perfection, and therefore only loves itself.[24] All love and longing that draw God's creatures find their origin and purpose in his love, and that is why God can love them too.

Here is the door through which violence creeps in again. No matter how sympathetic and realistic it may sound when Malebranche turns love into a matter of pleasure (*plaisir*) and well-being (*complaisance*), love is ultimately not about *our* pleasure, *our* well-being. The will that drives our love, the pleasure that accompanies this will, and the well-being that we rightly aim for: they ultimately trace back only to God. Love is not a matter of *my* will, as Fénelon claims; for Malebranche, my will is a matter of love, that is to say, of being affected by something or someone greater than myself. Love is basically loving God, being absorbed by his will and his love, a love that ultimately only loves itself and to which I can only give mine away completely.

Just as is the case for Fénelon's *pur amour*, Malebranchian love is all a matter of cleansing my share in that love. (The share that is only mine and to which figures such as Ananias still hold.) It is a matter of burning it in a deliberate "holocaust," so as to completely disappear in God's will and love. To lose oneself completely—Malebranche specifies—in the world as God wanted it, in his "unchangeable Order." To discard every form of (human) self and disappear into the perfect Self of God, of which the "unchanging Order" is the perfect expression.[25]

And of course, those worldly, mortal eyes of mine do not see the Order that well. They mainly see disorder, chaos, deficiency, sin, pain, and death—in short, the human condition of everyday life. But my love for God helps me to discover this Order in all the chaos, and to surrender myself to that Order, to lose my "self" in it and to disappear in the perfect One who loves Himself in a perfect way. In concrete terms, this means that I must actively ignore the imperfection of the earthly vale of tears in which I live every day. Only in and through this active negation of lack and pain do I acknowledge God's Order. Only when I take upon myself the "pain of being" do I acknowledge that being is carried by an Order that lies beyond all pain. Just like in Fénelon, here too, God's verdict condemning me does not prevent me from loving that very God. "A right-minded [person] must and can accept [their] annihilation, in case God has wanted it like this," so Malebranche writes on the same page we already quoted from *Traité de l'amour de Dieu*.[26] Even if it is God's will that eternal destruction awaits me, I must—and can—accept that *as such*. It is not because I, involved in it, do not see the logic, that it is not the logic of truth. Ultimately it is not about me, about my mortal "self," but about the divine Self in which I participate and through which, despite my longing for salvation, I can be destroyed if, in God's judgment, this benefits his glory.

Terrific Love . . .

Where does the violence come from that Christian writers link so closely to love? From the Christian straitjacket in which love is pressed? Or does it depend on love itself?

In any case it *also* depends on love itself, namely, the *eros* that flows through its veins. A quick look at world literature reveals descriptions of love's sunshine and roses, but also the various forms of its cruelty. It is cruel to be abandoned or deceived by the beloved, certainly. But also where the yearning that makes both lovers sigh to each other is described in positive terms, metaphors are rarely without a certain amount of violence. Love is cruel because the lover has to miss the sweetheart so, but also because they, even when they are together, suffer from not being completely absorbed in each other. The desire to completely give oneself to the other, to lose oneself in them, to no longer have to be a "self" but to be freed from all "self-love," to be absorbed in the other: it is found abundantly in the romantic poetry of all times and cultures.

In the strictly celibate love that Malebranche and Fénelon describe, this kind of "cruelly" delicious *eros* is not absent. It makes their texts readable and instructive for contemporary audiences, certainly for those who know how to read through the often-overheated surface of their reasoning. That heated surface—with the bombastic theater of "heaven against hell," "everything against nothing," "a thundering God against the mortal desire of earthworms"—allows one to paint a clear picture of what is at stake in every love: yearning lovers who, precisely because they love so much, realize that they are "nothing" compared to the perfection of their beloved. It is the kind of love that makes the same lovers, in close association with their beloved, complain that they are still "someone" and not "nobody" or "nothing," that they are not destroyed in the glorious "holocaust" of the abysmal enjoyment of their love.[27] Finally, being able to leave the own "self" behind and to be completely selfless: does all genuine love not finally want to end up there? "*Laisse moi devenir / l'ombre de ton ombre / l'ombre de ta main / l'ombre de ton chien*," Jacques Brel sings in the classic *Ne me quitte pas*.[28]

And yet the violence that Malebranche and Fénelon describe does not depend on the delicious cruelty of erotic love but precisely on its *denial*. Both Christian authors think of love by referring, not to its erotic and therefore inherently imperfect condition, but to its *agapeic* perfection. In the kind of love they advocate, people love as if they live in love's fulfillment, and this can have a crushing, disruptive influence on concrete love, on love in the sense of unfulfilled desire, of a never-ending play of pain and pleasure. It is the reference to agapeic, perfect love that is responsible for the cruelty that has caused monks and mystics to wander on the mystical path from deadlock to deadlock. When Jacques Lacan, in one of his seminars, links Christianity to an "apotheosis of sadism," he refers to this reality.[29] His characterization cannot be dismissed as a frivolous slip.

Neither in Fénelon's nor in Malebranche's theory is there space for a kind of love that is experienced from the full acknowledgment of its inherent deficiency and finitude. According to them, love's hunger must be comforted—read: denied—by those who satisfy this hunger. And that we feel we are completely lacking in love only means that we love from a fullness that we cannot deal with yet but into which we will soon be fully absorbed. This in fact implies that I have to deliver the "lack" on the basis of which I love entirely to the perfection in which I do not yet participate only because of my own sinfulness.

The problematic violence underlying this kind of love depends on the perfection attributed to the beloved God. Of course, in amorous love, the lover also glorifies the beloved. But in amorous love, the beloved too is driven by erotic desire. And if the beloved in turn metes out divine perfection to the lover, it is obvious that both "glories" meeting each other will soon be confronted with each one's "lack." And if the relationship persists, both will end up loving each other's "lack," each other's finitude. Lovers find each other on the basis of their mutual "lack," a "lack" that—in a never-ceasing loop of yearning and incomplete ful-fillment, of veil and disclosure—is acknowledged and outwitted by both.

In the course of an erotic relationship, the perfection of the beloved, which is an inevitable fantasy in every love, is gradually reduced to its realistic ground, and in the end indeed acknowledged as fantasy. So, love is given the opportunity to recognize its true ground, which is one of "lack," of deficiency and (unfulfilled) desire. In this sense, love is not just desire for satisfaction, but above all a desire for the *other's* desire,[30] and an ever-repeated recognition of—and play with—each other's "lack" and finitude.

The Christian culture of love is also characterized by this kind of erotic play between desire and counter-desire. There are numerous pages devoted to this in the oeuvre of John of the Cross or Jean de Saint-Sam-son, to name just these two.[31] But when that other form of love, *agape*, fully penetrates *eros*, the effect on the latter can be disruptive. *Agape* is incompatible with acknowledging any "lack" in the beloved (God, in this case). God is in no way marked by "lack," and therefore, unlike mortals, He does not love on the basis of (unfulfilled and unfulfillable) desire. If God loves, it is on the basis of an "excessive" abundance. Loving mortals, He overwhelms them with his perfect, by definition immeasurable, unilateral goodness. This is why the love we have for Him is by definition poor. My love does not share the same measure of its object. God's "everything" and my "nothing" have nothing in common.

But that is why I will focus even more on the "lack" from which I love, and in a way that simultaneously makes a denial of this acknowl-edgment. With respect to the perfect lover that is God, I am "nothing," and I can only become worthy of loving Him if I incessantly push myself forward precisely as a "nothing." *Pur amour* is an extreme attempt to realize that. This acknowledgment, as has become clear, at the same time functions as a denial. Precisely the acknowledged "nothing" of my love proves that God is everything and that the Order of his creation is not marked by any shortage. Shortage, lack, and desire are only illusions. Everything that exists is one great divine fullness. It is precisely the "nothing" that I am in my love for God that proves there is nothing beyond God and His Order.

By taking up position at the place of nothingness and deficiency—by lovingly embracing my damnation (Fénelon), or by lovingly giving way to the pleasure God experiences for Himself (Malebranche)—I deny the fact that reality is marked by deficiency and so restore the fullness of God and his Order. Yet, I have secretly pushed myself to the fore as the person responsible for this recovery; therefore, it is I who offers the ultimate guarantee for the fullness of God and his Order. It is thanks to *my* sacrifice that God's perfection can remain perfect and that He can retain His function as the foundation of reality. At the end of the day, it is I who enables God to be the perfect creator of a perfect universe.

. . . for the State and for the People

Reality has a divine ground, and we want to relate to reality on the basis of that ground. This is the main concern of both Fénelon and Malebranche. But the more you want it, the more you have to get rid of yourself in order to give that "ground" the space it deserves. And with both authors it turns out that you inevitably become the victim of the perfect order that you want to keep perfect through your own actions—through your pure love.

Stated in the Christian terms both authors use, it all seems very far away for us. And yet, the tendency to get rid of oneself and become selfless in order to give the world the "ground" it needs is far from absent, even in our post-Christian times.

In early post-Christian times, we came up with a world where all people would be free, equal, and brothers or sisters. And even though we considered that desired world to be not without ground in itself, we realized that it was up to us to make it real. This resulted in the French Revolution and the first freedom-based society in modern Europe. In 1789, the French revolutionaries declared all citizens in their country to be "free, equal, and brothers" and to constitute the political foundation of their society.

However, in the free society established in France, it quickly became difficult or even dangerous to have *individual* freedom, a freedom that feels free *with regard to* fellow citizens. Those allowing themselves individual freedom (and the least private act could be interpreted in that sense) were suspected of pretending to be freer than others, allowing themselves privileges typical of the Ancient Regime's nobility—privileges that had been banned from the new revolutionary, equality-based society.

By 1793, the French Revolution had changed into the so-called Reign of Terror: in the name of equality, all who allowed themselves to be different were viewed with suspicion by the authorities. Freedom became almost impossible in reality and changed into a kind of theatrical duty. All citizens were supposed to act *as if* they were free, *as if* they were equal to all their brothers and sisters. The result was that everyone was struck by the fear of taking action or expressing an opinion that seemed unequal to those of others. Freedom became a mere *idea*—an idea that everyone constantly had to pretend to be a reality, while everyone in fact sacrificed their personal freedom to that idea.

Pur amour is not as far off as it may seem at first sight. Just like God at the end of the seventeenth century, free society at the end of the eighteenth existed mainly as something that was *loved*, and here, also, with a love requiring everyone to resign themselves—i.e., their personal freedom, their *amour-propre*. Only when citizens sacrificed their individual self (this sacrifice is what Robespierre called *vertu*, virtue), were they considered to be loyal to the new society founded on liberty, equality, and fraternity.

Modern society is free: it has no ground in itself; it is free from any predetermined foundation. This means, however, that it is up to us to actively give ground to such society. That this turns into a situation where everyone has to sacrifice their personal freedom to a society that is only free *ideally* is not absolutely absurd. The history of the past few centuries offers numerous illustrations. The project of a truly social society on which all hopes had been pinned after the Russian Revolution of 1917 soon changed into a society in which citizens saw no other way out than to *pretend* that they were social and created an atmosphere of "as if" that kept the whole social system in a grip of terror. The only way to prove one was a real communist soon turned out to be sacrificing oneself in favor of the Party and even self-effacing this sacrifice.

Think of Nikolai Bukharin who, in his notorious 1937 Moscow show trial, did not even get the chance to express the slightest hint of his willingness to sacrifice himself to the Party and to the communist project in general. Despite his innocence, he wanted to confess all false accusations, and he declared to do this out of love for the Party. He had been loyal to the revolution all his life and now wanted to seal this by deliberately agreeing with his condemnation, despite the false charges. He could commit suicide, he explained to his comrades, but he refused to do so in order not to damage the reputation of the Party and the communist project. Even in the moment of his death, however unjustified it may have been, he refused to put his own "self" before that of the Party. So *pure* was his love for the "holy" cause of communism. The only thing he asked of the Party members gathered in court was that they understand and appreciate his act of sacrifice, done for their and for the Party's sake. He expected a minimal sign of recognition from them. A small passage from the minutes of the trial is sufficient to make clear that he was in no way granted this.

BUKHARIN: I won't shoot myself because then people will say that I killed myself so as to harm the party. But if I die, as it were, from an illness, then what will you lose by it? (*Laughter*)

VOICES: Blackmailer!

VOROSHILOV: You scoundrel! Keep your trap shut! How vile! How dare you speak like that!

BUKHARIN: But you must understand—it's very hard for me to go on living.

STALIN: And it's easy for us?!

VOROSHILOV: Did you hear that: "I won't shoot myself, but I will die?!"

BUKHARIN: It's easy for you to talk about me. What will you lose, after all? Look, if I am a saboteur, a son of a bitch, then why spare me? I make no claims to anything. I am just describing what's on my mind, what I am going through. If this in any way entails any political damage, however minute, then, no question about it, I'll do whatever you say. (*Laughter*) Why are you laughing? There is absolutely nothing funny about any of this.[32]

Of Bukharin a love was demanded that was so *pure*, so devoid of every "bourgeois" *amour-propre*, that it could no longer count on even the slightest recognition. From the very beginning, the love for communist society demanded of its foreman that he purify himself away entirely: that he does not shoot himself in the head, that he does not commit suicide out of love for the Party, but that he lets himself willingly be executed by it: even of this last bit of self-respect Bukharin had to purify himself. Only by that act of unrecognized self-sacrifice (or, let us say, of unseen "holocaust") could the communist project maintain that it was founded on sound, solid foundations.

The early Christian *agape*-communities denied the concrete dimension of "lack" and desire. Where this "lack" became manifest, they immediately eliminated it with the seal of death. Similarly, the "perfect" form of modern free society denies the "lack"—read: the freedom—upon which it is based. And so this denial too implies that this society eliminates its subject—i.e., the free citizen—or, more precisely, forces its subject into a state of pure, that is awfully selfless, love.

Whether violence in our relation to society and to one another can be completely eliminated is by no means certain. What is certain is that, if one thinks of this relationship as love, it should rather take shape as *eros* than as *agape*. In *eros*, as has been shown earlier, the violence will not be absent, but at least it will not be increased by the selflessly agapeic violence that pretends to deliver us from all violence. Until today, however, the agapeic ideal of love is firmly nestled in our culture and will also assert its influence in the future. This influence will be beneficial in as far as an eroticization of this ideal can assert itself. It is here that the rich mystical tradition known and nurtured by Christianity could be beneficial. As a cult of longing and desire it could protect us from the secret violence that dwells in our most idealistic aspirations.

2

Selfless

Eckhart, Fénelon, and the Modern Subject

Then again I said that if it were possible that I might return to nothing, just as I came from nothing, so that he might be avenged upon me; if it pleased Him, it would be pleasing to me.

—Marguerite Porete, *Mirror of Simple Souls*

Modern mysticism relates to the Ego. We cannot get away from it. We are sick or have to defend ourselves.

—Hugo Ball, *Flight out of Time*

Of all the obstacles characterizing the path of the mystic, the own Ego is by far the largest. It is a given in all mystical literature. In the yearning for the divine, it comes down to eliminating every semblance of egoism. In fact: also, the Ego that, with the best intentions, steers the sanitized yearning needs to be conquered. The mystical experience is selfless, or it is not. And yet it is difficult to imagine that someone walking the path to radical selflessness has no strong self-awareness. How would a weak Ego be able to walk this difficult path at all? The *corpus mysticum* of the Christian tradition is a big incentive to—a celebration of and exercise in—radical selflessness, but that does not prevent it from being written by authors who were all big personalities with clear will power.

What is evident here is the core as well as the paradox of mysticism. Everything revolves around a fight against the self, but this struggle

39

invariably shows the particularly strong self that concerns it. The Ego is the biggest obstacle, but who else but the Ego is able to clear this obstacle?

This chapter offers a close reading of some fragments of works of two mystical authors, the one premodern, the other modern. It will become clear how each has a different experience of the paradox of mysticism. This difference, it turns out, is precisely due to the paradigm each of these mysticisms presupposes. The slowness and patience that come with a close reading also allow the reader to penetrate the sharp line of reasoning that characterizes many mystical texts. Despite the reputation that precedes these texts, the rationality they demonstrate is often just as unfathomable as it is sharp-witted.

Eckhartian Selflessness . . .

No one except the self can walk the path of selflessness. This enigma can be read on almost every page of one of the most fascinating oeuvres in the mystical tradition, that of Meister Eckhart (1260–1328). Sometimes the paradox is laid bare and relentlessly commented on and questioned. This is the case in the well-known sermon *Beati pauperes spiritu*, about a verse from the gospel of Matthew (5,3): "Blessed are the poor in spirit, for theirs is the kingdom of heaven."[1]

Eckhart indicates that he will only speak about "*interior* poverty." In a typically scholastic way, he defines this concept from three perspectives that he will successively deal with. "A poor man," we read, "is one who [1] wants nothing, [2] knows nothing, and [3] has nothing."[2] In the treatment of the first element—poverty as "not wanting anything"—the Ego is already targeted as the biggest obstacle to be overcome. And Eckhart would not be Eckhart if it were not all a bit more complicated than the already punchy first few sentences of his sermon suggest; that many people do not quite understand poverty as not-wanting still seems a conceivable thought.

> Firstly, we say that a poor man is one who *wants* nothing. There are some who do not properly understand the meaning of this: these are the people who cling with attachment [*die sich behaltent mit eigenschaft in pênitencie und ûzwendiger üebunge*][3] to penances and outward practices, making much of these. May God have mercy on such folk for understanding so

little of divine truth! These people are called holy from their outward appearances, but inwardly they are asses, for they are ignorant of the actual nature of divine truth.[4]

For the reader it is clear: the Master turns from the outward display of those who pretend to be holy, while inside they are anything but. Rather, they are still too attached to their own Ego, to what is their own (*eigenschaft*) and not to what refers to God and what is God's own. But what does Eckhart want the listener/reader to understand? About the would-be saints, the "asses," he writes: "These people say that a poor man is one who wants nothing and they explain it this way: A man should so live that he never does his own will in anything, but should strive to do the dearest will of God."[5] Poverty—defined as "wanting nothing"—characterizes those who do not aim their will on anything or anybody but God; who want nothing more for themselves, but make every effort to exclusively "do the dearest will of God." Note, this is according to the "asses," who "are ignorant." But what is wrong with that? What these "asses" claim about spiritual poverty is surely not so superficial, so "outward"? Is it not simply an unadulterated version of the Christian ideal—including its mystical version? Eckhart is, incidentally, all too aware that this is the case. This is already evident from the next sentence. Those who live like this, he writes, deserve his (Eckhart's) praise and, God willing, even a place in the kingdom of heaven; but it does not prevent him from immediately adding that such a person has not understood a thing about spiritual poverty.

> It is well with these people [the asses] because their intention is right, and we commend them for it. May God in His mercy grant them the kingdom of heaven! But by God's wisdom I declare that these folk are not poor men or similar to poor men. They are much admired by those who know no better, but I say that they are asses with no understanding of God's truth. Perhaps they will gain heaven for their good intentions, but of the poverty we shall now speak of they have no idea.[6]

The "asses" are right, yet they do not know what spiritual poverty is, and if they deserve divine bliss on this basis, it is because God is indeed all "mercy." Of the truth coming from the same Merciful One, they have not understood anything.

And Eckhart can say this because he understands it, since he speaks
in no other name than that of the divine truth itself. He already warned
his listener in the first line of his sermon when he said that he had
heard the beatification he was going to discuss from "beatitude itself"
and "its . . . wisdom ("Beatitude itself opened its mouth of wisdom and
said, 'Blessed are the poor in spirit . . . '"). And he added that in the
face of the truth spoken here, all the wisdom of people, saints, and angels
together sinks into nothing: "All angels, all saints, and everything that
was ever born must keep silent when the wisdom of the Father speaks:
for all the wisdom of angels and all creatures is pure folly before the
unfathomable wisdom of God. This wisdom has declared that the poor
are blessed."[7]

Not only have the listeners/readers been warned, they are, moreover, also forgiven in advance should they not understand the divine
truth (thus belonging to the "asses" against whom they hear the Master
ranting). Right before Eckhart starts his exposé about his threefold poverty theory, we read: "We shall now speak of these three points, and I
beg you for the love of God to understand this wisdom if you can; but
if you can't understand it, don't worry, because I am going to speak of
such truth that few good people can understand."[8] The listeners/readers
now know where they are up against, when they thought they had well
understood the beginning of the actual argument. What they considered
to be at the heart of the Christian message—no longer thinking about
yourself and only seeking to fulfill God's will—is not at all what "poor
in spirit" is all about. But what is it about then? Eckhart:

> If, then, I were asked what is a poor man who wants nothing,
> I should reply as follows. As long as a man is so disposed that
> it is his will with which he would do the most beloved will
> of God, that man has not the poverty we are speaking about:
> for that man has a will to serve God's will—and that is not
> true poverty! For a man to possess true poverty he must be
> as free of his created will as he was when he was not. For I
> declare by the eternal truth, as long as you have the will to
> do the will of God, and longing for eternity and God, you
> are not poor: for a poor man is one who wills nothing and
> desires nothing.[9]

Who is poor in spirit? Who has the right attitude and way of living
that is expected from a Christian? Not they who fully direct their will

at God (even if this is in accordance with Christian teaching and can ensure eternal bliss granted by God) but the person "who has a will and longing for nothing." Eckhart's words here can best be taken in all their radicality. Poor in spirit is not the one who wants nothing. Neither is it the one who wants *the* nothing and/or wants nothing more and wants to erase every form of Ego in the self. Poor in spirit is the one who wants *not*; one who, for example, does *not* want to erase the own Ego. Not because they want something else, but because they do not want at all. The poor in spirit no longer has any will, not even the will to have none.

Here, Eckhart touches on the paradox of mysticism, as mentioned above. Because how does the "poor" ever get this far? How else but by *wanting* to no longer want? How do you eliminate your will without *willing* to eliminate it? If you are going down the mystical path and want to end up in a state where there is no longer any Ego or will, you still just need a strong Ego and a strong will. And, once more, how exactly does one overcome that which makes it possible for the "poor in spirit" to finally be what, who, and where they must be? Or, to formulate it more abstractly but perhaps more clearly: the mystical paradox touches on the *subject* of the mystical experience—and, if it were up to Eckhart, simultaneously on the *subject* of being human as a whole.

The term *subject* must be understood in terms of its abstract, formal meaning: that which is cast (*iectum > iacere*) under (*sub-*) something—in Latin: *subiectum*, which is a literal translation of the Greek *hupokeime-non*. The term is derived from Aristotelian logic, where it represents a "bearer," to which "attributes" are then ascribed. Translated by the Latin *subiectum*, the term acquired an ontological meaning in Late Antiquity: bearer/support/ground *of reality*. Subject becomes the term for being as such or, in Christian philosophy, for God, bearer-because-Creator of being.[10]

In the mystical experience, where I touch the ground and support of my existence, *I* am no longer ground and support—*subiectum*, in other words—of that "touching" or that "being"—or of anything that happens or is there. But where then does this experience have its "bearer," its "subject"?

. . . as "Subject"

The concept of "subject" can indeed cast an illuminating light on the mystical paradox that is a theme here. In the following paragraphs of his sermon, Eckhart puts into position his whole theology and philosophy, and hidden therein lies (albeit not mentioned as such) a subject theory that makes the mystical paradox indicated here somewhat more comprehensible and at the same time less paradoxical. Eckhart's sermon continues:

> While I yet stood in my first cause, I had no God [*Dô ich stuont in mîner êrsten sache, dô enhâte ich keinen got*] and was my own cause: then I wanted nothing and desired nothing, for I was bare being and the knower of myself in the enjoyment of truth. Then I wanted myself and wanted no other thing: what I wanted I was and what I was I wanted, and thus I was free of God and all things. But when I left my free will behind and received my created being, then I had a God. For before there were creatures, God was not "God": He was That which He was. But when creatures came into existence and received their created being, then God was not "God" in Himself He was "God" in creatures.[11]

It is impossible to explain all the facets of Eckhart's sophisticated theological system hidden behind these few sentences, but a number of general lines are nevertheless essential. We immediately come across the bold claim that "I had no 'God'" and—in the same breath: "I was my own cause." "Being the cause of oneself" thus seems to define the state Eckart focuses on here, the state where the Ego "desires nothing," where it is "bare being." Is this not the exact opposite of someone who is "poor in spirit"? Is it not the richest Ego thinkable, even to be able to be its own cause?

Eckhart's logic here is more consistent than it appears on first glance. In these sentences, all elements refer to a pre-creational state, a state in which everything already existed in the wisdom of God but had not yet been created. Everything existed, albeit not caused *by*, but still residing *in* the "first cause." In this respect, there was as little distinction between everything that existed and the divine, as between beings themselves. It is in this sense that Eckhart can write that "I had no God." God as such arises only *after* the first cause has come into effect—therefore, *after* creation. Before creation there was no distinction, no God, and also no Ego. Or, what amounts to the same thing, the Ego was not yet characterized by a difference from something else. In that sense, Eckhart can write that it was entirely the "cause of itself," with the understanding that there was neither a "self" that was distinct from another "self" nor one distinct from the divine Self.

In this state, "I wanted what I was, and what I was I wanted." This is as good as saying that I was not characterized by will or desire at all, because these would imply that difference and time were at play. So, in this state, God was also not God, but "he was That which he was." Numerous are Eckhart's reflections about the dictum that Exodus 3:14 puts in the mouth of Yahweh-God: "I am who I am." God is a being before there are any distinct beings, a being that, seen from our post-creation point of view, could be defined as much as a nonbeing as—what amounts to the same thing in negative theology—a more-than-being. Only with creation did beings come into existence, including my Ego and also God. Then, everything that previously existed undifferentiatedly in the divine became a universe full of separate beings, each of whom was therefore able to receive their being from God's hand. For human beings, this receiving implies that they were free, or, as Eckhart writes (in a sentence that perhaps contains the most enigmatic knot of his theology), that they "went out of [their] own free will and received [their] created being [dô ich ûzginc von mînen vrîen willen und ich empfienc mîn geschaffen wezen]."

It is, in other words, of my own free will that I was created—that is to say, received my created being from God's hand. When the creature that I am—prepared to be "poor in spirit" in accordance with God's word—looks to a state that fully brings me back to God, my Ego must get past this God, beyond the state of difference. There it will arrive at what it was before creation. And therefore the Ego must renounce its "free will." In itself, "free will" is good, noble, and holy, because it makes it possible for me to receive my created being from God's hand. But should I want to return to a not-created state, this same "free will" is the ultimate obstacle, and for the "poor in spirit," which I am in essence, it comes down to being without "will" and without "ego," and even without "God."

This is repeated in the paragraph with which Eckhart concludes his first point—poor in spirit defined as "to be poor by not wanting": "Now we say that God, inasmuch as He is 'God,' is not the supreme goal of creatures, for the same lofty status is possessed by the least of creatures in God."[12] How great is "the least of creatures in God"? Greater than God, greater than the image or "non-image" could contain that is called "God" in the human word. This "God" cannot fulfill the human being's desire (for God). And He would not even be able to with the desire of the least of these beings—of flies, for instance. Here, Eckhart's discourse becomes quite plastic: "And if it were the case that a fly had reason and could intellectually plumb the eternal abysm of God's being out of which it came, we would have to say that God with all that makes Him 'God' would be unable to fulfil and satisfy that fly."[13] And he concludes his first argument:

> Therefore let us pray to God that we may be free of "God" that we may gain the truth and enjoy it eternally, there where the highest angel, the fly, and the soul are equal, there where I stood and wanted what was, and was what I wanted. We conclude, then: if a man is to be poor of will, he must will and desire as little as he willed and desired when he was not. And this is the way for a man to be poor by not wanting.[14]

The human being "must will and desire as little as he willed and desired when he was not." That is, in a nutshell, Eckhart's "solution" for the mystical paradox. The Ego can handle its destruction because it is in this way returned to when it "did not exist," when it was there where "what I wanted I was and what I was I wanted." "There," that is to say: in the state before creation, the state before differentiation, before there was difference—difference among creatures, difference between God and beings, difference between me and myself (where "Ego" was, in other words, not yet marked by lack, desire, or will or, what amounts to the same thing, where it coincided with my fulfilled desire or will).

"There," in this place, the "subject"—which means that which lies at the basis of everything that is, including myself and what I call God—positions itself. For Eckhart, this absence of differentiation pre-ceding every origin is the *bearer* (*subiectum, hupokeimenon*) of everything that is. Our entire existence should, in other words, be considered as grounded in this absence of differentiation. From the sublime "nothing" of this absence, the infinite range of differentiated beings was created (or "emanated," in Neoplatonic terms). And all things, longing to be what they are, want to return to this state, to what Eckhart calls "the eternal abyss of the divine being [*den êwigen abgrunt götlîches wesens*]."

The ground is an "abyss." The Ego's ground too. Within this (in this case Neoplatonic, negative theological) conceptual framework, it is not entirely illogical or paradoxical to argue that the hankering of the

Ego for its ground of being is a hankering for self-destruction, for the disappearance into this ground that, from the created position from which one considers things, could be conceived of as nothing but an abyss.

The paradoxes and contradictions of which every page in Eckhart's oeuvre testifies are no break from rational logic, no leap from the straitjacket of the narrow boundaries of thought. On the contrary, they are staged only to impel us to follow the trail of true logic and correct thought, a logic and thought that become clear only when we reach the trail's end, where everything becomes clear, in other words: when we find the true *subject* from which we have to approach everything and in which we find the true ground of thought as well as of being. This ground is the divine, the pre-creational undifferentiated, the abyss into which the differentiated, in its desire to be what it is, wants to disappear and annul itself. The real (divine) Self to which each self returns is this radical selflessness. There lies the subject, the "bearer" of ourselves and of everything that is.

Modernity: A Change of Subject

What we humans ultimately seek, and what a mystical experience confronts us with in an eminent way, is an unfathomable abyss. Only now does it become clear that this abyss concerns nothing less than the ground of both ourselves and reality in general. That we see it as an abyss can be fully attributed to our created state, delineated by sin and finitude. But those who think and believe (and for Eckhart and medieval thought generally, these are in line with each other) know that truth cannot be taken from this finite position but should be considered from the true ground that is the divine. This ground is indeed dark, mysterious, and "mystical," but nevertheless we know that it concerns ground and no abyss, and, what is more, that it is all goodness and grace. For the medieval understanding, that "ground" or "subject" is God. As obscure and unfathomable and groundless as He might be, God is the name for the "base" of everything that is. Moreover, he is the point from which we can say something truthfully about everything that is. We can say something about reality because we speak from the ground of reality—a ground that is at the same time ours. The subject/support/ground of our relationship to the world is at the same time the subject/support/ground of the world itself.

Modernity can be defined as the demise of *this* "subject."[15] That is
what is behind the famous dictum of "the death of God." What disappears
is not the Godhead as such but the function it holds in self-understanding
in Western thought. Previously, the self was understood *from* God. God
was the Creator of reality and of us. We and the reality confronting us
were all tied up with each other since we were given to each other by the
same Giver named God. That is the realism of medieval thought: human
knowledge was understood to be founded on the fact of everything that
is. Everything is "given" because created by the same *Creator*, just as we
ourselves are "given" to reality because created by its *Creator*. Hence,
our ability to know reality in its essence, an essence that we share with
each other because ours as well as that of things is the work of the same
Creator. And this knowledge knows its subject/bearer/ground in God.
Knowledge is fundamentally "theo-logy." Not in the sense of knowledge
of God, knowledge that has God as object. Knowledge is theology because
it has its point of departure/subject in God. Human knowing is a *logos*
whose bearer—subject—exists in the equality between the essence of *those
who* know and the essence of *what* they know, an essence that for both
acknowledges its foundation—in other words, its subject—in God.

The demise of the medieval subject—or in more dramatic terms,
the "death of God"—took place during the sixteenth and seventeenth
centuries. All of this comes back to the Reformation and the religious
wars.[16] During that 150-years' struggle, the basic assumption from which
people had, until then, understood themselves and the world, and had
therefore also waged wars and experienced peace, became undermined.
Indeed, as strange as it may sound to the modern ear: in the Middle
Ages, God made even war possible, He provided the framework for it,
and in the end, the warring factions might find themselves under a seal
subjecting them both to the same God. For this reason, the critique of
God *as such*, although never completely absent, never dominated during
the Middle Ages. The binding principle—the collective basic assumption, supposition, *subiectum*—survived any criticism and succeeded in
maintaining its binding role.

With the Reformation, radical criticism of God and religion suddenly
obtained free rein, not least because it became politically valorized. After
Luther's protest against the pope's indulgence policy in 1517, Frederick
the Wise quickly realized that he could deploy the Lutheran reformatory
God to loosen the ties between his electorate and Emperor Charles's
Holy Roman Empire. In this way, the long-simmering criticism of God

as such received strong political support. In fact, it made God the object of massive criticism, of strife—and soon also of outright war.

The fact that these religious wars lasted 150 years—culminating in the unprecedentedly cruel Thirty Years' War, which only came to an end in 1648—accounts for God no longer being able to be "subject." No culture can fight about its own *subiectum* (basis, foundation, basic assumption, starting point) for a century-and-a-half and keep that *subiectum* in function. This is the backdrop to the so-called skepticism that characterized the second half of the sixteenth century. The *Essays* of Montaigne provide one of the most stylized reflections thereof.[17] An even stronger display of the prevailing skepticism of the time comes from Montaigne's contemporary, Francisco Sánches. The title of the book already speaks for itself: *Quod nihil scitur*: that nothing can be known, that knowledge is impossible.[18] Impossible since its basis and starting point have fallen away, because "God is dead," because there is no longer such a thing as a *subiectum*.

From this perspective, the importance of Descartes's intervention cannot be overestimated. It is precisely by taking skepticism completely seriously, by systematizing the prevailing doubt and transforming it into the sole way of thinking, that he managed to discern a new *subiectum*. That nothing is certain anymore, that I can doubt whether God is indeed God and the world is the world I see, that nothing escapes doubt: that is precisely where the new certainty lies. Because the fact *that* there is doubt and that there must consequently be a foundation or subject underlying this doubt: that is indisputable. Along these lines, doubt itself proves its "self," its "subject."

This new subject forms the basic assumption for what would soon become a new culture that would go down in history as "modernity." The "modern" person no longer defines himself from his being "given" to reality—created, as both he and reality are, by the same "giving" ground of being. From now on, the modern person defines himself as *free*, in the sense of independent from reality, free to doubt it. And he finds his foundation and starting point precisely in this doubt, precisely in the certainty of the *cogito* that proves itself in and through this doubt.

Is the *cogito* the *subiectum* of reality? Does it replace the medieval God *in that sense*? Not at all. For Descartes, it remains clear that God is the basis of all that exists; He is and remains the Creator. But the Creator is subject no more in the sense that he is no longer the point from which the human being relates to the world. This role now goes to the *cogito*, which in this sense—and *only* in this sense—becomes the subject of modernity. Descartes ascribes an ontological status to this *cogito/* subject: for him it is a *res*, a being. The only thing is that the being of *cogito*, as free as it has positioned itself through methodical doubt, is so separated from reality that it no longer shares being with the latter. The free *res cogitans* has nothing in common with the law-determined *res extensa*. After Descartes, the being of this *cogito/*subject would increasingly be questioned, until Kant declares it to be a simple hypothesis.[19] But as point from which we relate to the world, that subject continues to function to the current day. We relate "freely" to reality, which means from a place that has nothing to do, in principle, with that reality. Where this place still had the substance of a being for Descartes, it has gradually lost every substance. As "basis" from which we relate to reality, it is itself "abysmal," without grounds.

Mysticism and Modernity

Before the Ego installs itself as a new subject with Descartes, it fully shares in the crisis in which the ruling (divine) *subiectum* finds itself. In the Middle Ages, under the regime of the divine subject, the Ego experiences itself as groundless, but it could relate that groundlessness to that of reality itself. No matter how painful this experience was for the people in question, they still knew they were being carried by—and grounded in—that very groundlessness. After all, for the finite human being, groundlessness was the ultimate sign of the true ground upon which reality rests, ground as provided by the infinite God.

However, in the sixteenth century, this "ground" ended up being the issue of a hopeless battle. For the sake of that God, war after war was waged, and gradually, less and less of the visible reality showed the presence of that God and, which amounts to the same thing, the con-nection with the groundless goodness that lies at the basis of all that exists. No wonder the faithful fell back on the interiority of their own "self." Long before Descartes moved the human being to the fore as subject, the Reformation already did something similar in its own way. The *sola fide* it preached simultaneously pushed forward a strong Ego. I, and not the Church or any other intermediary, am the basis for my relationship with God, thus rang the new Protestant creed.

It is remarkable that alongside the promotion of this strong religious Ego, the Ego at the same time became the object of critical investigation. The Ego was, after all, no subject of our relation to God; that was God Himself. How could the Ego then fall back on itself? More precisely: How could I find God in myself, in my Ego? It is in this context that we should situate the lasting and ever-growing interest, during the course of the sixteenth century, in mystics from the Low Countries and the Rhineland as well as in new mystical movements that emerged all over and reached new heights with the Spanish mysticism of Teresa of Ávila and John of the Cross among others.

It was already the end of the century when the mystical wave reached France. Only then did French religious culture become interested in the mystical traditions from the north and the south. From the outset, this interest could count on the skeptical gaze of the Church and other authorities, if only because that mystical wave arrived in the country together with Protestantism. This movement, soon baptized as *spiritualité*, would therefore—also because of its clear success—never quite escape the suspicions of official institutions.

It was in the spirit of this *spiritualité* that mysticism would see its first *modern* bloom. The *modern* would be expressed in the specific way in which the mystical focused on the own Ego in order to overcome the obstacle it presents. But the battle the seventeenth-century mystics waged against their own Ego would mainly betray the grammar of the *modern* in which these mystics moved. Even though he would strongly resist a time that no longer acknowledged God as the *subiectum* of our relationship with reality, the early modern mystic, without saying it in so many words, would often come close to the new, modern subject position. As so many contemporaries, these mystics would also often be more Cartesian than they realized. But their inner struggle while going down their "inner path" brought the anomalies of the new, modern subject into sharper focus than Descartes himself would be able to do— anomalies that, for instance, had always found elegant solutions within the religious-intellectual universe in which Eckhart lived.

For this reason, we turn to Fénelon again. In a number of texts from his pen, this problem surfaces particularly sharply.[20] The effort is worth it in order to observe how, in the very attempt to rigorously consider the mystical ideal of mystical selflessness, the Ego or the self surfaces as an untouchable, foundational certainty.

"On the Renunciation of the Self"

In my hankering for God, it is not about me but about God; every form of Ego-involvement or self-love stands in the way and should be eliminated. That is what Eckhart's sermon about poverty amounts to. It is no different in the writing of Fénelon. Drawn by the attitude of Madame Guyon, the young court prelate was completely captivated by the mystical movement engulfing France during the seventeenth century under the term *spiritualité*. His oeuvre reads like an intermittent attempt to show that this relatively new and in many ways suspicious *spiritualité* was perfectly in line with Christian orthodoxy.[21] The fact that Fénelon's attempt met with condemnation by the Vatican in 1699 did not prevent him from continuing to write, and thousands of pages of in-depth reflections on the mystic way were published posthumously.

One of his countless smaller "spiritual writings and letters" is entitled *Sur le renoncement à soi-même*, "On the renunciation of oneself."[22] In sharpness, Fénelon's analysis is not inferior to Eckhart's *Beati pauperes spiritu*. For Fénelon, too, it is clear that self-renunciation could in many cases be a hidden way to still satisfy one's egoism. The most selfless of dedication might lead to extreme satisfaction and the stroking of the ego. As early as the first page of this letter (which is in fact addressed to Madame de Maintenon, the "unofficial" spouse of Louis XIV),[23] he writes:

> The origin of our trouble is, that we love ourselves with a blind passion that amounts to idolatry. If we love anything beyond, it is only for our own sake. We must be undeceived respecting all those generous friendships, in which it appears as though we so far forgot ourselves as to think only of the interests of our friend. If the motive of our friendship be not low and gross, it is nevertheless still selfish; and the more delicate, the more concealed, and the more proper in the eyes of the world it is, the more dangerous does it become, and the more likely to poison us by feeding our self-love. . . .
>
> [Such a person] does not indeed accept payment in as gross coin as others; it does not desire insipid praise, or money, or that good fortune. . . . It must be paid, nevertheless; it is greedy of the esteem of good people; it loves that it may be loved again and be admired for its disinterestedness; it seems

to forget self, that by that means, it may draw the attention of the whole world upon self alone.[24]

And where can we find a remedy for this malignant self-love that para-sitizes our disinterested love? Not with ourselves, it appears. That would only serve to confirm our sense of self and our self-love. Where then do we find grounds or support to leave all egoism and self-love behind? Fénelon and most of his Christian contemporaries find this in what still serves as *subiectum*—in God. In the words of Fénelon:

> We may be sure, then, that it is not the love of God only that can make us come out of self [*il n'y a que l'amour de Dieu qui puisse nous faire sortir de nous*]. If his powerful hand did not sustain us, we should not know how to take the first step in that direction.
>
> There is no middle course [*Il n'y a point de milieu*]; we must refer everything either to God or to self; if to self, we have no other God than *self* [*moi*]; if to God, we are then in order, and regarding ourselves only as one among the other creatures of God, with selfish interests, and with a single eye to accomplish his will, we enter into that self-abandonment which you desire so earnestly to understand.[25]

How does this kind of radical self-abandonment work? How can God be the ground from which our action to abandon ourself has any chance at success? Beside God's overwhelming revelation, meant to enlighten our "spirit," Fénelon mentions—incidentally, entirely in line with Augus-tine[26]—the "miraculous" fact that God Himself has laid down in our "heart" his desire for Him. "The second miracle which God works is, to operate in our hearts that which He pleases, after having enlightened our understanding. He is not satisfied with having displayed his own charms; He makes us love Him by producing, by his grace, his love in our hearts; and He thus himself performs within us, what He makes us see we owe to Him [*ainsi il exécute lui-même en nous ce qu'il nous fait voir que nous lui devons*]."[27] "He thus performs within us, what He makes us see we owe to Him." What do we owe Him? Everything we have and are, including our love for Him and thus also the radical *renoncement de soi* (self-abandonment) that we do for His sake. The sentence says

even more: we also owe Him that through which the *renoncement* can be
executed. A thoroughly abysmal line of reasoning announces itself here.

This is what Fénelon must have been thinking while he was writing, because in the next sentence, he directly addresses the reader, in
this case Madame de Maintenon, and promises to clarify the matter.[28]
He slows down, it seems, and explains that she must renounce evil, of
course, and with horror (*horreur*). She also needs to renounce what is
good, it is argued straight away, but not with repugnance, nor abruptly
and hastily, but patiently, moderately, incrementally. Maintenon lives in
the lap of luxury, after all, and Fénelon is realistic enough not to demand
her to break with all that "good" overnight. But in the long run, it is
indeed what he—or rather, God—demands of her. On the very same
page, Fénelon cites Luke 14: 33: "So therefore, none of you can become
my disciple if you do not give up all your possessions."[29] And soon the
tone sharpens again and the earlier abysmal reasoning reappears.

"Each Christian," he writes, has to renounce the care they have
for loved ones, family, and their own reputation. "He must give up those
whom he loves best"

> and his renouncement of them consists in this: that he is to
> love them for God only; to make use of the consolation of
> their friendship soberly, and for the supply of his wants; to be
> ready to part with them whenever God wills it, and never to
> seek in them the true repose of his heart. This is that chastity
> of true Christian friendship which seeks in the mortal and
> earthly friend, only the heavenly spouse. It is thus that we
> *use the world and the creature as not abusing them*, according to
> Saint Paul (1 Cor. vii. 31.) We do not desire to take pleasure
> in them; we only use what God gives us, what He wills that
> we should love, and what we accept with the reserve of a
> heart, receiving it only for necessity's sake, and keeping itself
> for a more worthy object. It is in this sense that Christ would
> have us *leave father and mother, brothers and sisters, and friends*,
> and that *he is come to bring a sword upon earth*.[30]

And why should you be *reserved* in using what God gave you and not
enjoy it fully? Because it is an amorously envious God, as we read in the
following sentence: "God is a jealous God; if, in the recesses of your soul,
you are attached to any creature, your heart is not worthy of Him: He must

reject it as a spouse that divides her affections between her bridegroom and a stranger."[31] God is jealous. Why? Because we have the tendency, no matter how well intended we are, to cling to what we received from God and not to God Himself. Therefore, as Fénelon explains in more detail in the following, we have to abandon all that is material, as well as—and this is more difficult—the spiritual. We even have to renounce our own spirit as such: "*renoncer à son esprit.*"[32] We must even renounce our renunciation, our asceticism as such: "We renounce with courageous moderation the most flattering temptations of the world, and content us with the satisfaction derived from a conviction of our self-control. . . . You must renounce all satisfaction and all natural complacency in your own wisdom and virtue."[33] You must therefore, and above all, renounce the positive feeling of having achieved something on the "spiritual path" to selflessness. As such, *spiritual* satisfaction is evil. The following sentence directly addresses this warning to Madame de Maintenon:

> Remember, the purer and more excellent the gifts of God, the more jealous He is of them. . . . He would have us attached to nothing but Himself, and to regard his gifts, however excellent, as only the means of uniting us more easily and intimately to Him. Whoever contemplates the grace of God with a satisfaction and sort of pleasure of ownership, turns it into poison. Never appropriate exterior things to yourself then, such as favor or talents, nor even things the most interior. Your good will is no less a gift of God's mercy, than the life and being which you receive direct from his hands. Live, as it were, on trust; all that is in you, and all that you are, is only loaned you; make use of it according to the will of Him who lends it, but never regard it for a moment as your own. Herein consists true self-abandonment; it is this spirit of *self-divesting*, this use of ourselves and of ours with a single eye to the movements of God, who alone is the true proprietor of his creatures.[34]

Put in a more abstract way, Fénelon argues that you have to renounce the *false subject* of renunciation. Only then can you make space for the *true subject* and does your renunciation take you where you want to go: to a pure love for God that has renounced every bit of self-love. In your strongest attempts to give yourself to God and completely renounce yourself, God is envious as long as *you* still want it; in other words, as long as you do not allow Him to be the subject of your self-renunciation and your love for Him.

But how must I make God the subject of my love for Him and my self-renunciation? Everything I have and am, I have and am because I have received it from Him. To honor Him, to profess to Him my love, I must therefore accept His gifts, but then—as it turns out—without actually accepting them. I should, writes Fénelon, see them as borrowed. But not so much in the sense of giving them back because God ever needed them or will ever have them. Even if, in my renunciation of the world and myself, I return to God everything He has given me, it is not what He is ultimately asking of me; He demands love from me—a love in which I acknowledge that in everything the *giving* lies completely on His side, also regarding "my" love for Him.

In what still follows in this "letter" to Madame de Maintenon, Fénelon sticks to a number of reminders: do not be too hasty, and do not work entirely on your own, but remain patient and let God do his work. The opening page of the letter suggests that Maintenon had asked him the precise meaning of self-renunciation. In this letter, Fénelon only briefly touches on the abysmal of what it means to let God Himself be the subject of this renunciation. He is more explicit about it in a number of other letters he writes to her. Some fragments of these letters are included in the *opuscule* "About the interior voice" ("De la parole intérieure").[35]

"The interior voice"

This *opuscule* directly addresses the problematically abysmal that we are up against here. The subject of our self-renunciation does not correspond with our "self." On the contrary. And yet it resides in us. It is the "interior voice," according to Fénelon, that by way of which "the Spirit of God dwells within us," or also, as he mentions farther on, "the soul of our soul."[36] That does not make the problem any smaller. Because this latter "soul," that which inspires us here and now, is self-interest. That soul needs to die to itself, and it has to perform that act of dying itself: therein lies the challenge of the mystical path that it goes. And so, again: How can it do that? How can a "self" actively cause its "self" to die, without performing its very "self"? How can a self *itself* make space for the selfless, true Self, for the Holy Spirit, for the "interior voice"?

We already know the answer. This is what God does. When someone who wants to love God obeys his interior voice, his Ego is "wrested away from the center of [his] love." "In this state, God takes care of everything necessary to detach this person from [his] 'self.'"[37] Fénelon does not get tired of repeating this and providing new supporting arguments. But these arguments never quite succeed in being completely conclusive. For as God completes the work in which He tears the Ego from the center of the human soul, a similar Ego also seems to impose itself again and again, admittedly not as the subject of self-love but nevertheless as the subject of its own "de-selving," of its own renunciation. A little earlier in this same *opuscule*, we read:

> As to the external mortification [*mortification extérieure*] of the senses, He causes us to accomplish it be certain courageous efforts against ourselves. The more the senses are destroyed [*amortis*] by the courage of the soul, the more highly does the soul estimate its own virtue, and live by its own labor [*plus l'âme voit sa vertu, et se soutient par son travail*]. But in process of time, God reserves for his own hand the work of attacking the soul in its depths, and depriving it finally of the last vestige of the life of Self. It is no longer the strength of the soul that is then employed against the things without, but its weakness that is turned against itself. It looks at self; it is shocked at what it sees: it remains faithful, but it no longer beholds its own fidelity. Every defect in its previous history rises up to view, and often new faults, of which it had never before even suspected the existence. It no longer finds those supports of fervor and courage which formerly nourished it. It faints; like Jesus, it is heavy even unto death. All is taken away but the will to retain nothing, and to let God work without reservation.[38]

In its yearning for God, the soul abandoned itself and left everything to God. But God does not fail to carefully hold it up to the soul once more: to confront it with the fact that it has lost all grip on itself and to force it to still be the bearer—the subject—of this loss and the existential inability that comes with it. Facing its successful loss of self, the soul is confronted with the fact that it consciously chooses it; that, no longer wanting anything or anyone, it *wants* this. "All is taken away but the will." And what kind of "will" is at play here? "It is no longer a perceptible, designed will [*volonté sensible et réfléchie*], but simple, without reflex acts [*volonté simple, sans retour sur elle-même*], and so much the more hidden, as it is deeper and more intimate in the soul. In such a state, God sees to everything that is necessary to detach the soul from self."[39] A will that is no longer "reflective," no longer "reflexive," but is—if you like—purely "flexive": a "flexion" ("bend," "fold") without "re-" without folding back on itself, and in this sense radically "simple," unambiguous; a will that simply unfolds, away from itself, to God. The moment someone's will is in this state, God is able "to detach it from itself."

Is, then, God the *subject* of this mystical event? Does the point from which one relates to God here correspond to that God? The will, however "simple," seems to contradict this. The will admittedly leaves everything to God and refuses to fold back on itself, but the will, therefore, is not yet without will; or more cryptically but perhaps more precisely: its installed will-lessness is in itself not altogether will-less. And this is exactly what God wants: the moment where one has completely surrendered to God and one's will is pointed one-dimensionally in the direction of God, God still folds the human will back on itself. The moment the God-lovers finally no longer see themselves but only God, God reveals precisely *this*. They *then watch* how they do not see themselves but God. And that subsequently means that *they* are the ones who see this and that the subject still lies with themselves and not with God. As if God in a way casts them back on a subject that is not Himself! As if the true subject (God) can only be discerned in the falling back on the "false" human subject.

Fénelon, of course, does not come to this conclusion in such terms. And yet the reasoning in which his meandering discourse unfolds constantly rubs up against a similar conclusion.

In the course of this *opuscule*—to name another example—Fénelon describes in detail how the soul goes the "inner path," effectively completely eliminating itself or, better still, allowing God to eliminate every self-reference of the soul—until God, as outlined above, confronts the soul therewith, thus bringing it into a profound crisis. Now it becomes clear to the soul that the courage it has to abandon all that is self is not even its own courage but goes back entirely to what God does with it. It is only at this moment that courage is *really* lost.

> Our courage fails; frivolous excuses are suggested to flatter
> our feeble and tempted souls; then we hesitate and doubt

whether it is our duty to obey; we do only the half of what God requires of us, and we mix with the divine influence a something of self [*un certain mouvement propre*], trying still to secure some nutriment for that corrupt interior which wills not to die [*pour conserver quelque resource à ce fond corrompu, qui ne veut point mourir*]. A jealous God retires: the soul begins to shut its eyes, that it may not see that it has no longer the courage to act, and God leaves it to its weakness and corruption, because it will be so left. But think of the magnitude of its error! The more we have received of God, the more ought we to render. We have received prevenient love and singular grace: we have received the gift of pure and unselfish love, which so many pious souls have never tasted; God has spared nothing to possess us wholly; He has become the interior Bridegroom; He has taken pains to do everything for his bride—but He is infinitely jealous. . . .[40]

The selflessness to which the soul has surrendered now becomes—by God's envious hand—the subject of fear and doubt. It once again forces the soul that has become selfless to a selfhood, to a subject or "ground" that lies with itself, since it and no one else feels this doubt. No, it is no longer itself, it has lost itself in God, but God lets it feel how that loss is not even its own and forces the mystic to be the bearer or subject of this doubled loss. This is what the mercy of God's jealousy accomplishes—as Fénelon writes in the sentence that immediately succeeds the previous citation:

Do not wonder at the exacting nature of his jealousy! What is its object? Is it talents, illuminations, the regular practice of external virtues? Not at all; He is easy and condescending in such matters. Love is only jealous about love; the whole of his scrutiny falls upon the state of the will. He cannot share the heart of the spouse with any other; still less can He tolerate the excuses by which she would convince herself that her heart is justly divided.[41]

God's will is straightforward: He is fixed 100 percent on his spouse, that is, the soul going the mystical path. Therefore, He demands the same from the latter: it must choose God. But unlike with God, for the soul this comes down to choosing against the self. And it does so, which finally results in eliminating the self. Once the soul feels it has come this far, God throws it back on itself, however, on the subject of this feeling, and it realizes that it also has to eliminate that subject. And then the will appears: it can do nothing but want to eliminate that feeling. And in turn it seems impossible to eliminate that will—including the subject it implies—once more. That will is what the circular reasoning Fénelon employs to chart the logic of the path to selflessness, encounters time and again.

As soon as the state of selflessness is achieved, it remains in the last instance a matter of the will and thus of a subject that agrees with what happens to the mystic when they turn themselves into God as "clay [that] must suffer itself to be shaped at the will of the potter"![42] Ultimately the "clay" must *want* it: this is what, in the end, the experience of mystical selflessness is all about in Fénelon.

Unlike with Eckhart, the liberating state of *theosis* ("becoming God,"[43] a phrase so typical of the mystical tradition) will leave behind a *willing* Ego, thus assuming a subject that does not, like in the Middle Ages, correspond with God. Farther down, when Fénelon is talking about the culmination of the mystic way, he writes:

> O bridegroom of souls! even in this life, a foretaste of this felicity. They will all things and nothing. As it is things created which hem up the heart, these souls, being restrained by no attachment to the creature, and no reflections of self, enter as it were into thine immensity! Nothing stops them; they become continually more and more lost; but though their capacity should increase to an infinite extent, Thou wouldst fill it; they are always satisfied. They do not say that they are happy, but feel that they are so; they do not possess happiness, but their happiness possesses them. Let anyone ask them at any moment, Do you will to suffer what you suffer? Would you have what you have not? They will answer without hesitation and without reflection, I will to suffer what I suffer, and to want that which I have not; I will everything which God wills; I will nothing else.[44]

Here, too, the same paradox: the Ego is completely selfless, having disappeared in God; but in the final analysis a will—and consequently an Ego—emerges again. In the mystical apotheosis of disappearance, Fénelon apparently has no alternative but to identify a will, because he still needs an endorsement that has its subject precisely not in God but in the human being itself. In this way, the radical selflessness with which his argument wants to conclude runs aground time and again.

The result is that selflessness is affirmed, not so much in a state *beyond* the self as in the infinitely continuous destruction of the self, in a never-ending *will* to be or remain destroyed: "I want to suffer what I suffer, and I do not want what I have not got; I want everything, I want nothing."

"Pure Love"

The persistence of the will in Fénelon's mystical theory is linked to the cruelty to which his ideal of *pur amour* can lead. In the previous chapter, this was illustrated by the "holocaust" Fénelon encouraged among those he accompanied on the spiritual path.[45] For this reason, I focus on an *opuscule* entitled *Sur le pur amour (On Pure Love)*.[46] This is a short dissertation that, according to Fénelonian Jacques Le Brun, dates back to the time of the *Querelle du Quiétisme*.[47] Here, Fénelon meditates about a verse from Proverbs (16:4) that notes that God made everything for his own glory.[48] But what about the eternal beatitude that God promises us and which we as His creatures desire? Is this desire compatible with the glorification God demands of us? Fénelon writes:

> It is not that the man who loves without interest does not care for the reward. He cares for it in so far as it is of God, and not in so far as it is his own interest. He wants it because God wants him to want it. It is the order, not his own interest, that he seeks in it. He cares for himself, but he only cares for himself for love of God, as a stranger would, and for the sake of loving what God has made.[49]

We do not want our happiness because *we* want it, but because God wants us to want it. Note: human beings were made for happiness, and that we long for it is, for Fénelon, the "foundation" of his being human. Yet this foundation is a question of mercy, of a gratuitous gift, which is based in God's sovereign will. "The promise [of beatitude] itself, which

is the foundation of all, is supported by the pure mercy of God, on his
good pleasure, and on the good purpose of his will [*sur son bon plaisir et
sur le bon propos de sa volonté*]. In this order of blessings, everything is
plainly reduced to a supreme free will."[50] Here again Fénelon's reasoning
tips to the contrary. From the sentences following, it will become clear
that not God's will but that of the human being constitutes the basis
of *pur amour*. It is here that he comes up with the "supposition" mentioned in the previous chapter that serves—certainly in the reception
of his oeuvre—as hallmark for the Fénelonian *pur amour*. The section
immediately succeeding says:

> Having presented these indisputable principles, I make a sup-
> position. I suppose that God wants to annihilate my soul at
> the moment that it escapes from my body. This supposition is
> only impossible because of the entirely free promise. God could
> have excepted my particular soul from his general promise for
> others. Who will dare deny that God could not annihilate
> my soul following my supposition? . . . I suppose then a very
> possible thing, since I only suppose a simple exception to
> the purely free and arbitrary rule. I suppose that God, who
> makes all other souls immortal, will finish the duration of
> mine at the moment of my death. I suppose again that God
> has revealed: his design to me. No one would dare say that
> God could not do this.[51]

What Fénelon holds up is a situation in which my every prospect of bliss
has been denied in advance, and I also know this. I know that God,
at the moment in which I lose myself in Him, will not admit me to
Him. I know that, when I will be radically selfless and "liberated" from
my false subject, no grounding subject (God's mercy) awaits me but the
abysmal nothingness of a radical subjectlessness. What then? Fénelon
brings out his sharpest rhetoric to bring the question down as hard as
possible on the reader's head.

> I suppose that I am about to die. Only one moment of life
> remains of a life, which is to be followed by fatal and eternal
> extinction. How shall I use this moment? I urge my reader to
> answer me with the most exact precision. In this last instant,
> shall I give up loving God, because of not being able to think

of Him as a reward? Shall I renounce Him since He will no longer be my salvation? Shall I abandon the main true end of my creation? Could God, in excluding me from the joys of eternity, which He was under no obligation to give me, divest Himself of what so essentially belongs to Him? Has He ceased to work for His own glory? Has He lost the right of the Creator in creating me? Has He freed me from the obligations of the creature, which owes necessarily all its existence to Him by whom it exists? Is it not evident that in this very possible supposition I ought to love God for Himself alone, without expecting any reward for my love, and with a certain exclusion from all beatitude, so that this last moment of my life, which will be followed by eternal annihilation, ought to be necessarily filled by an act of love, pure and completely disinterested? . . .

I am going to be annihilated right now. Never shall I see God. He refuses me His kingdom which He gives to others. He does not want either to love me or to be loved by me forever. I am obliged, nevertheless, in dying, still to love Him with all my heart and all my strength. If I fail Him in this, I am a monster and an unnatural creature.[52]

Is what Fénelon's "supposition" describes the last step on the mystical path? Or is it already interpreting the state one is in after having reached the end of this path? Fénelon himself does not pose this question, not in these terms. Someone who has occupied this hypothetical position would not pose the question either. For whoever arrives at that point, it no longer matters whether there is a step that follows. In that sense, Fénelon's "supposition" fully describes the point where the mystical longing knows its end. Those walking the path are now where their yearning led them: pure love. A love that is pure, also in the sense that yearning and satisfaction are no longer distinguished from each other.[53] That God does *not* satisfy my desire is experienced as satisfaction itself, as ultimate selflessness.

But is it a coincidence that Fénelon's "hypothesis" is bathed in an atmosphere of extreme suffering? After all, it appears as if only a state of direct pain can keep a love pure in the sense that Fénelon envisages. Pain and suffering, in any case, offer the structure in which selflessness manages to chime with a *will* to selflessness.

Let us briefly list the steps of reasoning. My amorous longing for God makes me, after the long mystical path I have trodden, endlessly selfless. But precisely for the sake of keeping my love that way, God once again explicitly confronts me with that selflessness. Therefore, the latter finds itself under pressure. How can I keep it intact at all? Fénelon's answer: by expressly affirming—by *willingly wanting*—that selflessness and the deplorable, utterly deprived state to which it brings me. But—here the same question that has its cadence in the entire mystical tradition emerges again—does this not precisely presuppose the recycling of a self? In order to maintain my selflessness, according to Fénelon, I have no other choice but to actively long for my complete destruction. I do know that God does not allow me that (the desire for beatitude is, after all, my foundation), but how else can I keep my love selfless, now that it still finds its ground in the self of a will? The only way out is no longer actively and willingly wanting a self: consciously and with all inner strength that I have left willing my powers and my entire self to be unceasingly and actively destroyed. Only then can my will arrive at a selflessness of which God demands that I consciously observe it.

Even though I am selfless, God does not allow me, as mortal creature, to disappear into the beatitude of selflessness. He forces me to face my beatitude as that into which I have disappeared. He forces me to be continue looking at my disappearance—not at my being gone but at the act of my disappearing *as such*, in other words: as an act that never reaches completion.

I can only do so by continuously and actively willing my disappearance. Which is concretely only possible by actively and continuously, willingly wanting to suffer. Not for the sake of suffering itself but precisely to prove that it does not affect me, that I nevertheless love God—that *despite* my disappearance into a state that I cannot assume to be blissful, I still love God.

I need this "despite"—and therefore this suffering; it allows me to see that I no longer belong to the world, even though I am still in it. The world—even though it is pure pain and precisely *now* that it is pure pain—no longer concerns me, because I am already elsewhere, in the divine. But already enjoying the divine here would destroy the victory over my self-love—and therefore my pure love. For this reason, I embrace this pain, as it gives me the opportunity to still experience my achieved selfless disinterestedness here, in the world of *amour-propre*. I testify to my state of beatitude, which I will not feel in heaven, by showing, in the midst of the pool of pain that urges me to self-love, that I am not affected by it.

The Pain of the Modern *Martyrium*

Embracing pain on the mystical way: it is not unheard of for Eckhart either. In the sermon *Mulier, venit hora et nunc est,* we read: "A master says, 'He who has once been touched by truth, justice, and goodness, though it entailed all the pangs of hell, that man could never turn from them even for an instant.' "[54] Even if "it entailed all the pangs of hell," those who were touched by God's truth would take it. What Eckhart takes from the mouth of a teacher and presents to his reader/listener, seems to echo the bath of pain in which Fénelon preeminently sees *pur amour* being present. And yet there is a difference.

With Eckhart, the context is radical selflessness as well. The sermon concerns what it means "when true worshippers shall worship the Father in spirit and in truth."[55] And this truth implies that you worship God for no other motive than for God Himself and that you therefore have to abandon every focus on yourself. "I have sometimes said," Eckhart writes, "whoever seeks God and seeks anything with God, does not find God; . . . If you seek God and seek Him for your own profit and bliss, then in truth you are not seeking God."[56] So here, just as with Fénelon, beatitude in itself cannot be the motive to love God. That this love brings pain, does not matter. I love God because of God, because of a why that is its own answer. Eckhart writes:

> All things that are in time have a "Why?" Ask a man why he eats: "For strength." —"Why do you sleep?" —"For the same reason." And so on with all things that are in time. But if you should ask a good man, "Why do you love God?" —"I don't know—for God's sake." "Why do you love truth?" —"For truth's sake." —"Why do you love righteousness?" —"For righteousness' sake." —"Why do you live?" —"Indeed I don't know—I like living!"[57]

You will not find anything like the latter with Fénelon and his contemporaries. They love God because of God Himself, but that this equals lust for life, with love for life because of life itself: that idea is no longer well received in seventeenth-century France. Malebranche is the only one to come close, but he has to mobilize all the registers of his theoretical apparatus to ensure that the idea is not immediately rejected. "Why do you live? I do not know, I like to live," and therefore I also love God: Eckhart could dish up something like this for his listener/reader as if it were entirely self-evident.

And that is, strictly speaking, also what it was in the fourteenth century. With Eckhart, too, the idea assumes a heavy theoretical apparatus, but then precisely to explain that this idea is fundamentally evident. The truth itself is without why or, what amounts to the same thing, it has its why in God, in God's love—which is, in turn, also without why and is therefore divine, pure love.[58] By analogy, my love for God also does not need a single why. The pain that might theoretically come with it would not make it less sovereign and without-why. Of course, it is painful if I have to abandon or completely empty the temporary, including my own self. But such an attitude toward God, stripped of any self-centered rationality, is nothing other than a reconnection with the ground of creation, with the why-less (and in this sense abysmal) ground in which reality rests. And if the latter has something to do with pain, it is because pain, after all, belongs to life and its zest for life.

Fénelon, too, loves God only for the sake of God Himself, but his love is no longer of such a nature that it can be expressed as the spontaneous love for life that is innate in all creatures. For Eckhart there is admittedly an abyss between creation and God, but that abyss is simultaneously the true ground, the ground in as far as it speaks from every fiber of creation—if only we were willing to listen carefully, in other words, listen *beyond* the vanity characterizing our mortality, to the eternity of which that creation testifies. For Fénelon, too, there is an abyss between creation and God, and he believes that this is the ground of reality, but unlike Eckhart, he can no longer assume that for everyone the abysmal ground merely speaks out of creation. And this because he himself no longer speaks *from* that ground. He would like that, but modernity prevents him. It is not his modern *ideas* that prevent him (because modern they are not), but indeed the *point* from which he holds ideas, the point from which he relates to creation. This point—the modern Cartesian subject—has been separated from creation.

On the level of content, everything in Fénelon's thinking resists this modern proposition. On the contrary, the mystic way he propagates with his *vie intérieur* wants to indicate that human beings, like other creatures, live from their Creator. But he in fact repeatedly clashes with himself as the ultimate obstacle to reaching this point. Time and again, he is thrown back on a modern self or subject, and the true *subiectum*, God, lies beyond. But unlike with Eckhart, this "beyond" does not assume the incorporation of the finite subject into its infinite ground. Instead of such an incorporation, the modern subject can ultimately only see its love for God realized in its own destruction. No creature can absorb it in its selflessness, or, to use Ruusbroec's terms: there is no "shiny stone" whose glow and luster gives it the assurance that it selflessly shares in the sovereign, "why-less" selflessness on which the whole creation rests. The only certainty the human being has is its destruction as modern Cartesian subject. Or, expressed in the religious narrative: the distance that separates the sinner from the Creator is so insurmountable that, ultimately, only the voluntarily taken punishment and the enduring love therein gives the Creator the honor He deserves from that sinner. Only the *martyrium* of pain and suffering can bear witness to the fact that humankind and the world are grounded in a God who has been separated from them since modernity.

3

Love Thy Neighbor Purely

Mysticism and Politics in Fénelon

Unfortunately, you do not understand these truths. How could you appreciate them? You do not know God at all. You do not love Him at all. You do not pray to Him at all with all your heart, and you do nothing to try to know Him.

—Fénelon to Louis XIV

Christian love is thoroughly social. Since its very beginning, Christianity has been imbued with the ideal of *agape*, the term for the way the first Christians organized their communities. In these, so to speak, proto-communist societies no one was poor because all possessions were common property and all lived in perfect harmony. Such were the consequences of the fact that the participants defined God as love, as *agape*. The "Kingdom of God," which Christians believed was about to be realized on earth, was meant to be the reign of love. "Love thy neighbor as thyself": this biblical commandment was practised in a radical way, so we read in the Acts of the Apostles.[1] When, later on, Christianity had become part of society's official power, that power was again and again criticized by reference to the very idea of *agape*. Under all kinds of Christian regimes, "love" was part of the slogans by which the sharpest criticism against them was expressed. To this day, Christian love has always been a motor behind all kinds of social revolt and political change.

However, is Christian love not, rather, the name for that intimate relation the faithful have with God? Is love for God not first of all what

69

matters to the soul—the soul considered neither in its relation to other souls nor in some social or political commitment, but the soul on its own, hoping to find in that loneliness a direct intimacy with God. Here, love is not something social, let alone political. Here, love is explicitly solitary and intimate, a matter of introspection, of inner life.

This kind of love, too, has a long tradition in Christianity. Here, however, the background is not only *agape*, but *eros* as well. Man's intimate love for God is highly erotic, albeit in a sublimated way: "carnal" long-ing is transformed into spiritual desire for truth or, what amounts to the same thing, for God. In other terms, it is Platonic *eros* that is at stake in this tradition, a tradition that started with Origen's commentary on the Song of Songs, plays a dominant role in the entire narrative, and is most explicitly expressed in what is commonly known as Christian mysticism.[2]

Christian mystics love God by going along the inner path of their soul. And yet, at the same time, they pretend that this love is not in contradiction with explicitly social love. Mystical love, they say, is perfectly compatible with neighborly love and with social commitment in general.

This chapter, too, focuses on François de Fénelon (1651–1715) and reflects upon the way he considers mystical—or, as he calls it, spiritual—love to be compatible with social and political commitment. Even though my conclusion will be critical of the theoretical possibility of this compatibility, it must be said that, in fact, Fénelon combined an extremely intimate conceptualization of the love for God with one of the sharpest critiques of the political absolutism of his time. Fénelon did not succeed, however, in properly arguing the compatibility of the two kinds of Christian love he both practised: the intimate love and the social one. What is at stake in this failure, is—as I will show—the impact of the then emerging Cartesian *cogito* that became the new, typically *modern* subject. I will argue that the modernity of the subject position is problematic, both at the level of intimate love and at that of social love. In this sense, the social problem of Fénelonian love can shed light on the profoundly problematic character of the way modernity considers the social and the political.

Pur Amour and Neighborly Love

In the previous chapters we discussed Fénelon's ideas about the ultimate form of Christian love: the *pur amour*. It is "pure" because it is deprived of selfishness, of *amour-propre*. It is purified even of the loving person's "self." In a passage from one of Fénelon's *Lettres spirituelles*, the God-loving readers were invited, so we quoted in chapter 1, to "be really nothing, in all and everywhere." A few lines farther, we read: "Let us be the holocaust which love's fire reduces to ashes."[3] This context, however, did not prevent Fénelon from making a small remark referring to man's love for his fellows: "Receive from the hands of men the comfort that God will give you through them. You must receive it not from them, but through them from Him."[4] We all live in the love of God. We share that love. On this basis, we have to love one another and be grateful for the love we receive from others as well as for the love we give them. But, if we follow Fénelon in this, we must love one another *purely*: not because of the benefit we gain from it, not because of the love we receive from one another. We receive all benefits and all love from God, and only from Him. It is *through* Him that we give and receive one another's love. Here, God functions as a purifier. He purifies us from the self-interest involved in our mutual love. He makes us love others not for what we get from that love, but for the sake of love as such, of pure love, *pur amour*.

We have to love one another unselfishly, without any return to the self that is almost inevitably involved in that love. Is such a thing possible at all? Is it, more precisely, possible within the context of neighborly love? Is it not, rather, the ultimate obstruction for love between people, for love as the basis upon which a society can be built? Pure love is unselfish love. Yet, precisely therefore, it requires an attentiveness with respect to the self, for this is what is to be destroyed for the sake of love's purity. I must be preoccupied with the self in me. Especially when we are together with others, we have to be preoccupied with our "self," with that self of ours that must be tamed and put away.

Of course, it is God who is between my fellows and me. It is his love that brings us together and only via Him are we able to love one another purely. But God at the same time obliges us to be occupied with the purification—and finally the annihilation—of our "self." Does this, however, not imply that in the first place, we have to be preoccupied with ourselves and not with our fellow men and with the wider society around us? And, in the end, when our love has finally reached the state of pureness, is this love not exclusively for God, a love in which there is not only no longer any self, but no other, no society either?

So, if society is based on love—the premise that is implied in the Fénelonian thesis—and love's paradigm is the love of/for God (and the *pur amour* that this requires from us), is society then not based upon what in fact disintegrates it? Between my neighbor and me, there is God, and finally it is not one another we have to love, but God.[5] In the end, there is no "we" to love God, there is rather a, so to say, randomly gathered set of individuals that love God, each one going an inner path that tries to destroy his own ego.

The Fénelonian *pur amour* appears to be an excellent precept for a kind of asocial and apolitical Christianity. Though loving his fellow men, the Christian is finally oriented toward a solitary relationship entirely submerged within a God to whom he has sacrificed his very self. Here, all social and political activism seems to be neutralized or even made impossible.

Fénelon: Political

And yet, both Fénelon's life and his writings are far from asocial and apolitical. On the contrary, his writings contain some of the sharpest criticism of the absolutist regime of his time. Decades after his death, his reputation was such that the protagonists of the French Revolution toyed a while with the idea of honoring this Catholic priest as one of their inspiring geniuses by giving him an official tomb in the "Temple of the Revolution," the Pantheon in Paris, beside the ones of Rousseau and Voltaire.[6]

Fénelon did not primarily owe this reputation to his most remarkable *Lettre à Louis XIV*, in which he criticizes vehemently the belligerent politics of the Sun King as well as the scandalous luxury of the Versailles Court and the French nobility in general, unconcerned as the entire political power was about the cruel poverty in which the masses found themselves. The *Lettre* was a private document,[7] certainly not meant to be read by the king in person, but probably by his unofficial (but extremely influential) wife, Madame de Maintenon, in order to nourish the advice—sometimes also political—that she provided to the king.[8]

Fénelon undoubtedly owed his success in the enlightened circles of prerevolutionary France to his novel *Les aventures de Télémaque* (1699).[9] This novel, too, is addressed to someone in the center of French political power, the *Duc de Bourgogne*, the Dauphin's son and, consequently, the possible heir to the French throne after Louis's death. At the time when he was writing the novel, Fénelon was his *récepteur*, responsible for his education. The novel's plot follows Telemachus, son of Ulysses, traveling around in search of his father. He is accompanied by Mentor, Fénelon's alter ego, who instructs him how to respond to all the difficulties they encounter, providing in the meantime an entire course on politics—instructing the possible future king about how to install and guarantee a state ruled by justice and virtue. No reader—and certainly not Louis XIV himself—could have missed the criticism the novel leveled at the current situation in France.

To summarize Fénelon's ideas about politics, one can say—with Patrick Riley—that he pleads for a kind of "republican monarchy," a political order that "combines monarchical *rule* with republican *virtues*."[10] In the eyes of Fénelon, the king's power is not absolute, since he is not above the laws of the state.[11] Together with his aristocracy and his people, he must cultivate such qualities as "simplicity, labour, the virtues of agriculture, the absence of luxury and splendour, and the elevation of peace over war and aggrandizement."[12] So, the "republican" dimension of Fénelonian politics is above all of an ethical nature, and compatible with the morality as expressed in the Gospel.[13] The power is with the king and his aristocracy, but both must behave according to Christian and republican virtues. They must set aside their personal interest and act in favor of the *res publica,* the common good. In the small dissertation commented upon in previous chapter (*Sur le pur amour, On Pure Love*), after having explained his famous "supposition," Fénelon underlines his thesis by referring to antique society. There, he writes:

> The idea of perfect disinterest ruled the politics of all ancient legislators. The laws and the fatherland must be preferred to oneself, for this is what justice wants; and one must prefer to oneself what is called beauty, good, just, perfect. . . . It is not a matter of being happy by adapting oneself to that order. On the contrary, out of love for that order, one must negate oneself, perish, and not keep any resource. This is the way in which, in Plato's *Crito*, Socrates prefers dying to running away, fearing to disobey the laws that held him in prison.[14]

Setting aside personal interest: this is what connects Fénelonian politics to the kind of mysticism he defends, the *pur amour*. In the *pur amour*, those who are in a position of power can find an excellent directive for their political engagement. Already, the first lines in Fénelon's *Letter* to *Louis XIV* point in this direction. The idea of *pur amour* guides the entire argument, and yet, as I will show, that is precisely why it reaches an impasse. The letter begins as follows:

> The person, Sir, who takes the liberty of writing you this letter, has no interest in the world. He writes it neither from hurt nor from ambition, nor from any desire to become involved in the affairs of the state. He loves you without being known by you. He sees God in your person. With all your might, you cannot give him any reward that he desires, and there is no pain that he would not suffer willingly in order to make you understand the truths necessary for your salvation.[15]

The first thing that stands out is Fénelon's astonishing lack of subservience. Rather than with the king, here the "absolute" is obviously with Fénelon. And this is definitely due to the position of *pur amour* that Fénelon pretends to occupy. Hence, the "freedom" he mentions in the first sentence. He addresses himself to the king in "liberty." Why?

Because he is free from all interest, he says, he has no ambition, no desire whatsoever—except the desire to love God or, which amounts to the same thing, to love *purely*. And, so he adds, this is precisely the way I love *you*, my king. I expect no reward from you, whatever you can give me with all your might. It is not might or power that connects us, but love. You do not know me, which makes it impossible that you reward my love for you, but this is the very reason why I love you *purely*. It is the very reason as well why I see God in you—God whom I love purely. Even if you should know me and should not be pleased by my love for you, even if you should punish me severely for the immodesty of my love for you, I from my side would continue to love you. And I would continue to do everything in order to bring you in line with God, to make you love God and your people as purely as I love God and, through him, my fellow men and your people.

Fénelon, then, anticipates the negative reaction of his addressee. Talking about himself in the third person, he continues the passage quoted above: "If he speaks to you forcefully, do not be amazed; it is that the truth is free and strong. You are hardly accustomed to hearing it. People accustomed to being flattered easily mistake for spite, for bitterness, and for exaggeration that which is only the pure truth."[16] With these sentences, Fénelon starts to develop the list of criticizable points in the way Louis XIV rules his country. The Sun King should resist the flattery in which he has grown up and in which the royal court in Versailles continues to live. Instead of putting his own person in the state's center, he should follow the selflessness as present in the ideal of *pur amour* and concentrate himself on the well-being of his subjects: not on the nobility's prosperity, but on that of the majority of the population, who are being exploited by the gentry.

In all this, the *pur amour* is central. It allows Fénelon to practise an astonishing freedom of speech, for it enables freedom in the locus from where he addresses the king. He loves the king *purely*, precisely because he is not bound to him by any interest. And this is how the king must love his people: not for his own interest, but for that of the people. The freedom Fénelon takes to criticize his king is precisely the freedom he wants his king to take: the king, too, must be free—free of himself, of his self-interest, of his *amour-propre*. This is, Fénelon adds, why the truth is also free. Just like God, the truth is sovereign; it has no need of anything in order to be what it is. So a king must be: sovereign for the very reason that he needs nothing. This is to say that he does not give in to the slightest of his own needs or desires, that he does not give way to the temptation of taking advantage of his royal position and, thus, of giving in to *selfish love*. God—or, what amounts to the same thing, truth—is sovereign in the sense that He coincides with the perfection of his being, that He is not marked by lack or desire, that He is so much Himself that He does not need to be selfish at all. Society must be led by this God, by this truth. People must live together and build up a society "in truth"—which for Fénelon means "in love," in *pur amour* for God. But, so Fénelon observes, this truth has been neglected, and even denied by the king. It is up to Fénelon—and to his confessant and spiritual pupil Madame de Maintenon—to bring it to him.

But not without the help of God! For God is indeed needed here, so Fénelon concludes in one of the most direct and hard attacks on Louis XIV in person. I quote it at length, also to illustrate the vigorous tone of Fénelon's critique:

> God will finally be able to remove the veil that covers your eyes and show you what you avoid to see. It has been a long time since He laid hands on you. But He is not quick to punishment, because He has compassion with a prince who has been obsessed by flatterers for his entire life, and because

your enemies are also His. But He will know to separate his just cause from yours, which is not just, and to humiliate you in order to convert you, for you will only be Christian in the humiliation. You do not love God. You only fear Him with the fear of a slave. Your religion only consists of superstitions, of small superficial practices. You are like the Jews of whom God says: while their lips honour Me, their heart is far from Me. . . . You only love your glory and your comfort. You return everything to you as if you were the God of the earth and as if all the rest is but created in order to be sacrificed to you. On the contrary, God has created you for the sake of your people. Unfortunately, you do not understand these truths. How could you appreciate them? You do not know God at all. You do not love Him at all. You do not pray to Him at all with all your heart, and you do nothing to try to know Him.[17]

King Louis must "know" God, which is to say that he must recognize Him as the principle that de-possesses him of any kind of false, egocentric self, from the illusive glory in which his *amour-propre* holds him captive. He has again to learn the truth, which is not in selfish but in pure love: in the love that kills the ego in order to enable the love for the people. Fénelon writes these hard words in the hope that they are at least clear in the ears of Madame de Maintenon, so that they can one day, in a more diplomatic way, enter those of Louis XIV himself.

The Pure Basis of Politics

What, according to Fénelon, is wrong with Louis XIV's politics? Is it the absolutist character of his regime that represses even the tiniest form of democratic participation? Not exactly, for "democracy" is of no concern to Fénelon. In no sense does he turn against monarchy *as such*. What is wrong with Louis XIV is that he does not "know" God and does not recognize Him as the unique basis of a just political order.

And what does it mean that God constitutes the basis of a just political order? To answer this question, Fénelon does not refer to the early Christian idea of *agape* and the "perfect communities" based on this principle. When he (rarely) mentions *agape*, he reduces its meaning to the Eucharistic practice, and simply omits the social and political dimension as described in the Acts of the Apostles.[18]

If the basis of politics is love, which in the eyes of Fénelon is indeed the case, then it is not brotherly love, but love for God. Brotherly love is only the effect of the more basic love for God. Without that love for God, we would not be able to love one another in a proper and just way. Why not? Because then we should love the other for the love we expect from him in return or for other benefits that this implies. And in fact we normally do so. Such is our natural condition. However, this is precisely why that natural condition is a bad and wrong basis for society. It grounds our living together in the selfish love—the *amour-propre*—of each of us.

Fénelon can understand that most people stick to selfish love or, despite their attempts, never get beyond it. Human nature is selfish, and only a few, elected by God Himself, are supposed to go the "inner path" that conquers all *amour-propre*, and reach the state of *pur amour*. It is not ordinary people who constitute the target of Fénelon's political critique. Targeted are those who have power over them, those who are responsible for society as a whole. When they relate to their subjects, even when they claim to do so out of love, they are guided by selfish love. And unlike the love of ordinary people, *their* selfish love has a direct and disastrous effect on the entire population, on society as such. This is why they must do everything to limit the selfishness of their natural condition. More than anyone else, they must "know" God and be aware that it is God who constitutes the basis of society.

So, if there is one person who has to "know" God, it is the one pretending to be the substitute of the heavenly ruler on earth: the king. To call his power "absolute" can only signify that, in his position as king (as father and guard of his kingdom), he is absolutely unselfish. Being king in a "just" way implies loving his people in a *pure* way, that is to say, in the way of *pur amour*.

If, for his people, the king is like God, this does not mean that his personal will shall be their law—as Louis XIV himself explicitly suggests in his *Mémoires*.[19] What does God stand for? According to Fénelon, He stands for the principle of man's essence as being his very "self-destruction." Man only exists by the love of God, and he only finds this truth when emptying himself from any human self in order to make room for the real Self that he belongs to, which is God. This kind of *pure love* has its social implications. What enables human beings to relate to one another in a *true* and *just* way requires the elimination of their selfish reflexes. Absence of selfishness: this is society's real basis. It is in this sense that society is grounded in God, and that no society is possible without God's substitute, namely, a king.

Hence, Fénelon's monarchism, despite the republican virtues that he puts forward both for those who have power and for those who live under it. The powerful basis of society can be nothing else but God or—what amounts to the same thing—the king. Only, the king must "know" God, which is to say that, in his quality of sovereign, he can only be "selfish" in the way that God is "selfish," which means: not marked by needs and desires—as a "self" that, within the earthly world of needs and desires which is his kingdom, acts out of mere selflessness.

In a way, the Fénelonian king shares a basic characteristic with the Hobbesian "sovereign." Of course, Fénelon would never agree with Hobbes that the sovereign of a state (a "commonwealth," in Hobbes's term) has a mortal basis, since for Fénelon, state and sociability in general are based in the immortal God. And yet, there is a common feature. For, despite the violence of the Leviathan being the origin of his power,[20] the Hobbesian sovereign is supposed to be free from any personal violence, if only because he is free from interest in the society he rules. Located by "social contract" in a position radically outside society and the mutual interests reigning there, the sovereign himself is free from any interest and therefore able to install an order of law that counts equally for everyone. It is his unselfishness that legitimizes him as sovereign. And on the part of his subjects, a similar unselfishness is required: that they put aside their own personal interests is the condition *sine qua non* to obey the law and to be proper subjects (i.e., to be *justly* subjected to the sovereign's law). A "commonwealth" is only possible when each of its subjects has renounced his natural rights and transferred them to the sovereign, and when the latter acts not on the basis of his own natural "Rights" (his personal interests), but only on the basis of the rights that he has received from them and transformed into "Laws." On this basis only, the sovereign is able to create a just order of law.[21]

That the difference between unselfishness and its opposite plays a basic role in the foundations of society is an idea that can be found in Rousseau as well, despite his severe criticism on Hobbes. According to Rousseau, too, selfishness, considered socially, is a most profound vice. It is at the very basis of society, although society is not the basis of the human as such. Man is not basically—in the words of Rousseau, "naturally"—social. In the state of Nature, there are no societies, not however because—as Hobbes teaches—these are made impossible by the war of everyone against everyone. The state of Nature is the opposite of that of war, Rousseau explains, since there, in his needs and desires, man is directly provided for by Nature herself. There, life with others is really free and really peaceful at the same time because no one needs the other. This is why, in the state of Nature, selfish relations to others and selfishness as such are simply absent. Only when society comes into being, *amour-propre* emerges. And the social contract is there to repress that *amour-propre* and change it into a real social love, a love for the community.

All three authors, Rousseau, Hobbes, and Fénelon, have the idea in common that at the basis of society, unselfishness is indispensable and that even the basis as such is unselfish. For Rousseau it is Nature, for Hobbes the Sovereign, and for Fénelon God. Each of them has a different conception of the way man should relate to this basis. For Rousseau, he should take that unselfish state of nature into account as being impossible to re-establish *and,* at the same time, as the regulative idea upon which society's social contract is built. For Hobbes, the selfishness that dominates society should be repressed by the unselfish sovereign to whom the subjects should relate in absolute obedience. Fénelon locates just politics in the selfless way the king and all men of power relate to their subjects as well as to society's ground, which is God.

Yet, Fénelon is the only one who really goes into the selflessness required here. He does that not so much in his political, as well as in his spiritual writings. In order to train themselves in "loving" their subjects, men of power can use his long and numerous reflections on the *pur amour*—so Fénelon implicitly suggests on almost every page of his *Lettres spirituelles*, if only because these are for the most part addressed to people belonging to the center of France's political power, the Versailles Court. Madame de Maintenon is but one example—though an important one, since Fénelon wrote many letters to her and, by doing so, tried to influence directly the very heart of political France, Louis XIV.

There, in the *Lettres spirituelles*, the reflection on selflessness is much more elaborate and more acutely problematized than in Hobbes or Rousseau, where it is hardly touched upon. What is more, in Fénelon's reflection the paradox of the intention to be selfless comes to the surface. And, as we will explain, the paradox sheds light on the paradoxical basis of the modern political subject in general—a subject that in Fénelon's time is about to emerge.

What is this paradox? That the attempt to get rid of the self, installs this very self. Remember the elementary line of Fénelon's argument: No, it is not I who want to be the basis of my being; I no longer want to live on the basis of that mortal self of mine. I want to live on God's basis, and love is the way to achieve this goal: pure love, love purified from the self and its interests, even purified from the benefits God promises me. Suppose I know that I will be condemned to the eternal pains of hell, even then, and precisely then, I will love God, for then and only then, my love is really pure, truly unselfish.

Is it? Is that self of mine no longer operational here? Has it been overcome? As already explained, this is not at all the case.[22] For my so-called unselfish love, contrary to what it pretends, does not depend on God, but only on myself. I, and no one else, give ground to my love for God. Even if God condemns me to hell, even if heaven is a mere chimaera, even if God does not exist at all, my love for God remains, for it depends only on me.

Contrary to his own intentions to make God the source from where man relates to Him, Fénelon turns out to be himself that source, which can only keep its original intention by endlessly trying to destroy the source that he is himself. Despite his own objective, he turns out to be a modern, Cartesian subject: the point from where he relates to the world is no longer God, but Fénelon himself. He allows for the doubt whether God will keep his promise of heavenly beatitude and makes that doubt his very method. And where does he find the certainty overcoming this doubt? In the doubt itself, in the uncertainty of God's promise. In this methodically maintained uncertainty, he finds the only certainty that remains: the absolute freedom of his will to love God.

Modern politics is no longer grounded in God, but in the human. The citizen himself is supposed to be the basis of his society. Hobbes was one of the first to think this through. In a different way, Rousseau did something similar a century later. But even if man himself is the basis of his society, a kind of unselfishness is required. This was clear to both Hobbes and Rousseau. Social coherence cannot be based on self-interest. Fénelon is interesting here in the sense that he radically opts for unselfishness as the very basis of society. Yet, considering this unselfishness by reflecting upon the inner path on which the mystics go, he runs into a persisting self. He more precisely runs into the Cartesian ego that turns out to be the basis even of the *pur amour*. From this perspective, one can find in Fénelon all elements to criticize the naive idea of selflessness as understood by Hobbes and Rousseau. To sacrifice the individual (natural) self in order to ground the social "self" is not only far from easy, it is tricky as well, because it nonetheless installs a strong (Cartesian) self. Hence, the absolutist character that persists in Hobbes and even in Rousseau.

And yet, notwithstanding its tricky character, the kind of unself-ishness that is at play here is indispensable in politics. More than in Hobbes and Rousseau, it shows its power in Fénelon. What else gives him the strength to stand up against the absolutist power of Louis XIV? Of course, it is the strength of his own self that is at the basis of his critical stance—a self clearly taking the position of a Cartesian ego. And yet, this criticizing ego owes its power and its authority from the idea of a radical unselfishness. It is this unselfishness that is responsible for Fénelon's political courage.

A huge field of research appears here, an inquiry into the problematic entanglement of self and selflessness in the way in which we are modern subjects, both in how we go the inner path in search of our real self (referring in this to the mystical tradition) and in the way we try to live together on the basis of mutual respect, precisely, for each other's self.

4

Nothing Writes

On Madame Guyon

Ideas come and settle in my mind by mistake, then, realizing their mistake, they absolutely insist on coming out. I do not know where they come from, or what they are worth, but, whatever the risk, I do not think I have the right to prevent this operation.

—Simone Weil, *Waiting for God*

The seventeenth-century French idea of *pur amour* for God involves the voluntary annihilation of the human loving subject. Remember Fénelon's famous "impossible supposition," discussed in the second chapter.[1] Even if you know with absolute certainty that God will not reward your love for Him but, instead, will condemn you to hell, you still can—and must—love Him. This unselfish, radical love must be. But does it really annihilate one's loving ego? In fact, it does not. As explained, even in Fénelonian *pur amour*, one's love is not based in God—as Fénelon would like to have it. Such annihilation still supposes a *human* subject, which is nowhere else than in the self of the loving person. As shown in chapter 2, despite his own claims, Fénelon ends up being a hard-core Cartesian.

The "holy indifference" assumed by Fénelon and so many other seventeenth-century spiritual authors—indifference to the pains of hell as well as to the promise of eternal bliss—is supposed to imply the becoming "nothing" of the "pure lover." In fact, however, it puts the pure lover in a radically independent position vis-à-vis God, a position of which, instead of God, he himself is the subject.

We know that Fénelon owes his interest in *pur amour* to Madame Guyon. She is the one who introduced the young priest to texts by spiritual authors of their own time as well as to those by Flemish, Rhenish, and Spanish mystics of earlier centuries. The large correspondence between the two shows that they shared the same *pure love* spirituality. And yet, although Fénelon's "impossible supposition" is mentioned in Guyon's oeuvre, she makes it function in a different way. Nor does she support the idea of "holy indifference." For her, loving God without hope of being saved by his grace is an indefensible and intolerable thought. How then does she conceive of the annihilation of the ego? How can one hope for eternal salvation and at the same time, as the mystic path requires, disappear as the "subject" for whom this salvation is meant?

In this chapter, I read and comment on a few passages in Guyon's work. First, a passage where she criticizes the idea that one can love God without hoping for salvation, but nonetheless embraces the possibility—even the necessity—of annihilating the self. The passage that I read next shows that she situates this annihilation neither in hell nor in heaven (unification with God) but, more down-to-earth, in the act itself of reporting it, of writing about it. The Guyonan "selflessness" is to be situated in the pen that writes her texts. "She" does not "write." In her texts, "nothing writes."

This scribal annihilation makes Guyon's texts anticipate the literary writings of three centuries later. Many twentieth-century avant-garde authors would do everything to free their texts from any intervention of the writing "I" or "self." Speaking or writing without an "I": that was what Guyon wanted to do in the seventeenth century, and that is what so many literary authors of the previous century also explicitly intended to do.

Against "Holy Indifference"

In one of her *Discours spirituels*, "Sur le sacrifice absolu et l'indifférence du salut [On the Absolute Sacrifice and the Indifference of Salvation]," Guyon seems at first to embrace Fénelon's *supposition impossible*.

> It is said of Saint Francis de Sales that, having been subject to a severe temptation for three years, during which he thought he was damned, he said to God: "Although I must be eternally unhappy, I still want to love You and serve You." . . . Did [he]

not say in his conversations: "If my damnation were a little more agreeable to God than my salvation, I should prefer my damnation to my salvation because of this good pleasure of God [*bon plaisir de Dieu*]"?[2]

Guyon here quotes a sentence from Book IX of the *Treatise on the Love of God* where Francis de Sales defends his thesis on "holy indifference." The soul who loves God must be indifferent to everything because she is allowed to be preoccupied with only one thing: "the good pleasure of God." "In short," he writes, "the good pleasure of God is the sovereign object of the indifferent soul."[3] A few lines farther on, we read the sentence quoted by Guyon—a sentence that is perfectly in line with Fénelon's "impossible supposition." In the rest of her *Discours spirituel*, Guyon affirms one of the great tropes of pure love spirituality, which perfectly illustrates the Fénelonian thesis.

> It is noted in the Life of Saint Louis, written by M. de Joinville, that Saint Louis, having gone to the Holy Land, met in the city of Acre a woman who, holding a torch in one hand and a jug of water in the other, was going through town like this. A good clergyman who saw her asked her what she wanted to do with this water and this fire. "It is," she said, "to burn heaven and extinguish hell, so that there will never be either heaven or hell again." And when the religious asked her why she had said these words, she replied: "Because I no longer want anyone to ever do good in this world to earn heaven as a reward, nor also that we beware of sinning for fear of hell; we must, however, do so for the full and perfect love that we must have for our Creator God, who is the sovereign good."[4]

What is *pure love*? It is love that has delivered itself from all interests, positive as well as negative ones. This love is indifferent to hellish punishments, should the devotee be judged imperfect. And it is just as indifferent to heavenly rewards if the worshiper is flawless.

Is this what Madame Guyon means, quoting Francis de Sales and the history of Saint Louis? Does she share Francis de Sales's idea of "holy indifference"?

It is curious that she wholeheartedly approves of these quotes while also pleading *against* the idea of "holy indifference." Already the first sentence of her *Discours spirituel* leaves no doubt: "To speak against the indifference to salvation is to speak against a chimaera."[5] And hardly a few lines farther on: "The souls who are perfectly with God, are far removed from this monstrous indifference that is spoken of."[6] The whole of her *Discours* is intended to explain this. She proclaims that, yes, for his "good pleasure," God can condemn her to hell even if she only has "pure love" for Him. But that, no, by saying this, she is by no means "indifferent" to what God does to her.

A few lines farther on, Guyon repeats the "impossible supposition," not to argue in favor of "holy indifference" but of "the purest love," which for her is quite another thing:

> For those who are being tempted, their minds are so obfuscated and the apprehension of offending God is so great that there are some who say, "Damn me, and I will not sin. I know that hell is the punishment for sin, but I will ask for it to prevent sin." Who does not see that it is their purest love and respect for God that makes them make this sacrifice, without in any way considering the consequences? And if—impossible assumption—such a soul were sent to hell, she would bear the purest love there and the fire would not be able to reach her, since it can only burn sin.[7]

In this matter, Fénelon and so many other seventeenth-century spiritual writers affirm the "will" as the basis of love. God takes everything from me, and here I am who nevertheless loves—that is to say, wants—God. In Fénelon we read: "The *pur amour* is exclusively in the will alone; so, it is not a love of sentiments, for imagination is in no way a part of it; it is a love that loves without feeling, as pure faith believes without seeing."[8] For Fénelon, pure love is a matter of the will. It is a logical conclusion. Who else could be the "subject" of my love if God withdrew his support and condemned me to hell? This, however, is not the conclusion Guyon draws. In a letter to Fénelon, she writes: "The core of the state you are in, is the complete loss of all will, not only regarding its feelings, but in its totality."[9] Is it not indeed a matter of feeling, though? In her spiritual discourse against "holy indifference," Guyon does not use the word, but how else can we understand what she writes in the sentences following the last quotation extracted from the *Discours*?

> But one should not believe that a soul who makes this sacrifice with all her heart for the love she has for God and for fear

of displeasing Him, is in a condition to make any of these reflections. And this sacrifice is so pleasing to God, as I said, that the sorrows and temptations cease in the soul when she really and wholeheartedly makes it.[10]

A soul who loves God with pure love no longer makes reflections or returns to her own will. Such a soul no longer wants anything. Does she no longer feel anything? She no longer feels the pain that she undergoes. She immerses herself in the opposite feeling. She is mere joy, not her own joy but that of God. Her painful sacrifice is pleasing to God and her love coincides with this pleasing sacrifice, as she fully immerses herself in the joy of God.

But nowhere do we read that it is "she," the soul, who feels this joy. Where is "she" then in this divine experience of joy? Here, we touch Guyonian "nothingness." In the experience of divine joy, the soul has disappeared as a "she" and has become "nothing."

Rectifying Fénelon

In the passage we have read, Guyon does not thematize the "nothingness" she is as "subject" of this experience. She does it elsewhere, though, in one of her poems to Fénelon, for example. Guyon and Fénelon did not only correspond by letters, but by spiritual poems as well. Here is a poem by Fénelon to Guyon where he evokes the annihilation of his self in pure love for God:

O pur amour, achève de détruire	O pure love, finish destroying What you think is still left of me.
Ce qu'à tes yeux il reste encore de moi.	
Divin vouloir, daigne de me conduire ;	Divine will, deign to lead me;
Je m'abandonne à ton obscure foi.	I surrender to your obscure faith.
En quelque état que cet ordre me mette,	In whatever condition this order puts me,
Les yeux fermés, pleinement j'y consens :	With my eyes closed, I fully agree:

C'est pour lui seul que mon
  âme fut faite,
C'est à lui seul que j'offre
  mon encens.
Je ne suis plus désormais à
  moi-même ;
Dieu me possède et je ne
  sens que lui ;
L'éternel en mon cœur vit
  et s'aime,
Il en arrache et bannit tout
  appui.[11]

It was for Him alone that
  my soul was made,
It is to Him alone that I
  offer my incense.
I no longer belong to myself;

God possesses me and I feel
  only Him;
The Eternal One lives in
  my heart and loves Himself,
He snatches and banishes
  from it all support.

In his "pure love," Fénelon surrenders to God's "obscure faith." He is deprived of all that is left of himself and is fully possessed by God. It is in the empty mirror he has become after the destruction of his "self," that God now loves Himself. Fénelon has disappeared in his love for God. A purer love is unthinkable.

Except to Madame Guyon. Here is the poem by which she responds to that of Fénelon:

Vous vous croyez sans
  soutien, sans défense :
Vous êtes loin du parfait
  dénûment.
Que vous avez d'appui et
  d'assurance !
N'avez-vous plus ni goût,
  ni sentiment ?
Celui qui sent et voit
  encore qu'il aime,
O qu'il est loin de ce
  terrible RIEN,
Où l'on n'ose se regarder
  soi-même,
Tant on se voit éloigné
  de tout bien.

You believe yourself to be
  without help, without defense:
You are far from perfect
  destitution.
What support and confidence
  you have!
Do you no longer have taste or
  feeling?
He who still feels and sees that
  he loves,
Oh, he is far from this terrible
  NOTHING,
Where one does not dare to
  look at oneself,
So far does one see oneself
  distanced from everything.

Mais suivons Dieu, ne cherchons point de route,	But let us follow God, let us not look for away,
Contentons-nous de marcher sur ses pas,	Let us just walk in his footsteps.
S'il veut de nous une entière déroute,	If He wants a completely erratic journey for us,
Il le fera : nous ne le saurons pas.	He will make it so: we will not know.
Amour, Amour, si l'on croyait te suivre,	Love, Love, if we believed we follow You,
On marcherait sans cesse et sûrement.	We would walk relentlessly and surely.
Mais, lorsqu' Amour à l'ennemi nous livre,	But when Love delivers us to the enemy,
Si l'on se perd, c'est éternellement.	If we get lost, it is forever.
Du moins on croit qu'il en va de la sorte :	At least we think it is like this:
On n'en connaît plus ni sentier, ni lieu ;	We no longer know either path or place;
Et cependant l'âme alors se transporte	And yet the soul is transported then
Bien loin de soi, s'abîmant en son Dieu.[12]	Far from herself, sinking into her God.

The first lines already rectify Fénelon, but not by saying something different. Guyon says the same as Fénelon, maybe somewhat more accurately, more without compromise. What Fénelon says is in itself correct for her, but the mere fact that he writes it reveals a mistake. That he is able to say he is "without support" reveals too much support and shows that he is still far from a state of "perfect destitution." "What support and confidence you have!" she reproaches Fénelon. Whoever still *feels* that he loves—and therefore can write about it—is still infinitely distant from what he really loves, that is to say "this terrible NOTHING." This "NOTHING," in capitals, is the God who deserves only to be loved with "pure love."

This is not to say that God is "NOTHING." He is only so from the point of view of our *amour-propre*. We must love God to the extent that He no longer means anything for our self-love; it is in this sense that this kind of "NOTHING" is "terrible." Besides, it is also what we ourselves must be if we aspire to pure love. The slightest kind of self-love and even the "self" must be annihilated. To love purely, we have to be "NOTHING." It is the only way to coincide with the place reserved exclusively for God, where without hindrance He can love Himself and enjoy his glory. Only if we reach this place, God is at the same time both the subject and the object of our love. Here, our "I" is destroyed. In the "holocaust" of our love, we are finally lost in the One who is nothing but Love.

In fact, this "holocaust" no longer allows such love to be said or written. The very act of saying or writing still supposes too much an "I" and a "self." However, this does not mean that, for this reason, Guyon herself stops writing. What she objects to in Fénelon is just as true for herself, but that is not the conclusion she draws. In the rest of her poem she does what Fénelon also does: she talks about her abandonment of self in pure love, she describes her evaporation into "NOTHING." In doing so, she leaves out the "terrible" consequence of her act of speaking and writing.

In Fénelon's poem, Guyon sees the paradox of mystical love revealed. It shows how, while proclaiming the annihilation of the "self," he installs that very "self." She, however, does not recognize the paradox in her own poem. There, she leaves it unnoticed.

This is not the case in all of her work. In what follows, I analyze a few pages of Les torrents, one of her first books.[13] In these pages, she unambiguously runs up against the paradox of her own writing: How can someone, having lost herself in God and become "NOTHING," still *write* about this state of being NOTHING?

"I am not allowed to continue here"

The title Les torrents (The Torrents) excellently illustrates the core of Guyon's mysticism. To walk the spiritual path, you just have to surrender to God as to the flow of a wild torrent. The spiritual life comes down to the act of pouring oneself out into God—a perpetual act in which every form of "self" keeps getting lost in the ocean of divine infinity. The metaphor of the torrent suggests already that the mystical path is not the steep and difficult path that we know. This path is—on the contrary—radically simple: that of perpetual self-loss.

True, Guyonian mysticism, too, describes stages in the mystical development, but in each stage the accent is put on simplicity, that is to say, on the fact that what we are seeking is always already there. Someone who is too focused on the path to God, and is too consciously worrying about the correct method to reach his goal, is too preoccupied with himself rather than with God. The path that leads beyond oneself must itself already be without "self"; so Guyon repeats in various ways.

But can this be said or written? Does not the act of saying or writing immediately destroy what it expresses? It was the paradox that Guyon discerned in her reply to one of Fénelon's poems. In *Les torrents*, there is a page where Guyon explicitly discerns the same paradox, this time in her own text. She has just explained the last of the mystical steps and here she is, who, without warning, resorts to her confessor, that is to say, to the one for whom she is writing this book:[14]

I am not allowed to continue here; all is missing. I think I took too much on my natural lights. [*Je crois avoir trop pris sur mes lumières naturelles.*] You will easily discern it. I made reflections; perhaps it was more by nature than by grace that I had the instinct to write; and I am willing to confess it here and to admit frankly that I even made some mistakes at the end, having, instead of losing them, retained in my mind certain lights [*certaines lumières*] which had come to me in prayer in this state. Furthermore, in the state in which I am, I have not distinguished at all between what is natural or divine, what is God or what is mine. I pray to God to let you know.

I did not read these pages after having written them and I was interrupted a lot. After I had left the argument halfway, I reread a line or two, or a few words, in order to continue. I do not know if I acted against your intention. It happened to me sometimes, but I have not reread anything since. I did not consider if I had said everything about each thing [I intended to say] or if I repeated myself. I leave all this to your lights [*à vos lumières*], praying Our Lord to enlighten you to make you discern the false from the true, and what

> my *amour-propre* would have wanted to mix with his lights
> [*avec ses lumières*].[15]

The lines preceding this long quote suggest that Guyon has reached the end of what she has to say and is about to finish her book. She has just explained the final mystical stage, which in the edition published by Dominique Tronc has the title "Fourth Degree of the Passive Way in Faith. Divine Life."[16] And, then, suddenly it turns out that Guyon remembers what "to write" means to her: it is to present, not what she herself is thinking about, but what God makes her write. For her, writing as such is meant to be a form of passivity, to let oneself be guided by what comes like that—like the flow of a torrent. In writing, she only wants to be the wild, impulsive yet hyper-obedient spokesperson for God.

At least, such was her intention. But now, as she is writing the "last" pages of her book, she realizes that things did not go exactly as she wanted them to go. This is why she again addresses her confessor, at whose request she has taken the initiative to write her book.[17] It is up to him to judge whether, in the pages she has written, her *ego* is not too present. And immediately she confesses: yes, I made mistakes in that sense, everything is still too much "me," too much "nature," and therefore not entirely "grace." It were "my natural lights" that disturbed my prayer and that I let enter into what I wrote here. So she confesses to her confessor, and asks him explicitly to read what she has written and to separate in it what is the result of her "natural lights" and what was written down by God's "grace."

Rereading what she wrote is what she purposely refused to do, even at times when she was often interrupted. She hardly reread more than a few words or lines before continuing, she confesses. It is not surprising, then, that her texts are so impulsive, capricious, and often difficult to follow. And here she is now, unequivocally declaring that she does not know whether she said everything she intended to say, or has been lost in useless repetition.

It is hardly surprising that she did not want to reread anything, since she does not suppose herself to be the author of what she writes. What appears on her pages is the result of a state of "passive prayer"—a state of praying during which all form of "self" is erased and absorbed by the "torrent" ceaselessly pouring into God. And now she confesses that she must stop writing because she realizes she might be too present in what she has written. If this is the case, she prevented God from speaking in the book He wanted to write by means of her humble human hand.

Writing Scripture

"Nothing" writes. There are other passages in her works where Guyon directly thematizes the "self-absence" that writes the texts bearing her signature. In *La vie par elle-même*, for example, her extensive autobiography written at the request of her spiritual director "to defend herself against Bossuet,"[18] she informs us of the way in which she wrote on the Bible. This work, immense in itself, commenting on each verse of each of the biblical books, was written over a remarkably short period of time: between April 1684 and March 1685. One of the eighteenth-century editions had twenty volumes. But it was not "she" who wrote those comments, as she admits in chapter XXI of the second part of *La vie par elle-même*. It is even too much to say that she has *read* the biblical text, let alone has *reflected* on the commented verses:

> As soon as I would begin to read the Holy Scriptures, I was led to write down the passage that I was reading, and soon after, to write an explanation of it. In writing down the passage, I did not have the least thought about the explanation, and as soon as it was written, I was led to explain it, writing with inconceivable speed. Before starting to write, I didn't know what I was going to say. While writing, I saw that I was writing things that I had never known, and light was given to me. At the time of this manifestation, I saw that I had treasures of erudition and knowledge within me that I did not know I had. After writing, I would not remember anything at all of what I had written, and neither forms nor images were left in me. I could not have used what I had written to help other souls, but when that moment came, Our Lord gave me what I would say to them and all that was necessary for them, without my trying at all.[19]

First she "writes down" the Scripture, in the sense that, verse by verse, she copies it. And then this copying act, performed by someone who is "nothing," shows that this "nothing" is abundantly fertile, and continues writing by commenting on what has been copied. In this activity, Guyon herself is but a witness: she sees herself writing, or more exactly: she sees a hand and a pen writing, and the question to whom this hand and this pen belong has lost all importance. The act of writing is in complete union with what is written: it is the Guyonian version of the *unio mystica*. This is the consequence of the state of "permanent prayer" she is in.

In this chapter of her autobiography, Guyon continues to explain the circumstances of her mystical writing. She had only the Bible and no other book to consult; she was sick and had no time to write except at night ("I only slept one or two hours every night, and along with that I had a fever nearly every day").[20] And, what is more, God was doing everything to make her lose her concentration (read: to prohibit her to be herself the agent of her writing).

> You made me write with such purity that it was necessary for me to stop and start again. . . . When I was writing during the day, I was consistently interrupted, and I often left my words half written, and You would give me what You wanted immediately afterward. What I wrote was not at all in my head, such that I had a head so free that it was in a complete void. I was so disengaged from what I was writing that it was like a stranger to me. It took me one moment of reflection to be punished; I was punished, my writing slowed down immediately, and I remained like an idiot until I was inspired from above. The least joy from the graces that You accorded me was very rigorously punished. All my faults that are in my writings come from . . . not being used to God's operation.[21]

Is there suffering in Madame Guyon's "automatic writing"? Absolutely. In chapter XI of the same second part, she describes one of the first moments in her life when "there was such a strong movement in my writing that I could not resist. . . . It was a simple instinct, with a full-ness that I could not bear. I was like those mothers who are too full of milk, who suffer a lot."[22] Why does she suffer? Because she is "too full of milk," though having no milk herself and not even having the right to have it herself. She has an instinctual ambition to write and at the same time she knows that she has nothing to write because she has nothing to say: "I do not know, I do not want anything, and I have no idea, and I would even think it very unfaithful to give myself one, or to think for a moment about what I could write."[23] And does the *grace* that makes her write anyway deliver her from this suffering? Not at all. This "automatic writing," deprived of its instinctual ease and replaced by an obligation on the part of God, is experienced only as a "test," a "trial." A few lines later in the passage quoted from chapter XXI, she writes, addressing God:

> Did You not take a hundred different forms for me in order to see if I was yours without reserve in every trial, and if I still had some little interest in myself? You always found this soul flexible and pliable to your desires. What have You not made me suffer? Into what humiliation have You not thrown me to counterbalance your graces? To what, my God, have You not delivered me, and through what painful straits have You not made me pass? . . . But I had no pain at all from what You did to me. I saw with pleasure and compliance, not taking any more interest in myself than in a dead dog, I truly saw your divine games with compliance. You raised me to the sky and right away threw me in the mud, then with the same hand, You picked me up from where You had thrown me. I saw that I was the game played by your love and by your will, the victim of your divine justice; and it was all the same to me. It seems to me, oh my God, that You treat your dearest friends as the sea treats its waves.[24]

We have read how Guyon opposes the idea of "holy indifference." What she writes here, however, does not really illustrate this opposition. On the contrary, it is rather difficult not to interpret this "compliance" in the terrible "trials" imposed by God as an indifference on the part of Guyon. Of course, she does not use the word. She uses words that express nonindifference: the feeling of "compliance," or, expressed negatively, not having "pain at all from what You did to me."

In any case, she does not conclude that being the "wave" constantly broken by the sea-which-is-God puts her in a position where it is her will that is the ultimate basis of her love for God. As is the case with Fénelon. Guyon coincides with a "compliance" without will and, therefore, without subject. She is but a broken "wave" or, more exactly,

she coincides with the very breaking of that wave: the nothingness that
is the real substance of this fragile and ephemeral phenomenon that is
a breaking "wave."

Here, we touch the importance of writing—both as a metaphor
and as an act—in Madame Guyon's mystical thought. To express the
"nothingness" that she is and affirms to be in her *pure love* for God,
she seeks metaphors that all end up being more or less invalid. What
most aptly expresses this "nothingness" is the act of expressing as such,
that is to say, an act of expression showing that, in full act, it fails in
expressing the "nothingness" it intends to express—which, precisely,
is its most adequate expression. Hence, the endless—because endlessly
repeated—writing of Guyon. It is a writing that functions on the basis
of its very failure, of its "stopping." As soon as she realizes that she is
the one writing, she stops writing and at the same time starts again to
leave the act of her writing to this "nothingness," realizing that it is
only "nothing" that expresses itself in the text, which, despite herself,
is signed with her proper name.

Nothing That Liberates

In Madame Guyon's texts, "nothingness" (the annihilation of the "I") is
both object and subject. This is her *formal* way of effectively articulating
this "nothingness." But what does this "nothingness" imply *in substance*?
What is it to live as "nothingness" that addresses God in *pure love*?

Let us return to *Les torrents*, the text in the middle of which Guyon
ceased writing, realizing that she had been too much the author of her
writing. In the lines immediately following our last quote from this
text, she writes that she "forgot" something. With what she "forgot,"
she will fill dozens of new pages—that is to say, the second half of the
little book. What had she forgotten? Nothing, in fact, as we will see,
because what she discusses in the following pages is not really new. She
talks about the same state she explained just before the break in her
writing process, that is to say, about the last step on the mystical path:
the step in which mystical desire has reached its goal and the soul feels
herself absorbed in God.

In the following lines, she approaches this theme by analyzing
the state in which humans will find themselves after having risen from
the dead. This state is heavenly. Surely it will be so in heaven. But is

this state possible under earthly conditions as well? When, for instance, the mystic experiences the grace of being lost in God? To explain this, Guyon takes as many pages as she has written so far.

This celestial state of "the risen," experienced under earthly conditions, is that of "freedom." Immediately after the passage quoted, we read: "I forgot to say that this is where real freedom is given: not a freedom, as some imagine, that deprives or exempts from doing things. . . . The freedom of which I speak is not of this nature: it facilitated all things which are in the order of God and of his state."[25] This freedom, she continues, characterizes the state of "a resurrected man," which according to her is equal to the state in which someone in "perpetual prayer" is. That "resurrected" state is not beyond life, but is to be situated within the fullness of life:

> The actions of a risen man are actions of life; if the soul after the resurrection remains lifeless, I say that it is dead or buried, but not risen. To be resurrected, the soul must do the same actions as she did before all her losses, and without any difficulty; but now she does them in God. Did not Lazarus, after his resurrection, perform all the functions of life as before? And Jesus Christ, after his resurrection, even wanted to eat and converse with people. This is an example. Also of those who believe in God and are impeded, who cannot pray, I say also that they are not risen.[26]

To support her arguments, Guyon refers to Job. He too experienced the phenomenon of "loss" in all its intensity: God deprived him of everything. He made it all "rot."[27] But none other than God gave him everything back. And what He gave back was life, a life similar to the one he had had before. Guyon continues:

> It is the same after the resurrection: everything is given back, with an admirable ease of making use of it without getting soiled, without getting attached to it, without appropriating it as in the past. We do everything in God, in a divine way, using things as if we were not using them. And that is where true freedom and true life are: If you have been similar to Jesus Christ in his death, you will also be similar to Him in his resurrection.[28] Are you free when you have inabilities,

restrictions? No. If the Son sets you free, you will be truly free,[29] but in his freedom.[30]

What Guyon describes as the final phase of spiritual life is not a moment of ecstasy; it is not the limit-experience in which during an instant the mystic feels united with God. The goal of spiritual life is a "state" in which one finds oneself for a whole period—or even forever. It is the state of "risen men," of those who died with Christ and who are—and remain—risen with Him. This state is not ecstatic in the sense that it is not different from an ordinary state: life just goes on, even the life of the mystic. Of course he is "in God," but he keeps on praying to Him just as before. What has changed is the state in which—or, more precisely, the point from which—he does so. What he does now, he does in complete freedom.

What, then, is freedom? It is not just doing what you prefer to do. Freedom breaks all attachment and radically detaches. Then, you do what you do, but the reason why you do it is free from any constraint, any need or necessity, any causal logic. You do something, not because you need it, but precisely because you do *not*. You use things as if you do not use them, as if you do not live on them. In other words, you have detached yourself from all things around you; if you make use of them, it is to show that you are no longer attached to them.

You do what you do, but there is no longer an "I" who does it. You do what you do, being detached from yourself. You are liberated even from your "self." You are free because you have become "NOTHING," because there is no longer any kind of "self" to intervene in what you do. In other words, you now live by the only sovereign freedom which is God's.

Like *love* (*agape*), *freedom* (*eleutheria*) is one of the basic ideas of Christianity.[31] As mentioned in the first chapter, Christians live in *agape* and, therefore, are "free" from the old Mosaic Law.[32] And since Christ had conquered sin and death, they are even free from the laws of mortality and finitude. At least *in principle*. The *real* liberation of sin and finitude will only take place at the end of times, when Christ will return to render the Last Judgment. In the meantime, Christians can only *testify* to that "freedom" to come.

The *agape*-communities of the early Christians were the first form of such a testimony. Soon, it were the "martyrs" who, in the midst of the apotheosis of finitude—the Roman circuses and their public cruelties—bore witness to a Life freed from finitude, mortality, and sin. After the fall of the Roman Empire, Christianity fulfilled the role of this testimony by establishing centers of evangelical life: the abbeys. At the beginning of the modern era, with the decline of Christian cultural hegemony, this testimony of Christian freedom became more and more the responsibility of the private individual. It was in the interior of his soul that the Christian found the messianic state where one is free from sin, death, and finitude. The mystical experience became the place par excellence to live this. The intimacy of each person's love for God became the most proper place where such radical "freedom" could be experienced: a freedom unchained from all that is finite, including the human ego.

This, then, is why that kind of love required the becoming "NOTHING" of the soul. It is "NOTHING" that can testify perfectly to God. As Guyon says, it is only as "NOTHING" that one can love God *purely*.

Nothingness as Place

By affirming that "NOTHING" conditions the radicality of Christian "freedom," Guyon touches on an idea that has always been rejected by Christian doctrine, but which, logically, nonetheless goes in the direction of the Christian idea of God as established in all rigor in Guyon's line of reasoning. If one lives in true freedom, that is to say, absorbed by the freedom of God, one is detached from all that exists, including evil. A few pages farther than the last quoted passage in *Les torrents*, we read:

> [T]his soul participates in the purity of God; or rather: any self-purity [*pureté propre*] . . . having been destroyed, only the purity of God in Himself subsists in this nothingness, but in a way so real that the soul is completely ignorant of evil and powerless to commit it. This does not prevent that we can always fall, but that hardly happens here because of the deep annihilation in which the soul is deprived of any selfhood [*où est l'âme qui ne lui laisse aucune propriété*]; and only selfhood [*et la seule propriété*] can cause sin; so what no longer exists, cannot sin.[33]

"What no longer exists, cannot sin." Being in state of perfection (as is Guyon) delivers us from sins, even from the possibility of committing them. Even if we actually commit sins. In the fifth century, Shenoute, one of the Egyptian Desert Fathers, once said: "There are no crimes for those who have Christ." It is not without reason that Michael Gaddis took this sentence as the title for his book on "religious violence in the Christian Roman Empire."[34] Whoever considers himself released from sin easily considers himself above it, and therefore allows himself to commit sins. Christianity has never approved of this attitude, but the history of violence committed by Christians in the fourth and fifth centuries throughout the Roman Empire shows that it was widespread at the time. And it has not been completely absent either in the subsequent history of Christianity.

Guyon does not go so far as to justify sin, certainly not. But one can understand that passages like the one just quoted aroused suspicion on the part of Bossuet and other ecclesiastical authorities. And even if Guyon does not justify sin, she nonetheless problematizes the confessional practice for "souls" who live as "risen" in "pure love" for God. Directly after the passage quoted, she writes:

> And this is so true that the souls I am talking about have much trouble when going to confession because, when they want to accuse themselves, they do not know what to accuse . . . being unable to find anything in them alive, [anything] that may have wanted to offend God, since their will is completely lost in God. And since God cannot want sin, neither can they want it. If they are told to confess, they do it because they are very submissive, but they say with their mouths what they are made to say, like a little child to whom one would say: "You must confess this"; he says it without knowing what he says, without knowing whether it is true or is not, without reproach or remorse. For, here, the soul is no longer to be aware of it, and everything about her is so lost in God that there is no longer an accuser in her: she remains happy, without seeking to be. But when we say to her: "You made this mistake," she finds nothing in her that made it; and if we say, "Say you did it," she will say it with the lips, without pain or repentance.[35]

Contrary to what Shenoute says, for Guyon, the one who lives in Christ—the "risen one"—would confess the sins of which he is accused, but he would only do it "with the lips" and would not be "aware of it."

Christian freedom, in its perfect state, is delivered from all "aware-ness" and "conscience." And, paradoxically, it is also delivered from the pretension of being above or beyond all conscience. It is neither touched nor touchable by sin, albeit without changing the behavior of the one who is in this state. Such a one acts as if he is guided by his conscience; he confesses when asked, without doing it consciously, without knowing what he is saying. We recognize the way in which Guyon writes her spiritual texts. Like her writing, such confession is without "I." It is a confession of "NOTHING," by "NOTHING": a "nothing" that is both subject and object.

This "NOTHING" can only be approached and defined as a place. It is the locus where the difference takes place between the world of sin and that of the deliverance from all sin, between the terrestrial life marked by finitude and the Eternal Life, between the mortal state and the risen state. It is an active place: the locus of an activity produced by someone's being without "I" and actively occupying this place as an absolute "NOTHING," a nothing not even attached to itself, to its own nullity, and therefore ready to confess sins that it never committed and of which it is not conscious.

That "NOTHING" operates under the condition of the "as if." It is the "as if" of a risen man who, in the world of mortals, acts as if he is not, and who, conversely, for those who would already hold him to be in the world of immortals, continues to live as a mortal. In the world of sin, death, and finitude, he pretends to be sinful, mortal, and finite. The "as if" mode is the only possible way of being perfect and of carrying out the witness that is the main mission of Christian life, that is to say, to bear witness, in full human condition, to Eternal Life, which is the true condition of man and of God's entire creation.

The most existential form of freedom for this holy "as if" is that of suffering. Suffering shows the reality and the truth of the "as if." Those who live as "risen" live in God, that is, in absolute peace. But how does this peace show itself? In full suffering—a suffering that one experiences *as if* one is suffering. The "peace" of the "risen ones," we read in the sentences that follow,

> is so invariable and unalterable that nothing in the world or in all of hell can alter it for a moment. The senses are always susceptible to suffering; and when a person is overwhelmed and cries like a child, if one asks her, and she searches in herself, she will find nothing in herself that is suffering: in

the midst of inconceivable pains, she says: "I do not suffer anything," without being able to say or admit that she suffers, because of the divine state and the bliss that she carries.[36]

It is only as if such persons are suffering. In reality, "NOTHING" suffers. Or, more accurately, those "saints" who suffer stand, precisely by the practice of suffering, in the midst of "NOTHING," in the abyss of nothingness. What is crucial, here, is that this nothingness is only possible thanks to an "abyss," thanks to the contours of a chasm in which the "NOTHING" can be given a place. Only its contours make the abyss possible. And so does the suffering to the holy nothingness. It is the suffering that, for the "risen one" living under earthly condition, makes possible the holy "as if"; it provides the "as if" with its reality, with its truth. Only thanks to suffering, the "risen one" can live as if he does not suffer, as if he is no longer subjected to the mortal condition and is already enjoying Eternal Life. Having only the "as if" to live his "peace" and his "resurrection," this "as if" cannot stand without the raw reality of suffering.

Nothing Writes

With Guyon, writing fulfills a role similar to that of suffering in the earthly life of the "risen." Guyon acts *as if* she is the one who writes, and this can only be experienced in scribal suffering. From time to time she explicitly realizes this, and at these moments she admits that, from her perspective, an absence, an abyss, a nothingness must be the agent of her act of writing. Although it is obvious to her that at the locus of this nothingness, God is doing the job; she above all has to keep this locus empty. That locus is not with God in the sky, but here on earth. It is down here that God must be prepared a place, a place that is none other than the place where we humans are. *Our* place must be emptied and left entirely to God. Without us to occupy it, this place has no substance, but we must empty it to return it to our true substance, which is God. This is why emptying this place requires an act, the only true act that man is capable of—an interminable act of self-effacing that coincides with the truth of his act of living.

Here, we touch on the beating heart of Guyon's writing. She writes from her own absence, but it is only through her writing that she can give a place to this absence. It is only by the "torrent" of her writing that she is able to make this writing empty and show that it is God who writes through the pen her hand is holding.

An absence that makes you write; an absence which at the same time needs writing to be the absence that it is. To the French literary critic Maurice Blanchot, this is exactly the kind of experience that is at the origin of modern literature. Time and space are lacking here to explore this Blanchotian thesis in light of the literary texts of the twentieth century.[37] Let us simply refer to the opening chapter of Blanchot's *The Space of Literature* (*L'espace littéraire*, 1955), in which he extensively develops this theme—a theme that permeates his entire work.

In this introductory chapter, Blanchot puts forward the idea of an "essential solitude" (the title of the chapter) that he believes characterizes modern literary works. This solitude, he explains, is not "existential," but "essential," which for Blanchot means that the author is *structurally* alone vis-à-vis his own work. It is *his* work, of course, but that work inevitably puts its author on leave. "He who writes the work is set aside; he who has written it is dismissed," Blanchot writes.[38]

The author was "fired" (*congédié*) from the very start, he adds. This is precisely the cause of his work: being at the origin of the work, he nonetheless was never there. His work is only the "substitute" of his impossible presence. Blanchot applies this thesis to the writing—as simple as it is basic—of the word "to be," or more precisely "it is."

> The writer writes a book, but the book is not yet the work. There is a work only when, through it, and with the violence of a beginning which is proper to it, the word *being* is pronounced. This event occurs when the work becomes the intimacy between someone who writes it and someone who reads it. One might, then, wonder: if solitude is the writer's risk, does it not express the fact that he is turned, oriented toward the open violence of the work, of which he never grasps anything but the substitute—the approach and the illusion in the form of the book?[39]

The origin of the work, the moment when a work changes from "non-being" into "being": this is where the author has a decisive role, but as absentee in this moment of origin. This is what makes him alone, "essentially."[40] This is also why the author can but assume that his work is not yet finished and that he must continue to work on it; which will force him to work on it endlessly. Blanchot continues:

> The writer belongs to the work, but what belongs to him is only a book, a mute collection of sterile words, the most insignificant thing in the world. The writer who experiences this void believes only that the work is unfinished, and he thinks that a little more effort, along with some propitious moments, will permit him and him alone to finish it. So he goes back to work. But what he wants to finish by himself remains interminable; it involves him in an illusory task. And the work, finally, knows him not. It closes in around his absence as the impersonal, anonymous affirmation that it is—and nothing more.[41]

The work of literary writing fails on principle. It lives from its failure, from its powerlessness to be present at its inaugural act, and from its desire to be there. To be present at what? At the origin of saying something; the origin of the act that says, "This is it"; the origin that links language to the world, words to things. This connection assumes a distance between two realities that are not evidently linked—two realities that are basically separated from each other. And these two are, precisely, words and things, language and the world. What makes people talk, what is the origin of saying "This is that," is the absence of a connection between this and that, between the word and the thing. The intention to touch this origin is the intention to touch the word or language as such, the intention to touch the being of language, that is to say, of language as it is without connection with things.

Here is the emptiness of language encountered by the writer: emptiness, not as the absence of words, but as an endless stream of words all empty in the sense that they say nothing, that they have no connection with things and nevertheless speak, *only* speak—an endless stream of words that "are"; words that show, in a sovereign manner, only their "being there," their mere existence. What speaks through literature is speaking as such, words in their sovereign power to be—not being grounded in their meaning, that is to say, in their connection with things. A language that whispers, endlessly, regardless of what the words say, regardless of who has them on his lips or makes them flow from his pen. Language in its "impersonal, anonymous affirmation," as the quote says. Literature is by definition a language without "I":

> To write is to break the bond that unites the word with myself. . . . To write is to break this bond. To write is, moreover, to withdraw language from the world, to detach it from what makes it a power according to which, when I speak, it is the world that declares itself. . . . Where he [the writer] is, only being speaks—which means that language doesn't speak any more, but is. It devotes itself to the pure passivity of being. If to write is to surrender to the interminable, the writer who consents to sustain writing's essence loses the power to say "I."[42]

Writing without "I" and without knowing what is being written: this is, as we have seen, the condition of writing in Madame Guyon's spiritual oeuvre. With her, all the paradoxes that this writing implies lead to God. Through the absence of Guyon's "I," her writing writes down what God tells her. Rather than being the solution to all of these paradoxes, God above all provides a context allowing Guyon to develop and formulate them in an accurate way.

In Blanchot, we read nowhere that it is God who organizes the paradoxes of writing. For him, God would just be an imagined, literary idea. But in his view, the effects of this imagination do not differ very much formally from what Guyon describes as effects of God. For Blanchot, too, it is not the "I" that writes. What is written cannot be traced back to an instance of self-awareness or self-control.

In Blanchot's eyes, it is not God, but the imagination that writes: an imagination that does not have its source in the inventiveness of the subject, but in the "image character" of language. Language is "image" before being the image *of* something, and it is this "pure being" of language that speaks and writes in literary texts.

In Guyonian spirituality, it is God who takes up the pen; in literary writing as Blanchot conceives it, it is the imaginary (in the "materialist" sense of the term: the "mere being" of the image). This is not the place to explore this parallel further, either in Blanchot's work or in modern literature in general, but it is clear that in both cases it is "nothing" that writes.

And this writing by "nothing" invades the existential being of humans, even their "pain of being," their "pain of existence." There is, to cite just one example, this famous poem by Fernando Pessoa, "Auto-psychography," the first verse of which says:

> The poet is a faker
> Who's so good at his act
> He even fakes the pain
> Of pain he feels in fact.[43]

To compare the way in which Guyon experiences suffering as "not living" it, with the way in which the suffering imagined in this poem is experienced "as real," would require a new essay. But by now, it is at least clear that the formal dispositives of modern literature can be found in seventeenth-century spiritual writings, as evidenced by Madame Guyon's texts.

The Mystical (of the) Self

5

The Power to say I

On Simone Weil

. . . there is not enough *I* in us to love,
to abandon the I by means of love.

[. . . *il n'y aurait pas assez de je en nous pour aimer,*
pour abandoner le je par amour.]

—Simone Weil, Œuvres complètes VI/3

What is at stake in Simone Weil's shift to Christianity? Is it only the story of a modern agnostic intellectual who discovers and reinvents the old religious tradition? What if, under the surface of that move, modernity itself is at stake just as much? What if Weil's mystical thought conceals a profound reflection on the modern subject? It is true, in line with almost the entire premodern and modern mystical tradition, her thought is a full-blown attack against the Cartesian ego and its pretention to be the solid and free basis of our modern relation to reality. And yet, what if the most interesting aspect of Weil's thought is that she *fails* in that attack, and that, despite all her efforts to destroy the modern subject, that subject resists even in the very heart of both the mystical truth she describes and her theoretical thought about that truth. What if Weil's move to Christianity does not say as much about Christianity, or about the Christian side of modernity, as it does about the abysmal basis of modernity's subject?

In this chapter, I focus on Weil's first posthumous publication, *Gravity and Grace*, an anthology of her reflections written down in the notebooks that she left in France when, in 1942, she left for America in order—being Jewish—to escape Nazi Europe. I will start with an interpretation of some of her notes on the "I" (*le moi*) in *Gravity and Grace*. Some main points of her general theory must be understood in order to comprehend the paradoxes that characterize the "I" in her mystical thought. Only then will it be possible to understand the critical potential of her oeuvre with respect to modernity and its problematic subject.

Nothing but the I

Modernity can be defined as the age of the I.[1] As explained in chapter 2, the modern subject supposes itself to be free *from* the world, *disconnected* from it. It believes that, on this free basis, it relates to the world as to an infinite set of "objects," as to the *res extensa* (Descartes), as to the "mechanical" universe, the world of modern Newtonian physics. Everything has become "objective," except us, that is to say, the "things" thinking this. God, too, has become "object." Functioning as "subject" in the Middle Ages, at the dawn of modernity God changed position and became "object": object of doubt and object of faith. The *subject* of faith as well as of science and of any other relation to reality is henceforth man himself. The ego, the I: this is the subject, that is, the "first certainty," the solid ground upon which man's relation to reality is based.[2]

Weil's thought, as expressed, for instance, in the notes gathered in *Gravity and Grace*, put forward a world that, at first sight, is not quite modern in the sense outlined here. Weil's world is dominated by "gravity" or, which amounts to the same thing, by "necessity," that is, by laws independent from any human influence and to which humans are profoundly subjected.[3] If there is a kind of freedom with regard to the dominance of "gravity" and "necessity," it is located, not in the human subject, but in God and his "Grace"—both being mainly present by means of radical absence. Thus, the paradox that is central to *Gravity and Grace* as well as to all of Simone Weil's writings: though seemingly its antipode, the necessity that rules the world *is* its freedom. The ruling necessity *is* a gift of Grace. Once someone is open to Grace, he lives necessity as given by Grace. So, if Weil discovers traces of Grace and God in our world, it is only as persistent absences. Moreover, as is explained farther on, her desire for God will therefore coincide with a desire to disappear—more exactly: to disappear as desiring I, as longing subject, as ego.

And yet, the ego, in its modern shape, is not simply absent in Weil's thought. In *Gravity and Grace*, and certainly in the chapter entitled "Le moi [The I]," the reader can easily discover clear traces of Cartesian modernity. Despite her intention to ascribe the totality of all that is to God, she clearly states that this does not go for the human subject, for man's "power to say 'I.'" "We possess nothing in the world—a mere chance can strip us of everything—except the power to say 'I.' That is what we have to give to God—in other words, to destroy. There is absolutely no other free act which it is given us to accomplish—only the destruction of the 'I.'"[4]

We are right in the middle of a typically Weilian reflection on the "divine" core of the human condition—a reflection that is known for the radicalism with which God is put in the first place, since, to her, He is in fact the only reality of all that is. God is everything and, therefore, the owner of all that is, so she believes. And yet, there is something that escapes God's ownership: the human "power to say 'I.'" That power and the I that are at stake in this saying are not God's property. So, if there is anything man can give to God that is not already God's own property, it is his I. In this case, to *give* means to *destroy*. Only by doing so can God be acknowledged in his quality of owner of everything. Whatever that may mean, it is clear that the power to say "I" is only man's property.

Can we not recognize a "Cartesian" movement underlying Weil's thought here? Of course, Weil's thinking seems to go in a direction opposite to Descartes's argument: it does not lead to the sovereignty of the human ego, but to that of God. God, being the sovereign of all that is, cannot avoid that the I has sovereign power over itself. At least it can *say* it has; at least that saying is beyond God's omnipotence. In this sense, one can state that Weil's thought puts the human subject in a Cartesian position, in principle escaping God's power. "Nothing in the world can rob us of the power to say 'I.'"

Really? Is that power so strong, so sovereign? Another note on the same page in *Gravity and Grace* nonetheless mentions an exception:

Nothing in the world can rob us of the power to say "I."[5] Nothing except extreme affliction. Nothing is worse than extreme affliction which destroys the "I" from outside, because after that we can no longer destroy it ourselves. What happens to those whose "I" has been destroyed from outside by affliction? It is not possible to imagine anything for them but annihilation according to the atheistic or materialistic conception.

Though they may have lost their "I," it does not mean that they have no more egoism. Quite the reverse. To be sure, this may occasionally happen when a dog-like devotion is brought about, but at other times the being is reduced to naked, vegetative egoism. An egoism without an "I."[6]

The "I" is not so strong and sovereign that it cannot be overthrown "from outside." The "I," which is to say the capacity for resistance by a power to say "I," can be annihilated by an "atheistic and materialistic conception." What Weil has in mind is modern science denying the existence of a proper "I" or "subject," on the supposition that all functions commonly ascribed to it can be reduced to bodily reactions. In addition, sadder than materialistic sciences as such, is the way they are applied in the social and political domain and, there, are able to support the cruelties of totalitarian regimes. A human being can truly be reduced to "dog-like devotion," unable to express the slightest kind of resistance. This is not to say that such a victim of totalitarianism has no ego and, consequently, no egoism at all. Its ego and egoism are reduced to a vegetative level, to an "egoism without ego," to a mere reflex of survival. Resistance is definitely beyond reach here.[7]

Moreover, so is the capacity to give up any resistance voluntarily and freely. For this is what Weil's argument is about here. She is looking for something we, as humans, can give to God that is not owned by Him beforehand. As we know already, there is only one thing eligible for that: our "power to say 'I.'" In another note on the same first page of the chapter "The Self [Le moi]" in Gravity and Grace, between the two notes already cited, we read:

> Offering: We cannot offer anything but the "I," and all we call an offering is merely a label attached to a compensatory assertion of the "I."[8]

The I is the only thing we can offer to God. As we already know, here offering equals destroying. The I must be destroyed for God's sake. However, it is not the destruction as such that counts, but the fact that it is I who destroys the I that I am. This is why we have to prevent my I from being destroyed "from outside." It must be destroyed "from within." The I must be destroyed by the I: this is what God deserves, what is at the level of his sovereignty. The note cited before the last one ends as follows:

> So long as we ourselves have begun the process of destroying the "I," we can prevent any affliction from causing harm. For the "I" is not destroyed by external pressure without a violent revolt. If for the love of God we refuse to give ourselves over to this revolt, the destruction does not take place from outside but from within.[9]

What a strange situation the "I" is in! It must protect itself from being destroyed "from outside." For what purpose? To be able to destroy itself "from within." What is the purpose of this self-destruction? To protect it against the harm threatening it. Or, as Weil writes: "to prevent any affliction from causing harm."

Here we face a central knot in the paradoxical texture of Weil's thought that in fact requires an extensive explanation of her entire "system" (or, as some say, "lack of system"). Though space is lacking here to develop the entire philosophical and theological theory that is behind Weil's notes, some main points can briefly be clarified.

Religion for Slaves

Simone Weil had herself lived situations in which the "I" was on the verge of being destroyed "from outside." In a letter to Father Perrin (included in *Waiting for God* under the title "Spiritual Autobiography"), she describes such an experience. She refers to the period[10] when she had left the comfort of her teaching position at the *Lycée* of Roanne in order to share the life of factory workers in the industry. That experience of "affliction," so she declares, is one of the three "contacts with Catholicism that really counted."[11] Confronted with the sufferings caused by the industrial labor condition, she writes:

> That contact with affliction [*douleur*] had killed my youth. Until then I had not had any experience of affliction. . . . I knew quite well that there was a great deal of affliction in

the world, I was obsessed with the idea, but I had not had prolonged and first-hand experience of it. As I worked in the factory, indistinguishable to all eyes, including my own, from the anonymous mass, the affliction of others entered into my flesh and my soul. Nothing separated me from it, for I had really forgotten my past and I looked forward to no future, finding it difficult to imagine the possibility of surviving all the fatigue. . . . There I received forever the mark of a slave, like the branding of the red-hot iron the Romans put on the foreheads of their most despised slaves. Since then I have always regarded myself as a slave.[12]

She does not write that her "I" really was destroyed, but the risk that such could happen was definitely there. What is more, in Weil's view, this risk is always there. It hallmarks our human condition. That is why experiences of "affliction" do not incite her to avoid them or to look for "nonafflicted" situations. According to Weil, we are *always* in an afflicted condition. Why? Because we live under the regime of "necessity," of "gravity." That is what she means when she declares herself to be a slave, and slavery to be our common condition. In another text in *Waiting for God*, entitled "The Love of God and Affliction," she writes:

As for us, we are nailed down to the spot, only free to choose which way we look [*libres seulement de nos regards*], ruled by necessity. A blind mechanism, heedless of degrees of spiritual perfection, continually tosses men. . . . If the mechanism were not blind, there would not be any affliction. Affliction is anonymous before all things; it deprives its victims of their personality and makes them into things. It is indifferent; and it is the coldness of this indifference—a metallic coldness—that freezes all those it touches right to the depths of their souls. They will never find warmth again. They will never believe any more that they are anyone.[13]

The note is on affliction in general, but she talks about herself as well: about her terrible headaches, for instance, that never left her and got worse the older she became. Moreover, she talks about the outside world full of affliction: about society under the pressure of social conflicts

and wars that "afflict" our culture in crisis. There is a blind and fatal
necessity to all of this. As such, we cannot really change it, since even
our actions against it are ruled by the very necessity they are fighting.
If there is freedom in all of this, it is the freedom "to choose which
way we look." We are *libres seulement de nos regards.* This *"regard,"*
this "gaze," is the only means by which, in the realm of "gravity," one
can experience "grace."

This "gaze" is the basis of Weil's Christianity. It is, however,
not what made her convert to this religion. What she discovered in
Christianity is, rather, the conversion that is in the gaze itself. The
gaze itself has a capacity to produce a change, not in what it looks at,
but in the act of looking itself.[14] It is what happens in the gaze of the
amor fati, as practiced by antique stoic philosophers as well as by Weil
herself before her turn to Christianity. Confronted with a world that
goes its own way, ruled by laws of strict necessity and showing radical
indifference to our individual aspirations and sufferings, we must realize
we are excluded from it—so Weil argues. Whatever we think, feel, or
want, none of our acts will have impact whatsoever on a world that
goes its way in radical indifference, in metallically cold necessity. Yet
our gaze upon the world still has the capacity to protest against this
"metallic coldness" or, since that is senseless, to approve and to love it.
With iron certainty, we are able to acknowledge that. There is absolutely
no place in this world for us as independent and free persons, except
by fully accepting and loving it.

Redemptive Suffering

Weil lived her life that way. It is what, as a student of Alain, she already
adored in Homer's *Iliad*;[15] it is what she learned from Greek stoicism; and
it is what she discovered in Christianity. She did not so much convert to
Christianity; she rather discovered the *conversional* power of the human
gaze as practiced in Christian religion. This is how we should read the
well-known passage in *Waiting for God* that describes the "second" of
her "important contacts" with Catholicism. It reports an experience
during the Portuguese journey she made with her parents a few weeks
after the terrible time she had as a worker at the assembly line in the
Renault factory near Paris.

In this state of mind then, and in a wretched condition physically, I entered the little Portuguese village, which, alas, was very wretched too, on the very day of the festival of its patron saint. I was alone. It was the evening and there was a full moon over the sea. The wives of the fishermen were, in procession, making a tour of all the ships, carrying candles and singing what must certainly be very ancient hymns of a heart-rending sadness. Nothing can give any idea of it. I have never heard anything so poignant unless it were the song of the boatmen on the Volga. There the conviction was suddenly borne in upon me that Christianity is pre-eminently the religion of slaves, that slaves cannot help belonging to it, and I among others.[16]

Weil's Christianity is not that of salvation, of delivering the "slaves" we are from the chains of pain, sin, and finitude. According to her, we are and will forever remain slaves and, in that sense, we will never stop living lives full of affliction under the "gravitational" laws of necessity. Of course, we are looking for the opposite, for grace, freedom, and light. This, too, is our condition. It is so in an even more basic way, for it is the desire for grace, freedom, and light that keeps us alive. In essence, our life is to be defined as a desire for God. This is what Christianity teaches and why it is a religion that "slaves" need. Subjected to the afflicted condition of gravity and necessity, they need an orientation toward grace and light, that is, toward God. Yet, Weil argues, God is to be found not *beyond* the pains of affliction, but *through*—and even *in*—them. We are slaves, and only through—and in—the affliction of our slavery we can find God. So we read in the third of the "three important contacts with Catholicism" she sums up in her "Spiritual Autobiography":

In 1938, I spent ten days at Solesmes, from Palm Sunday to Easter Tuesday, following all the liturgical services. I was suffering from splitting headaches; each sound hurt me like a blow; by an extreme effort of concentration I was able to rise above this wretched flesh, to leave it to suffer by itself, heaped up in a corner, and to find a pure and perfect joy in the unimaginable beauty of the chanting and the words. This experience enabled me by analogy to get a better understanding of the possibility of loving divine love in the midst of affliction. It goes without saying that in the course of these services the thought of the Passion of Christ entered into my being once and for all.[17]

During her mystical experience in Solesmes, Christ's passion "entered" into Weil's "being." And *only* his passion. If, according to Weil, there is something redemptive in Christ, it is not the fact that He redeemed us from suffering and evil; it is suffering itself, evil itself, which is redemptive.[18]

Christ suffered, not simply from being tortured to death, but also from being abandoned by God. "Why hast Thou forsaken me": again and again this phrase reappears in Weil's notebooks.[19] What Weil admires in Christ is that, in this most Godforsaken moment ever that was his dying on the cross, there was absolutely no consolation. This is why she, a slave like everyone else, loves Christ: his divine suffering was without the slightest consolation, and to us, mortals in misery, his divine suffering does not give any consolation either. Christ does not deliver us from suffering. He rather shows us what it means that suffering itself delivers, renders free. Free from what? Not from suffering as such, but from its subject, from the "I" that suffers. This is at least the case with the one who has reached the level of spiritual perfection and who has succeeded in destroying his I "from within." Such a "destroyed" I lives the suffering it bears as redemptive. Christ suffers, suffers from affliction, suffers from the absence of consolation, and suffers from God's absence. And yet, he can bear that unbearable suffering because he has destroyed its "bearer," its subject.

His "I" is not destroyed "from outside," but "from within." It is in that sense—and solely in that sense—that, according to Weil, his suffering is redemptive. The fourth reflection that follows the first three that I have quoted from the chapter "The Self" in *Gravity and Grace* starts as follows:

> Redemptive suffering. If a human being who is in a state of perfection and has through grace completely destroyed the "I" in himself, falls into that degree of affliction which corresponds for him to the destruction of the "I" from outside—we have there the cross in its fullness. Affliction can no longer destroy the "I" in him for the "I" in him no longer exists, having completely disappeared and left the place to God. But affliction produces an effect which is equivalent, on the plane of

perfection, to the exterior destruction of the "I." It produces
the absence of God. "My God, why hast Thou forsaken me?"[20]

What is left when, in a state of affliction, the I is destroyed "from
within"? Nothing but affliction—affliction similar to the one caused by
a destruction of the I "from outside," affliction in the broad sense of
the word, which according to Weil also includes evil. What is left after
the I has been destroyed and perfection has been reached, is a universe
of pain and evil—a universe where God is terribly absent. A few lines
farther on, we read:

> Redemptive suffering is that by which evil really has fullness
> of being to the utmost extent of its capacity. By redemptive
> suffering, God is present in extreme evil. For the absence
> of God is the mode of divine presence which corresponds
> to evil—absence which is felt. He who has not God within
> himself cannot feel his absence.[21]

The I is destroyed "from inside," and what is left is a universe of pain
and affliction, where God is completely absent and where that absence
takes the shape of evil's dominion. However, according to Weil, *this* is
redemptive; it is the real way of God's presence.[22]

Weil's thesis is as strong as it is strange: this is the least one can
say. What does she try to say here? Why are suffering and (even) evil
by themselves redemptive? Answer: because they bring me back to
what I am, and this is nothing. Confronted with extreme suffering and
facing evil that destroys me, since I am destroyed from within, I finally
realize I am no longer that which is in between God and his creature.
I realize that, having become nothing, I have stopped disturbing that
relation and soiling the perfect beauty of God's creature. I see now that
I am but "nothing," and that this very nothingness allows God and his
creature to be in direct mutual contact with one another. This idea is
everywhere in Weil's notes. In *Gravity and Grace*, it is especially present
in the chapter "Self-Effacement":

> I am not the maiden who awaits her betrothed, but the unwel-
> come third who is with two betrothed lovers and ought to go
> away so that they can really be together. If only I knew how
> to disappear there would be a perfect union of love between
> God and the earth I tread, the sea I hear. . . .

> May I disappear in order that those things that I see may become perfect in their beauty from the very fact that they are no longer things that I see. . . .
>
> I do not in the least wish that this created world should fade from my view, but that it should no longer be to me personally that it shows itself. To me it cannot tell its secret which is too high. If I go, then the creator and the creature will exchange their secrets. To see a landscape as it is when I am not there. . . . When I am in any place, I disturb the silence of heaven and earth by my breathing and the beating of my heart.[23]

Once the I has been destroyed in a proper way (from within, not from outside), the relation between God and his creature is restored. Yet there is a question that cannot but be raised here: Why does all this result in a universe that is as full of affliction and evil as before? Why does the universe of the I that has been destroyed "from within" show no difference at all with the universe of the I that has been destroyed "from outside"? In the answer lies Weil's basic intuition. She locates the change that is at stake here neither in the outside world nor in God, but solely in the "gaze" (*regard*) with which the world and God are looked at. The change is solely in the self, in the "I." Once my I has been destroyed, I see that the world of necessity from which I suffer so much only made me suffer because I tried to be someone in it. Now that I see I am nothing, I see that the world of necessity is in prefect relation with the divine source of grace, with God. I experience now that the world of necessity *is* the one of grace. I praise God for his creation, also for the hard, metallically cold laws by which it is ruled, also for the blind fate of which I am the suffering victim. Yet Weil's universe is not one of praise. For that, God remains too absent. He is only present in his absence. Just as redemption is not beyond suffering, but suffering itself. Why, then, are suffering, pain, and affliction in no way to be overcome? Why does the solution for suffering require nothing else than suffering—except that now, I accept it, and even support it?

"The irreducible basis of my suffering"

Here, we face a paradox that Weil's mystical thinking shares with all mystical thought. It is a paradox concerning the I as the ultimate obstacle the mystic meets on his or her way to God. God can only be reached if the I is overcome, that is, destroyed. How and by whom must the I be destroyed? Weil's writings do not differ in this from the other writings in the mystical tradition: it is not "from outside" that the I can be destroyed. Why? In that case, it would *really* be destroyed in the sense that there would be simply no one left to even start reaching for God. Weil stresses that the I must be destroyed "from within." But who could do that job except the I? The I must empty itself, it must reduce itself to what it is, namely, to nothing. Yet, this nothing must be active, it must be an agency. How can this agency of nothingness realize its nothingness? This is only possible thanks to—and within—a context of contrast. Only the context of affliction—affliction that is destructive of the I "from outside"—can reveal an I that, "from within," bears this affliction because of its nothingness. A universe of pain is needed in order to allow the I to perform its nothingness.

The Weilian mystic would not be able to bear redemption from pain, affliction, or evil, for then he *really* would lose the nothingness he is supposed to be. His nothingness needs the contrasted context that keeps on saying to him that he is nothing. He exists by the grace of that message, that is, of the pain, affliction, and evil making clear to him that they do not take any account of him. Precisely this allows him to acknowledge his nothingness. It is only then that he, in his quality of nothingness, can testify to what the alternative to pain and evil is, that is to say, to the "light of salvation." In the chapter "The Cross," we read:

> An innocent being who suffers sheds the light of salvation
> upon evil [*répand sur le mal la lumière du salut*]. Such a one
> is the visible image of the innocent God. That is why a God
> who loves man and a man who loves God have to suffer.[24]

Suffering is needed, for salvation can only exist in the "nothing" that resists it. That is why this nothing, in Weil's writing, can only exist in the act of performing itself as being destroyed by the world of necessity, affliction, and evil, while that act, as a destruction "from within," again and again reaffirms that "irreducible I" that is at its basis.

In some notes, Weil almost uses these words. For instance, in a note of only one sentence: "This irreducible 'I' which is the irreducible basis of my suffering—I have to make this 'I' universal."[25] The I is nothing. This nothing can only be there in a context that attacks its false pretention to be something. It can only be there by the grace of an environment that afflicts it with "metallically cold" necessity. It needs affliction in order to perform that this affliction does do it any harm. It is the I's only way to show—and thus "to be"—the nothingness it is. It is its only way to realize itself as nothing. Yet, this is precisely the way in which that "self" is irreducible. The nothing that is the I uses the entire universe to posit itself as such. The irreducible I—which is nothing—uses the entire universe of affliction, pain, and necessity in order to perform itself as "irreducible." In the act of destroying itself, the I transfers its destructive force to the universe in order to let that universe destroy it. Why? To show that it is not the universe that destroys the I, but that it is the I that destroys itself, thus saving the universe, allowing it to be in direct contact again with its Creator. It is the self-destroying I that is the "irreducible basis," not only of its own suffering, but of the entire world—a world of mere necessity that has to afflict the I precisely in order to enable it to perform itself as "irreducible."

Like no other, Weil is a *modern* mystic—*modern* in the sense that she is fully aware of the "death of God." This means that God has ceased to be the "subject," that is to say, the "ground" on the basis of which we relate to reality. We no longer comprehend ourselves on the basis of participation in God's creation. Instead, we relate to reality on a basis that is nothing but ourselves. We consider ourselves to be the "subject" (basis, ground) of our relationship to the world, including its creator, God. Yet, the fact that we are the subject of our relationship to reality does not mean that we are the "subject" of reality as such. We clearly know we are not God. The modern turn does not prevent a significant number of modern people from believing that God keeps on being the subject/basis/ground of reality. However, the subject of *that* belief is not with God but with themselves.

Weil is definitely one of those who hold fast to God as the subject of reality. This is why, according to her, we must keep on looking for God in the reality we face. It is therefore obvious in her eyes that the real object of science is beauty, thus, the order of reality as it rests in itself.[26] In that sense, as she writes in one of her notes, "a science which does not bring us nearer to God is worthless."[27]

For Weil, science must touch God or, what amounts to the same thing, the iron laws of necessity which, in their pureness, are grace itself.[28] Science must touch the real subject, the subject of reality: God as reality's creator. Therefore, we must get beyond ourselves, beyond the false, modern idea of ourselves as subject. As Weil put it: the I must be destroyed "from within." Yet, if that destruction restores God in his original relation to reality, it might pretend to destroy the I, but that destruction itself requires a subject, an agent of that act. Weil's intention to go beyond the modern subject (the subject/ground of our relation to reality) and to restore the premodern, real subject (the subject of reality itself, God) fails. In a way, she gets stuck in the act *as such* of destroying the (modern) subject, an act that never stops being executed and which inevitably requires a subject. That subject is a *modern* subject, a subject, not of reality, but of man's relation to reality. In the act of destruction, the subject realizes that it coincides with an abyss. To embrace this abyss, to acknowledge the nothingness that separates reality from itself (i.e., from its Creator), that is the aim of life, according to Weil. This aim, however, needs what it contradicts: if not the I, at least "the power to say I."

Contra-Religious Religion

The Mystical Experience of a Modern Protestant Minister

Like a soup of rat's tails,
that is what all edifying literature is to me.

—K. H. Miskotte, *Uit de dagboeken*

But if faith itself is considered a
religion too, no breakthrough, no exodus
from the evil or cozy house of detention that is called tradition is
    possible.

—K. H. Miskotte, *Bijbels ABC*

A Religious Experience?

Between October 1923 and April 1925, Kornelis Heiko Miskotte, a minister in Kortgene in the Dutch province of Zeeland, wrote a weekly missive to the members of his community. In his weekly *Church News-letter* (in Dutch, *Gemeenteblaadje*) of December 13, 1924, he recounts a personal crisis of faith followed by a true "religious" experience:

> And how I was . . . afflicted! Because those who strenuously seek God suffer from this world, suffer from themselves, from their own inner discord. Afflicted by all doubt and agony,

afflicted then with a frenzy of happiness, so my life came and went. I also called out in the night: Why?—I, too, begged: Teach me your way! And I did find an answer, and a direction certainly appeared in my life, but *having* God inside, closer than my own heart: *that* I did not find. And that had been my dream: to feel eternity in every single moment of time, to tame and order all arbitrariness, and to spend every hour as a part of the perfect plan that God made appear within eternity—and see, it was not *allowed*: even if the intention was noble, it was not God's will. And my tormented heart . . . did not find God, and I was not allowed to sing his praises. . . . And then, as suddenly as a lightning bolt reveals hidden pastures to the watchful on a balmy night—it was in me like a big light that will never leave me: You have not yet sacrificed your *piety*; . . . in *your* consciousness must be the solution and in *your* soul the peace and enjoyment—and in that very moment something broke in me. . . . This has happened to me, that God has imprinted his miracle on me all the way into the depths of my soul: . . . I love you with an eternal love, [He says]. *Know*, once and for all, that you do not need to know it. Feel, once and for all, that you do not need to feel it, and that It is *still* there, the divine Presence, and that his faithfulness and his mercy are as eternal as his Being. And therein lies the peace that transcends all understanding. Parts of the soul that we do not know about are showered with blessings. It is all in Him who lives and gives life to my soul.[1]

Miskotte's biographer, Herman de Liagre Böhl, who has included this lengthy excerpt in his book, concludes: "This is the essence of experiential pietism.[2] The expression "you have not yet sacrificed your *piety*" could be read as proof that Miskotte had been under the influence of the critical theology of Barth: piety, too, offered no relief to man under God's judgment."[3] It is the "essence of experiential pietism" indeed. Struggling with himself, with his unruly congregation, and with God, the thirty-year-old minister is not exactly doing well in the remote village of Kortgene. He seeks strength in faith. In the troublesome pool of human, all too human needs, he wants to track down the Eternal. He wants to open himself to God and embrace with heart and soul that everything that exists comes from His hand. But as much as he desires it, as "noble" as his intentions are, "it was not *allowed*." He desires it *too* much; he relies too much on himself and on his will, therefore not on God. Only when he realizes that he himself, including his "piety," constitutes the obstacle on his path to God, he discovers that there is nothing to discover, that he should not go in search of anything, because everything has always been a given, the sought-after God has always been there, He has always been the "Presence," and he was not able to experience this precisely because he desired it too keenly. Nothing or no-one but he himself is the stumbling block on his path to experiencing grace. And only in himself, or more specifically, only there where he sets his "self" aside and makes space for what befalls him as pure grace, can he experience God. This "experience" is at the heart of what is called experiential pietism in the Protestant tradition.

Is that not also the core of every Christian religious experience—and of every religious experience, in any confession?

Would it be? Is the experience the young Miskotte describes here a "religious" one? Does the minister call it that? The word *religious* certainly does not appear in the "testimony" he gives of it, and that is no coincidence. The biographer is justified in emphasizing this. The sole thing Miskotte, in his yearning for "hidden communion" with God,[4] had not yet sacrificed was his piety, in other words: his "religion." He was still thinking that piety or any other religious attitude would help him to find God. However, the experience he speaks of here only proves possible after he had also let go of the typical "religious" anchor points of his yearning for God. "Experientially pious" is how Miskotte himself might have called the experience described here, but certainly not "religious." Rather, it is, in his words, an "antireligious" experience, an experience of religion as a barrier to our communion with and ascent to God—an experience that fits with what Miskotte, as well as for instance Bonhoeffer, would call a *religionloses Christentum* (religionless Christianity).[5]

Viewed from a broader perspective, Miskotte is describing a typically monotheistic experience of God here. It is "antireligious" in the sense that it is "anti" everything that leans toward idolatry, "anti" everything to which one likes to cling, in the relationship with the divine, in order to still have an individual hold on Him. "God is not who or what you think He is; only God is God": thus rings the strict definition monotheism has bestowed upon the divine.[6] That is why monotheism is never simply an achievement. The inclination to domesticate God, to involve Him in a relationship in which we ourselves can influence Him in one way or another, in which our "piety" becomes a weight that we can put in the balance to compel God to benevolence toward us—this inclination is timeless, it is ineradicable, and it is called "religion." The core mission of monotheism lies in the struggle against "religion."

Miskotte experiences the overwhelmingness of grace; he experiences how life is the result and the place of pure gift giving—a gift giving to which he can only surrender in the full sense of the word. A massive religious-theoretical tradition recognizes in that experience the definition of the "religious" experience. According to the monotheist Miskotte, however, what he has lived is rather a *non*religious experience—an experience that unmasks all religion and nullifies it. Or, maybe more correctly: Miskotte speaks of a *true* religious experience, an experience of religious truth, and to him this means: of the truth through which religion is unmasked. It is the experience of a truth that separates the wheat from the chaff in the whole religious shebang, in order to be left only with the essence: that God is either truth or not. As long as God still has something to do with religiosity ("piety"), as long as you think that He is in the extension of the manipulable world around you, you are looking for a false God.[7] The divine is only to be found in—and without a doubt corresponds with—a nonmanipulable, sovereign (and thus) *true* god unaffected by illusion and confusion.

A Philosophical Experience?

Miskotte's "testimony" points to an experience of truth. But is it—despite Miskotte's reservations about the term—also a *religious* truth experience? What if the incident should be rather seen as a *philosophical* truth experience?

Of course, Miskotte's "tormented heart" explicitly addresses "God" and seeks "his praises" and his glory. Also, in the eyes of Miskotte, his story slots seamlessly into the long mystic-religious tradition known to Christianity.[8] But if religion is not the path to which the quest for God ends up leading, what, then, does the searching soul find at the end of this quest? Miskotte calls it "God" and "glory," but is it nothing other than *being as such*, "being" in as far as it is distinct from "not-being," from "lack-of-being" or "mere appearance"? Is Miskotte's "God" anything else than "eternal being," "being" in as far as it has not been affected by transience and death? "To feel eternity in every single moment of time, to tame and order all arbitrariness, and to spend every hour as a part of the perfect plan that God made appear within eternity." Thus, he expressed his "dream," his desire, as well as that which happens to him in his truth experience. *Being* as that which merely is what it is: this definition from the ancient philosopher Parmenides forms the basis of what we since call *thinking, knowledge,* and *science.* It is the discovery of the first rule of logic, that of noncontradiction. "Being is, not-being is not."[9] Powered purely by *logos*—that is to say, by the words you use and take seriously for what they say—you know that the word *being* regards a state of "being" that can never be "not-being," just as, when you say of something that it is not, it can ever be.

The counterintuitive certainty of a state of being that has no other time than the present, the eternal "now" beyond—or hidden deeply in—time: Miskotte experiences it as a gift. It is grace, something that gives being—or "gives life," as the final line of the long citation at the beginning of this chapter declares.

The words *grace* and *gift* sound religious, but in this context, they can just as well be read as "philosophical" terms. The image of being as an inexhaustible, self-sustaining source is Plato's. It is in his "allegory of the cave." Plato wholeheartedly goes along with Parmenides and his view that being can only be being and never not-being. This, however, does not alter the fact that this cave full of not-being in which we live every day has something to do with the eternal "Presence" of being. The myth of the cave—actually the myth of the light that penetrates the cave—should make this clear.[10] Ultimately, being is a source of light—thus a wonder of gift and grace—that never ceases to offer itself and for this reason allows being (in Plato's terminology, the "ideas") to exist, but also grants a certain existence to the cave's shadow realm of not-being. In the eyes of the person in the cave striving for truth, "thinking" for this reason means: being receptive to this gift of truth that is even present in the cave's shadows: in unproven opinions, in lies and illusions.

In the third century, another philosopher, Plotinus, lived a few very intense, personal experiences of this gracious gift, and made this ecstatic experience of being the starting point of a remarkable rearticulation of Platonic thinking. That articulation was later systematized by Proclus, among others, and became known as Neo-Platonism. Neither for Plotinus nor for Proclus is this experience of the pure gift of being—in their terms, the experience of the One—an experience of a personal god.

But so it is for Christianity of the third and fourth century, which swiftly formulates its doctrine in Neo-Platonic idiom. Christians experience being as the gift of a personal god. And to express and explain that gift and their relationship to it, they will rely on Neo-Platonic schemes. Those schemes will continue to persist even in and after the Aristotelian-Thomistic reformulation of Christianity in the thirteenth century.

God stands for the eternal being that remains hidden in the transient everyday world. There are moments, however, in which this eternal state of being allows itself to be experienced by those who are open to it and seek for it; it might, in other words, grant them an experience of "hidden communion" with the perpetually giving being that is God. God is not the farthest point that awaits the seeker at the very end of a long road; He is the always-present being that is also the foundation of our quest for Him. He is the being, also of our search for Him.

Miskotte's "experience," even if it concerns God, might be read on a strictly philosophical level here. What he experiences is being—being that, as he suddenly realizes, has always been at the basis of everything that exists, including the "thunderous, terrific questions" that torment us so.

Being and Question

In the fragment with which Miskotte, in his *Church Newsletter* of December 5, 1924, opens his series *On Hidden Communion*, he goes into the meaning of this title. First, he raises "thunderous questions" such as "the terrible question about suffering" and "What is actually God's plan for this world?"[11] But the fact that Scripture provides answers to these questions, as he argues, does not prevent him from immediately adding:

> And yet . . . *beneath* these questions is something else still . . . and *around* these answers yet another light quivers. . . . Oh! Why do we ask our terrific questions? Is it not because our *thinking* does not see the light, while constantly and almost provocatively, the *soul*, in secret, continues to rely on the hidden An-swer [*Ant-woord*] and is secretly assured of the Light.[12]

Why do we raise our questions? Because these questions are *given* to us—given by their "An-swer." Because present in the questions is the gift that makes everything what it is, including our questions.

Hidden Communion: that is the last and the deepest. We are never entirely *conscious* of this hidden Communion, but it is the *pre*supposition of our questions. And the answer is only understood in this Communion.[13]

"Communion" with God remains a "hidden" matter, also for the believer. Also believers have no understanding of the deepest ground of reality. It is as obscure for them as for nonbelievers. But unlike nonbelievers, believers are open to the revelation of "mystery as mystery."[14]

The believer is taken up in hiddenness. "We are 'inside,'" it is later said.[15] But for Miskotte, that does not mean that his questions have been answered, even if there is Scripture in which the answers are written. The God with which we have a "hidden Communion" makes us ask questions. Miskotte continues:

If He were not, we would not even ask, we would not suffer, and we would not struggle; we would have settled in reality a long time ago, we would have resigned ourselves to ourselves and made conscience into nothing but an earthly constable, so that we might live an undisturbed life and create a Land of Cockaigne, a paradise of mediocrity, a playground of empty satisfaction, to our eternal pleasure. All of life's questions would long have been buried with a eulogy expressing our sincere regret that the deceased had caused us so many unnecessary headaches. But no, we *ask*, don't we, even if we say nothing; beneath the threshold of conscience, an entire legion of questions swarms; like carrier pigeons, desires sail and wallow there, eagerly awaiting every message from the Other, the Essential, in order to convey it.[16]

If God had not been there, we would have posed no questions. In Miskotte's eyes, God is indeed the "An-swer." Only, notwithstanding the capital letter, this does not solve the questions but on the contrary ensures that they are there. The divine "An-swer" ensures that everything in us amounts to a question. Our nature is that of questioning (our nature). If God were not there, we would lead an "undisturbed life" in the "Land of Cockaigne" where life questions are off the table. But God is there, not to answer life questions, but to guarantee the existence of these kinds of questions and to keep us questioning. To also make a question of our silence: "We *ask*, don't we, even if we say nothing?"

In Miskotte's discourse, God in fact stands for the human condition. That condition consists in not coinciding with ourselves, in being a barrel of questions and in remaining a mystery even to ourselves. Our condition is the "An-swer" remaining obscure. The latter does teach us that there *is* an answer, but that it does not lie *ahead* of our questions but is hidden behind and under them. It forms the basis of our questions *as* questions. The basis is "an entire legion of questions" and "desires, eagerly awaiting every message from the Other, the Essential." An Other, again, who places the sought-after Essential in the never-ending way of questioning. The sentences immediately following the cited passage put it even more sharply:

> Why are we without hope? Because we cannot give up *hope*! Why do we feel so far from God? Because He is so terribly *close*! Why is our heart a single question? Because God is the *one* Answer, which we presume! Why are we sinners? Because God's holiness burns our soul! Why are we filled with desire? Because the Lover arouses us with his wandering voice close by our being! Why do we seek? Because we are found! Behold, all of this does not take place in *our* consciousness, it does not settle in *our* feeling, it does not become the bounty of *our* strained will. It comes to pass, it happens, it *is*. As they say: it rains, it snows, the weather is good, *regardless* of your mood, attitude, and will: *so* it is in the soul: Communion comes to pass, happens, *is*.[17]

We are seeking, not because we lack the answer, but because we always hold "Communion" with it; because through the being itself of what we seek, we have always been found and in its grace been given an existence: as hoping, as seeking, as questioning. Hoping, seeking, and questioning *are*, like "it snows," like "the weather is good."

And what is the way in which it snows, rains, and is good weather? Our existence. Ourselves. Ourselves as question, also as question for ourselves. That is our "being," and with that "being" we always have (or, more precisely, we always *are*) a "hidden Communion": hidden because we normally overlook it, because we look for the answer to our hoping/seeking/questioning beyond it, and do not see that it lies in these activities themselves. It comes down to taking a step back in our hoping/seeking/questioning and in this way embracing the being thereof. Not to bring that which we overlooked to light forever. The light itself shares in the mystery. Embracing being is a matter of experiencing the answer in its mystery, and this means: in the being itself of the question (about being).

Only now do we better understand what the account of Miskotte's "religious" experience in the first citation is all about. I cite the passage again, but now add the two fragments I left out the first time, when I copied the passage from the Liagre Böhl biography:

> [A]nd in that very moment something broke in me <u>and hidden Communion began?—No, of course not—but the knowing, then, of that Very Best?—No, on the contrary—but</u> this has happened to me, that God has imprinted his miracle on me all the way into the depths of my soul: <u>Communion *is*</u>, I love you with an eternal love, [He says]. *Know*, once and for all, that you do not need to know it, feel, once and for all, that you do not need to feel it, and that It is *still* there, the divine Presence, and that his faithfulness and His mercy are as eternal as his Being. And therein lies the peace that transcends all understanding. Parts of the soul that we do not know about are showered with blessings. It is all in Him who lives and gives life to my soul.[18]

What happens when the obstacles on Miskotte's way to God are overcome, when he finally feels "*having* God inside, closer than my own heart"?[19] Does he then finally have knowledge of God? Does he finally end up in "hidden Communion"? He does not end up anywhere and does not arrive anywhere; he is where he has always been, only it has now got through to him, existentially *and* intellectually. From what we read in sections from the *Church Newsletter* series of later date, we now have a better understanding of what is written here: "Communion *is*." God's "Presence," his "faithfulness," his mercy *is*. As the rain that falls.

But above all we have a better understanding of what Miskotte means when he lets God say: "*Know* once and for all, that you do not need to know it; feel, once and for all, that you do not need to feel it." This "not-feeling" and "not-knowing" that hides beneath and rests in every feeling and knowing is an "entire legion of questions," an active questioning that speaks even when no questions are asked, and everything is peacefully quiet.

What is this "peace that transcends all understanding"? Not resting on our laurels in a state of not-knowing in which all intellectual activity is considered superfluous. "Peace that transcends all understanding" is found not *beside* or *beyond*, but *in* intellectual activity, in mobilizing this "legion of questions." What the mind finds in this peace is its basis—a basis that, once discovered, does not admonish you to stop all thinking but rather incites you to think, to question, not to coincide with yourself, to hear a questioning voice even there where "we say nothing."

What Miskotte experiences is the *being* of his desire, the *being* of his questions. That is what "Communion" is about. Miskotte's questions themselves make him commune with the state of being of which he goes in search. The end of his search is the *Communion* that has always been there, the "hidden Communion" with the being of the question.

Contra-Religious . . .

The experience Miskotte speaks of in his *Church Newsletter* of December 13, 1924, reads like a *religious* experience. On closer inspection it can just as well—and perhaps even better—be read as a *philosophical* experience: an experience of what it means to *be*; or more specifically *and* philosophically: what it means to pose the *question* of being. The experience comes down to a happy confrontation, not as much with an answer *to*, as with the being *of* that question.

So, is religion philosophy for Miskotte? Or is philosophy religion? It certainly stands out that he neither calls his experience "religious" nor labels it "philosophical." But maybe he shuns both terms precisely because of that which religion and philosophy have in common. "Truth" is, after all, central to both, and perhaps it is in the name of this truth that Miskotte guards against calling it either "religious" or "philosophical."

Why does he not call it philosophical, while his story clearly points in that direction? One of the reasons might be that he associates "philosophy" with knowing and knowledge. He wants to indicate that the experience he describes lacks precisely these kinds of pretensions. What he experienced did concern the ground of knowing, that is, the gift that also underlies knowing; but that ground can never be appropriated by knowing—precisely because, rather than a "ground," it is a pure gift, a groundless gift-giving source. This is the reason why thinking—and by extension: mankind—remains all question.

Miskotte shares this reluctance against knowing with a number of philosophers. Martin Heidegger, for instance, saw in this a reason to speak of the "end of philosophy" and in this way to perceive a space for what he called "thinking." What Miskotte describes in his own experience is not incompatible with what this Heideggerian statement is all about.[20]

We already discussed why Miskotte does not call his experience of truth "religious." Religion is "unbelief," argues Karl Barth, whom Miskotte admired.[21] It acknowledges God not as the *true* God but as an idol, as a god with whom one can bargain, whom one can tempt with good deeds, religious actions, and sacramental gestures. Christianity is about truth, not about religion: this summarizes the key message of Miskotte's entire oeuvre. It also explains his emphasis, from his earliest writings onward, on the Old Testament, the ancient text that lies at the basis of the three great monotheistic traditions. "God is not what you think God is: only God is God." That is why God is the truth. That is what monotheism comes down to. Following Jan Assmann, you could define monotheism as the introduction of truth in what we usually call "religion."[22]

This statement only becomes clear when you realize that truth and religion are contradictory and for this reason completely incompatible. Religion—or, better yet, the phenomenon to which we ascribe this relatively late and exclusively Latin term[23]—has nothing to do with truth at first. Gods are neither true nor false. They juggle with true and false as humans do, but their existence does not depend on the criterion "true versus false." They are simply there. They stand for the domain *beyond* life, the domain that escapes our grip on life but that, in turn, asserts its grip on our life, even only by handing it over to death. This domain beyond life is that of death—or, more precisely,[24] that where the distinction between life and death does not count. In that unsteady domain where nothing is what it seems and differences are never sharply delineated, there the immortal gods dwell. From this capricious domain, life is *given to* but also *taken away from* us. For us it comes down to being on good terms with this hybrid domain filled with gods. "Religion" is the name of the complex set of ways in which we try to achieve this.

With this "religion," monotheism broke. Monotheism says that gods do not exist and makes it a core mission to unmask and destroy them. The domain from which we are given life is not the messy wilderness of unstable immortals but the heavenly garden of truth. "Religion" is no value as such; it only has value insofar as it answers to the criterion of truth and represents a relationship with the *true* God. Only truth deserves the label "divine"; only to the one true God must gratitude be given for life.[25] The other gods must be unmasked and denied in their existence.

Beside the "negative core" of monotheism—the *breaking of gods*—
it also has a "positive" core: you only serve the real God if you serve
humankind, if you do justice to the "widow and the orphan," if you
stand up for the oppressed and if you turn humanity into a haven of
justice.[26] This is the socioethical dimension that the biblical prophets
bring to the fore and that has become the positive message of the two
later monotheisms.

Communing with the true God breaks the sacral commerce that
is "religion." That is what is liberating about monotheism: it delivers
us from the "business" that has connected mortals and immortals since
time immemorial and that all too often comes at the expense of the
weakest in society. It liberates the weak: they now become the aim of
communion with God. God wants no sacrifices but righteousness; no
religion but social justice. That is *true* religion; this is the truth *of*—and
in this sense *beyond*—religion.

. . . Religion

And yet. It goes without saying that monotheistic religions are proper
religions. Admittedly idiosyncratic due to being contra-religious religions,
but religions, nonetheless. That is how they define themselves, and how
they function. Contrary to their message, they cling to "communion"—a
gift-and-countergift relationship[27]—with the divine. Islam, Christianity,
and Judaism have their holy figures and places, their pilgrimages, relics,
rituals, and ceremonies, and the effects of these on the divine are never
simply admitted (as, in their eyes, it would make them guilty of magic
or idolatry), but never completely denied either.

All monotheisms struggle with this ambiguity. With its incarnation
theory, Christianity does so in a specific way. Only God is God, indeed,
but this God at the same time became man. So man can commune with
God as with a human being, as an equal. And this concretely means that,
when man does good deeds to His honor and glory, God is sensitive to
that. He is susceptible to gifts from man's side. This is also why, during
its history, Christianity has had to repeatedly highlight the transcendent
holiness of God—and, subsequently, time and again to remove God from
His all-too-transcendental heaven.

In the contra-religious religion that is monotheism, there is a collision between two religious "paradigms": the (ancient, "pagan") paradigm

of the *gift*, on the one hand, and the (monotheistic) paradigm of *truth* on the other. That collision has crystallized in a specific idiosyncratic narrative in each of the three monotheist religions, in which the merging of the two mutually exclusive principles de facto constitutes the dynamic of that religion and its culture. At the core of each monotheism, both of these principles continue to clash, while the specific form of this battle guarantees the energetic, historical, flexible identity of each of these religions.

In spite of its critique of gift/countergift religions, monotheism still clings to the idea of human relationships with the divine being tuned to the principle of the gift. Gods were only gods in as far as they were acknowledged as such via gifts received from mortals (sacrifices, rituals, processions, prayers, songs, et cetera). In Aristophanes's speech in Plato's *Symposium*, we read how Zeus, in his jealous anger, cuts the powerful, four-armed, two-headed, and androgynous human in half. Yet, he refrains from slashing this already halved mortal in half again, fearing that this cripple will no longer be able to honor him through the sacrifices and other religious practices he needs to feel guaranteed of his divinity.[28]

It is quite the opposite in the case of the monotheistic God: to maintain the fullness of his divine state, He does not need our gifts at all. On the contrary, He only needs Himself to be who He is. This is why He is the Truth.

The monotheistic person acknowledges this truth, confesses it is God, rejects existing gods on this basis, and refuses to acknowledge the legitimacy of the gift/countergift relationship humans have with them? (In other words, he rejects "religion.") Only—and this is crucial—the monotheist offers his true God this contra-religious confession *as a gift*. That confession does not allow itself to be defined as merely dishing up knowledge. It is, ultimately, a *gift* the believer *offers* God. Here, in the very heart of this manifestly antireligious culture, "religion" comes up yet again.

"In the very heart" indeed. Because, in the final instance, the relationship with truth does not take the shape of knowledge, in any case not of completed knowledge. When monotheism calls God the Truth, it also specifically means that truth indeed reveals itself to us but never completely exhausts itself in this revelation. Truth signals itself but does not surrender itself completely in this "gift." In other words, it only shows itself as a truth that keeps *being given* and therefore can never completely be appropriated or known. Whoever keeps up that pretense does not see that his knowledge finds its source in this gracious gift. Our last resort in acknowledging the truth of this gift—the truth *as* gift—is offering that truth a countergift. This countergift, however, does everything to remain outside of the gift/countergift traffic, out of the "commercial" logic of *do ut des*. It offers something that does not correspond to this logic. The monotheistic gift to the true God acknowledges this very gift to be redundant, having always resulted from the gift given by the true God. However, it is and remains a gift, and in that sense shows that monotheism (which is, in principle, contra-religious) still continues to listen to the paradigm of religion.

Does that gift not also show us what lies at the core of philosophy? At least of a dominant line in its tradition—a line that resounds all the way to the "contra-religious" religious experience the young minister from Kortgene describes in his *Church Newsletter* of December 13, 1924.

Inspired by Platonism and Neo-Platonism, this whole tradition attempts to make it clear that the ground of being is not just a "ground," and that it even *is* not, because it finds itself "beyond being," since it is located, according to a well-known passage in Plato, *"epikeina tès ousias."*[29] The ground of being *is* not, but *gives* itself. Being is fundamentally a source that is never simply itself but unceasingly gives itself away—"unceasingly," because being ultimately only exists in the act of giving. Taking notice of being is finally acknowledging that my knowing also "is," and for this reason is founded on the ground of being that is nothing other than an inexhaustible deed of donation.

The Platonic philosopher longs for the true state of being, only to finally realize that his desire *as such* has always followed the way of that very being. In terms of the allegory of the cave, the philosopher's desire is to leave the cave and, there, lie down enjoying directly the light of truth. But once there, the philosopher has to take being seriously in that place too, and follow the light of its truth shining back into the cave. This means the philosopher has to go back into the realm of shadows and lies in order to encourage there his fellows to seek the truth. Once the true being has been reached, the philosopher must do what being does: give itself away and, like the light of truth, relentlessly lose itself in the shadow of the cave. Only in this way does the philosopher conform to the "selfless" that is the "ground" of being. Only in genuinely taking this act of giving upon himself is the philosopher truly (the ground of) what he is and really responds to his philosophical mission. Only this giving leads him to the ultimate insight that the true destination to which our human questioning leads, does not lie in the answer but in abiding in the questioning itself.

It is not difficult to recognize herein the "experience" Miskotte describes in one of his first fragments from the series *On Hidden Communion*. Longing for communion with the true source of reality, he subsequently realizes—after following an inevitably difficult path—that he has always already communed with it, as deviating from this path has everything in common with the way in which reality goes. And this Communion is "hidden," because the source only allows itself to be experienced in the inability to be appropriated or, what comes down to the same thing, in the realization—that inevitably comes *afterward*—that the desire for Communion has always been enabled by Communion itself, and that this desire itself *is* Communion.

> We gasp for the light, the big light. But the light is not the last. We desire the deed, the big deed, but the deed is not the deepest. The last and the deepest cannot be expressed, can only be indicated. *Hidden Communion*, that is the last and the deepest. We are never entirely *conscious* of this hidden Communion, but it is the *pre*supposition of our questions. And the answer is only understood in this Communion.[30]

Philosophy / Religion

Is philosophy, then, religious as well? Just as religion would also be philosophical?

A long tradition has fiercely guarded the distinction between both philosophy and religion. It still determines today's intellectual debates and public opinion. However, the fact that the distinction between the two *had*—and has—to be so fiercely guarded may point to it being everything but self-evident, and that both have more in common with each other than has been commonly thought. Anyway, Miskotte's above-mentioned "experience," as well as the reflections it elicited, points in this direction.

Our religion is no religion; it does not allow itself to be defined as a gift/countergift flow between the human and the divine. It is a monotheism that, in the name of truth, wages war on religion. This contra-religious mission, however, does not prevent it from approaching truth as a God who, contrary to the monotheistic paradigm, keeps being addressed in a "religious" way—a way relying on the gift-giving paradigm.

Philosophy, too, in the name of truth, breaks with the paradigm of the gift. Like monotheism, philosophy puts forward the truth as the criterion of being and therefore declares nonexistent the dark realm of the gods, from where we used to think our volatile and instable lives are given. The Pythia who delivers oracles in Apollo's temple in Delphi does not teach us who we are and how the world really works; only the *Logos*, logical thought, does that. And yet, philosophy resorted very quickly to the paradigm of the gift when it came to considering the ultimate basis of truth. Although grounded in itself, truth and being were thought of as resting in a "ground" that one can apparently only formulate in terms related to the gift paradigm.

Monotheism and philosophy both share a basic reference to truth as well as to gift giving, and are, therefore, much more closely intertwined than we usually tend to think. So it comes as no surprise that a religious experience—such as, for example, that of Miskotte—can also be read as a philosophical experience of being, and that, in the latter, "religious" (more specifically monotheistic) reminiscences are easily audible.

This reading is, however, also interesting in a broader context. The type of monotheistic religion that emerges from Miskotte's account seems to ultimately reduce itself to a cult of the question—the cult of the question that has its ultimate answer in the *being* of the question itself. Translated into the monotheistic narrative, it means that confessing the true God mainly takes shape in the critical question with which one tackles the supposed gods. Not whom or what you think God is, is God; only God is God. This critical slogan means that a "religious" preoccupation basically comprises criticizing every religious claim or activity. Honoring God means critically screening every possible god, including the God with a capital letter. "Religion" can only be contra-religious for Miskotte; it can only be defined as criticism, criticism of idolatry, criticism of whatever answer you suppose will end your critical questions forever. Therein hides the rigorously worldly character of Miskotte's monotheism, never mind how strongly he might emphasize God's transcendence. The relationship with God does not lead us to some otherworldliness but keeps both our feet on the ground: this relationship defines our whole being *here* and *now*. In Miskotte's eyes, God's transcendent name might purely and simply serve to keep us closer to the concrete reality of everyday life, to experience our human condition *as such* as God's mercy—or, in Platonic terms, to experience the "cave" itself as a gift of grace. Hence, once again, Miskotte's criticism of "religion," that is, of every penchant to view God as an escape route away from our "cave."

The paradox of this "contra-religious religious" approach is tangible in a fragment already quoted above, the passage with which Miskotte opens his series *Of Hidden Communion*. It is worth reading it again. Miskotte had just introduced this *hidden Communion* with God, notably as "the *pre*supposition of our questions." And then he writes, referring to God ("He"):

> If He were not, we would not even ask, we would not suffer, and we would not struggle; we would have settled in reality a long time ago, we would have resigned ourselves to ourselves and made conscience into nothing but an earthly constable, so that we might live an undisturbed life and create a Land of Cockaigne, a paradise of mediocrity, a playground of empty satisfaction, to our eternal pleasure. All of life's questions would long have been buried with a eulogy expressing our sincere regret that the deceased had caused us so many unnecessary headaches. But no, we *ask*, don't we, even if we say nothing; beneath the threshold of conscience, an entire legion of questions swarms; like carrier pigeons desires sail and wallow there, eagerly awaiting every message from the Other, the Essential, in order to convey it.[31]

"Not suffer," "not struggle," "live an undisturbed life," a Land of Cockaigne," "paradise," "playground of . . . satisfaction," "eternal pleasure," a state in which "[a]ll of life's questions would . . . have been buried." It does not take much to discern, in these metaphors, the celestial condition that an authentic desire for God also seeks. And do they not equally characterize the blissful place to which the true state of being would transport us once all questions about it were resolved?

And yet these metaphors represent the contrary here. Miskotte qualifies them as "empty." And, what is more, it is precisely how blissful, how fulfilled with "being" we would be if God were *not* there. But God is there, Miskotte says, and what does that imply? That "beneath the threshold of conscience, an entire legion of questions swarms"; that, in other words, the condition in which we exist is one of questions, one that lacks an answer—in such a way that we cannot even consider the factual nature of that lack an answer.

The name of God serves to keep the *question* about God on the table. And not because it asks *for* God, but because it is "asks," because it is a *question*. It is important to allow us to be ourselves and, precisely for that reason, rail against us if we delight in everything we take to be true. For the young minister that Miskotte still is in 1924, it comes down to pointing out to the members of his community that they *are* only a *question* about *hidden Communion*, and that their existence—their *being*—does not lie in expected, future Communion, but in the question *itself*; that the "An-swer" is the truth, because it allows them to be who they are: a question.

It is in this light that Miskotte's attention for general cultural education should be understood. What he is trying to impart to the members of his congregation is of course the Bible and real (read: contra-religious) religion, but at the same time, he does not shy away from recommending modern literature to them. In Kortgene, and also elsewhere later on, he established "Literary Circles," where he read Fyodor Dostoevsky, Franz Kafka, Thomas Mann, and others. And there is poetry aplenty in his *Church Newsletter*. Literature is no provider of role models for Miskotte. It, rather, turns the gaze toward hard reality—toward a reality that continues to raise questions.

Just like his religious/philosophical "experience," literature, too, returns us to the selflessness that is the foundation of our most intimate self. Neither of the two takes us away from this world to a transcendental heaven where selflessness is elevated to an intangible self. On the contrary, the selflessness with which they confront us puts us back on the ground. In a diary entry from 1924, Miskotte expressed it as follows: "Only heathens plunge into the void because they believed in the All. But we, we have the *earth*."[32]

7

The Path of Mercy Means Simply that You Abandon Self

On a Novel by Shūsaku Endō

The one who truly possesses the word of Jesus is able to hear his silence as well.

—Ignatius of Antioch, Letter to the Ephesians (circa AD 108)

Christianity has roots in a cultural system of pain and suffering.

—Henk Driessen, *Pijn en cultuur*

"The path of mercy means simply that you abandon self."

Does this sentence not succinctly summarize what a Christian way of life is about? God, not we, is the basis of our existence. The needs, ambitions, and pretentions we have, the self-esteem that we uphold: all of this blinds us to the unmistakable fact that we ourselves are not the foundation of our existence, but that this existence is the result of an untraceable given, of a generous act of gift giving that hides behind the term *mercy*. If I would like to surrender my blindness to this fundamental act of gift giving, if I want to live consciously from a realization of "being a gift," if I want to go "the path of mercy," "the way of grace," I must not only set aside all needs, ambitions, pretentions, and self-esteem, I must also and above all—in the strong sense of the word—give up my Ego. "The path of mercy means simply that you abandon self"; "The way of grace is to give up the ego": that is what Christianity boils down to in concrete terms.

141

But what if this sentence is the ultimate argument to convince someone to renounce their Christian way of life and Christianity itself? What if this sentence ultimately means that to go the required "path of mercy," one has to surrender one's self even as a Christian and deny one's Christian identity for good?

This argument is raised in a crucial scene at the end of Shūsaku Endō's novel *Silence* (1966)—the novel on which Martin Scorsese's eponymous film (released in 2016) is based.[1] The one to whom the sentence is addressed is asked to not even hold true to his Christian Ego, his religious identity, or, consequently, to his religion.

What follows shortly addresses this scene from *Silence*, before subsequently reflecting on the headstrong, contradictory condition into which the Christian narrative forces the Ego.

"Trample! Trample!"

Endō's novel takes us on a journey to Japan of the early 1640s. Under the influence of the Jesuits, Christianity had been able to gain a considerable following there over the previous decades, but during the years in which the story takes place, Christianity is expelled from Japan. Jesuits have become *personae non gratae*, and Japanese Christians are ruthlessly persecuted. *Silence* tells the story of a young Jesuit, Sebastian Rodrigues, who clandestinely enters the country with a companion to search for their older fellow brother and mentor, Padre Ferreira. According to rumors, he has succumbed to the torture of the Japanese and converted to the local Buddhist religion. Once Rodrigues and his companion arrive in Japan, both, as might be expected, are arrested. The companion does not survive, and Rodrigues is put under pressure to renounce Christianity in public. But he stays true to his faith and mission. Most of the torture he has to endure involves watching how Japanese converts die during torture. The message from the rulers is clear: "If your Good Tidings really are good to your Japanese brothers, renounce your faith, and no-one will be tortured or killed anymore."

The novel's climax is the moment when Rodrigues, though prisoner, still sees the goal of his mission realized and is given the opportunity to meet Ferreira. The latter has indeed converted to Buddhism, lives with a Japanese woman under a new Japanese name, Sawano Chuan, and now puts his scientific knowledge to the service of the Japanese people.

At a certain moment during that highly emotional confrontation between the two Portuguese priests, the interpreter intervenes to remind Ferreira of his duty and urges Rodrigues to follow the former's example and renounce his Christianity. It is the interpreter who, directly addressing Rodrigues, utters the sentence with which this chapter opens:

> "Think it over," went on the interpreter. "You're the only Christian priest left in this country. Now you're captured and there's no one left to teach the peasants and spread your doctrine. Aren't you useless?" . . . "You heard what Chuan said. He's translating books of astronomy and medicine; he's helping the sick; he's working for other people. Think of this too: as the old bonze keeps reminding Chuan, the path of mercy means simply that you abandon self. Nobody should worry about getting others into his religious sect. To help others is the way of the Buddha and the teaching of Christianity—in this point the two religions are the same. What matters is whether or not you walk the path of truth."[2]

Of course, Rodrigues understands the perversity of the argument, if only because it fits into a strategy of coercion and torture. But things change when, a little later, in a second meeting, it becomes clear how his former spiritual leader, Ferreira, has made this argument his own. When Rodrigues is told that, because of his attitude, Japanese Christians are tortured to death in the "pit,"[3] he replies by arguing that heaven awaits them. With that, Ferreira replies, Rodrigues first and foremost coldly camouflages his own narcissism:

> "You make yourself more important than them. You are preoccupied with your own salvation. If you say that you will apostatize, those people will be taken out of the pit. They will be saved from suffering. And you refuse to do so. It's because you dread to betray the Church. You dread to be the dregs of the Church, like me." . . . "Christ would certainly have apostatized to help men." . . . "For love Christ would have apostatized. Even if it meant giving up everything he had."[4]

Ferreira says this just as Rodrigues is confronted with the *fumi-e*, a metal plate bearing the likeness of Christ on which he has to tread. It is, in the eyes of the Japanese rulers, the official sign that someone renounces Christianity. When Rodrigues finally does tread, it is as if Christ himself speaks from beneath the plate, not to admonish him but to encourage him.

> And then the Christ in bronze speaks to the priest: "Trample! Trample! I more than anyone know of the pain in your foot. Trample! It was to be trampled on by men that I was born into this world. It was to share men's pain that I carried my cross."[5]

And it is not only "the Christ" who speaks so. The author of the novel turns out to concur. If we can at least interpret the "end" of the novel in this way ("end" between quotes, since an appendix follows with notes from the "Diary of an officer at the Christian residence"). The last words of the direct report of Rodrigues's fate reveal the fact that he, even after his apostasy, hears confession one last time, to forgive the one who, again and again, gave him up to the authorities.

> The priest had administered that sacrament that only the priest can administer. No doubt his fellow priests would condemn his act as sacrilege; but even if he was betraying them, he was not betraying his Lord. He loved him now in a different way from before. Everything that had taken place until now had been necessary to bring him to this love. "Even now I am the last priest in this land. But Our Lord was not silent. Even if he had been silent, the priest's life until this day would have spoken of him."[6]

In Rodrigues's apostasy, in this radical renunciation of his pious Ego, so Endō suggests, a God is revealed who no longer does what He did during the entire novel, that is, remain silent. Or, the author immediately adds, even if God does still remain silent, what the believer does nevertheless speaks of his presence.

A Brief Genealogy of the Christian Ego as Self-Denial

It is remarkable how the Christian message, as it is displayed here, culminates in an ultimate self-annihilation. It is as if the novel wants to show us how this message of love-giving ultimately also has to give *itself* away and to remove the need for itself. Or is it nothing but a consistent consequence? Does the basic logic underlying Christian love finally result in self-denial, in the denial of the Ego that professes Christianity, of the subject that bears it?

However, is giving up the Ego a Christian idea at all? Is Christianity not a religion of salvation? Does it not promise salvation for all those who suffer, and does salvation not suppose an Ego, a subject to enjoy it? Why else would the Japanese have been open to Christianity? The only suggestion the novel offers in this regard is that it concerns lowly, impoverished people who found support in Christianity, to assert themselves against the rich feudal lords oppressing them. What they expected of Christianity was, in the first place, a better life, not only in the spiritual sense, but in a concrete, economic sense as well, improving their individual and collective Ego.

The call to resist social oppression and exploitation is at the core of Christianity. It is the heart of its biblical message, summarized in the idea of the "Kingdom of God," the realization of what the Old Testament prophets called the Promised Land: a society of "righteousness," where justice is done to the disenfranchised, where "the wolf and the lamb" sleep with each other in peace, and where people "beat their swords into plowshares."[7] At the very least, the Japanese also discerned this vision of righteousness and social justice in the message with which the confreres of Francis Xavier bombarded them. But is the goal of justice not that people are granted a life where, free from oppression, they can finally feel at home and be what they are? Where one might, in other words, be the Ego that one is, freely and without restraint? So where does the demand come from to give up every form of Ego? If God's *Glad Tidings* free me, why should I then give up precisely that which can enjoy this freedom and without which this freedom could not be what it promises to be, namely that of a free Ego?

A number of elements from the genealogy of the Christian self-denying Ego will finally shed light on Rodrigues's struggle with his faith and his eventual apostasy. The idea of self-denial, though not absent,[8] is not the central issue in the earliest Christian narrative. On the contrary, the Christian message is first and foremost a positive one. It considers itself the very victory over all negativity. Its message is linked to the Messianic expectancy the Jewish people had started to cherish during the second and first centuries BC. Centuries earlier, to remedy the negative condition His "chosen people" were in (poverty, inequality, injustice, misery; in short, everything that is crooked and "sinful"), Yahweh/God had given them the Book of Law. Handed over to the people via Moses, that Law contained rules and guidelines required to enter the Promised Land—a "Land" that, more than a matter of politics and power, was a matter of a just and peaceful society. When, despite all efforts, that social ideal did not become reality, the idea entered the Jewish religious imagination that God, through the help of the Messiah, would directly intervene to deliver us from all sin and negativity. Where Judaism continued to cherish the coming of the Messiah as an *unfulfilled* expectancy, Christianity asserted that the Messianic "Kingdom of God" was a fact: by taking death upon him, by dying *and* returning from the dead, God (in Jesus) had redeemed the world of death and sin—and, consequently, of all negativity.

Claiming that sin was no longer at play and that death had been overcome did, however, not immediately imply that this was also the case *in reality*. Even after Christ had risen from the dead, as the first Christians believed, and death and sin had been defeated, those same Christians could not deny that people died, and sin and perdition were anything but gone from the world. A new narrative was needed to counter this difficulty. "Ascension" provided it. Christ had delivered us from sin and death, but He had to go back to the Father "for a while," in order, then, to return definitively and to complete, on a universal scale, the salvation He had begun to bring in his own person. The end of time, which in principle had already become a fact with Christ's resurrection, had actually only been set in motion in order to be definitively carried out when He returned from the Father. On his return, the risen Jesus, in the Last Judgment, would forever separate life from death, wholeness from sin, immortality from mortality and, in this way, make Eternal Life a full reality.

Meanwhile—i.e., in the period between Christ's first and second coming—Christians were supposed to see, *through* concrete, transient reality that remained full of sin, the eternal, immortal reality that had started its victory march with Christ's resurrection. The Plato-inspired philosophies of the time helped them explain this more or less coherently. In addition, they could also reach for the stoic idea of the *logos spermatikos*: the *logos*, that is to say, the print of eternal being, which—difficult to see, yet visible to believing eyes—had been sown even in the darkest corners of the imperfect material world.[9] So the Christians realized that they were still living in the visible world full of imperfection, death, and sin, but this did not prevent them, in their eyes, from already taking part in a perfect but invisible world that was present everywhere, albeit in embryonic, "spermatic" form. This is the way in which the Christian *agape* communities understood themselves: as anticipations—and embryonic forms—of the true Promised Land that would soon, after the Last Judgment, become a universal reality.[10]

The very point where the world rubbed the Christian's nose in mortality and death—read: where it led them to the lions at Circus Maximus and other public arenas—was also, according to the Christians themselves, where they most clearly testified of the world in which death and sin had already been vanquished. Being obliged to give up their Ego gave them the chance to show that their Ego was no longer subject to the regime of sin and death, and already partook of the eternity their Gospel proclaimed. They could easily sacrifice their mortal Ego; after all, they already partook of a heavenly Ego—or of a blissful state in which an Ego was no longer needed.

It is important to realize that this structure, which underpins this Christian understanding of the self, is responsible for the central place Christianity in general has allocated to suffering from its early beginnings to the present day.

As a religion of salvation, the aim of Christianity is to relieve suffering and to install a society beyond pain and misery. In this, Christianity is perfectly in line with the message the Old Testament prophets received from their monotheistic God. Christianity has never abandoned this social mission. But that same Christianity has regarded suffering not only as the to-be-opposed objective of its redemptive work. Paradoxically, suffering functioned at the same time as a means to identify attained salvation. The suffering they themselves bore gave Christians the opportunity to show that at the very moment of suffering, there was simultaneously an escape from that suffering. Immersed in pain, they endured it with heads held high, in this way showing that they no longer fell under the regime of suffering—that they, in other words, already partook of a life in which mortality had been overcome.

Experiencing suffering as that from which, at the very moment you experience it, you have been redeemed: this became the typically Christian way to define and experience the core of human existence. Until then, it had never occurred to a single culture to understand the core of human existence in this paradoxical way. This self-understanding was so far-reaching that it profoundly marked our culture for the next two millennia.

This paradox perfectly expresses the structure that lies at the basis of Christian asceticism. Only in deprivation and mortification does the ascetic find what matters in life. They have to meet the earthly, have to confront themselves with the irrefutable characteristics of their human condition (with hunger, thirst, cold, deprivation, need), but to refute them and to *deny* that this is our true condition. After all, our true condition is, the ascetic believes, eternal perfection and immaculate completion. But he can only experience these in a "negative way," namely, in denying their opposite, in the sad vale of tears full of hardship and deprivation. Only here can he suffer and at the same time testify of the realm beyond suffering, pain, and death.

At the crossroads of this human, all too human condition and its divine counterpart is where Christians position themselves. Just as they are *in*, but not *of* the world, they find themselves *in*, but not *of* the human condition. Concrete suffering keeps them in that position—that is why they also consciously seek it.

The Christian culture installed in the Middle Ages succeeded in giving this position, so to speak, a kind of comfort that kept it livable. In the destruction of his earthly Ego, the medieval monk was still aware of being borne by a God who might have been invisible and transcendent but who permeated nature and culture right down to the smallest details. In this way, even if one had left one's Ego behind, one was still accommodated in a community that, in its way, gave shape to the old dream of the Promised Land. Even "liberated" from his Ego, the monk was aware of his congregation's support, as the pious citizens inspired by the *Devotio moderna* knew that the urban Christian community in which they lived supported them. Here too, Christians were *in* and not *of* the world, and they stood at the intersection, painful by definition (for them), between this and the "other" world. But because the earthly world here and now was itself Christian, that place was not necessarily also *openly* and *effectively* painful for them.

With the emergence of modernity, in which world and culture ceased to be Christian per se, this changed. Standing at the place where this imperfect world cuts away from the perfect, Christians now find less solace from the culture around them. If they want to take their place as Christians in the world seriously, they are now forced, more than ever before, to deliberately seek out situations of suffering. It is no coincidence that, as is known, the "cruel" practices within the milieus of the religious "spiritual ones" and mystics only increased in number and size during the seventeenth and eighteenth centuries.[11]

Increasingly being rejected by a culture becoming less and less religious allowed early modern Christians to be, with renewed strength, the "displaced" they themselves claimed to be in this earthly world. And they could only experience this strength in the personal relationship with suffering that confronted them and which they, for this reason, also sought out and cultivated *as such*.

The missionary zeal that characterizes Christianity during this time might also be seen in this light. The deprivations the missionaries braved on far continents, and the uncooperative, often hostile audiences they had to endure there, could return them to the foundation of their Christian existential self-understanding. The very animosity of the world in which they spread the Good News only strengthened the existential position they measured out to themselves, namely, being associates of and witnesses to a truth that is not of this world.

However important they were for the promotion purposes of the time, the measure of the missionaries' Christian engagement was not so much the results of the missionary zeal but the often-infernal hardships and pain they had to endure. These were valued in themselves. More specifically, the "blissful" and "divine" way in which they were endured was de facto the only "testimony" of the perfect world with which the missionaries wanted to replace the imperfect pagan world.

Neither the number of conversions nor the extent to which the Promised Land of justice and peace was realized counted that much. Realizing that these would never really bring the promised Kingdom of God to earth, one would have to wait for the Last Judgment for this to happen. What counted was the inner attitude with which one acknowledged the project of the Promised Land, the zeal with which one embodied, in this wretched world, the Heavenly Jerusalem in embryonic form. And this attitude could only be revealed in the way in which one, unable to physically leave this world, did it *mentally*. The suffering one personally had to endure lent itself perfectly to this. This is also the reason why suffering is cultivated as something in itself, and at the expense of the message of salvation, which is also part of Christianity and calls for the concrete relief of everyday suffering as much as possible.

Rodrigues's Doubt

It is against this background that the fate of Rodrigues, the protagonist in Endō's *Silence*, should be understood. The novel tells the story of

the growing doubt to which the young *padre* falls prey, tormented by
the pressure of physical and mental torture to which he is subjected.
He cannot believe that his former colleague and mentor Ferreira succumbed to Japanese torture and renounced his Christian faith. That
is why—though almost certain that he will be captured, tortured, and
killed—he beseeches his superiors for a secret mission to Japan. To do
what? Not only to find out whether or not Ferreira had held on to his
faith, but also to attain that which Ferreira perhaps had not been able
to reach: martyrdom, which means *martyrium*, bearing witness to Eternal
Life at the most appropriate moment, namely, when existence itself is
reduced to what it seems to be: finitude and death. This is the kind of
death Rodrigues seeks, in order to testify to whom he has always been: a
Christian, which means a partaker of the Eternally Living One (Christ)
and, in this way, of the Heavenly Jerusalem.

The novel follows his doubt up until the moment when it has
also undermined the last of his coordinates, his testifying martyrdom.
To go the path of mercy, you have to abandon yourself, he is taught.
He understands this teaching against the background of how he has
been educated: You have to give up your Ego insofar as it is attached to
the earthly and perishable, for that Ego is itself earthly and perishable.
Against this background, doubt is a welcome instrument on your way
to surrendering yourself. The latter would not be possible if you did not
question all the false ways in which you pretend to do so. That is also
why Rodrigues went out in search of the situation in which he would
be certain of being confronted with this kind of doubt. The torture he
would face in Japan would undoubtedly lead him there.

But this torture proves trickier than he anticipated. The crux of
it lies in others, converted Japanese Christians, being tortured to death,
even if they stepped on the *fumi-e* and renounced their faith.[12] Not *his*
but *their* fate lies in Rodrigues's hands, the fate of those to whom he
preached the *Glad Tidings*, the promise that the Messiah had liberated
them—or would in the future, or in the afterlife, liberate them—from
all sin, evil, and other negative fortunes.

As perverse as it is, the torture method followed here touches the
core of Rodrigues's faith, precisely the point where his Christian narrative
is tied to the message of salvation he preaches. Does this message bring
salvation to the people? Does it bring the realm of justice and peace for
which they hope? Or does it bring mainly—or, even, only—salvation
for the preacher himself who, from the problems this impossible task

brings, draws the evidence that he already belongs to those for whom salvation has come? Put in a different way: Does the Christian give up his own Ego for the salvation of others, or does he abuse other people's unfulfilled desire for salvation to imagine himself as having achieved salvation? Is the fellow human being the instrument or is he the goal of the salvation that Christianity preaches?

In the first chapter, we already discussed Fénelon, who unequivocally states in one of his *Lettres spirituelles* that one's relation with a fellow human is never about what happens in that mutual relation itself, but only about what this might contribute to one's relationship to God: "Receive from the hands of men the comfort that God will give you through them. You must receive it not from them, but through them from Him."[13] My love for others is about God, and therefore about *me*, about *my* relationship with God, about the salvation that I expect for myself. And even if my own salvation leaves me indifferent, as is the case with Fénelon's *pur amour*, it is not less valid that love is a matter between God and me, and that my fellow human being is an instrument, even in my *moment suprême* of selflessness, to showcase the greatness of my Ego.

It is from the mouth of a pagan that Rodrigues hears that "the path of mercy is that you abandon self." It is not inconceivable that at this moment the Fénelonian reasoning goes through his mind and he succumbs to the doubt that has been festering in him for a long time. The path to Christian selflessness culminates in an unparalleled affirmation of the own self, and this explicitly at the expense of others—at the expense of the Promised Land or the agapeic community that Rodrigues's monotheistic Christian message is all about.

Endō's novel does not comment on how Christianity itself might refute this impasse. Rodrigues solves it by simply turning his back on Christianity and embracing the religion of his torturers, even if, the novel suggests, he nevertheless remains faithful to Christianity. When, years after his apostasy, he still hears the confession (and consequently runs the risk of being betrayed for it) of the contemptible man who repeatedly betrayed and continued to stalk him, the former priest experiences it as a real sacrament. In any case, he is at this moment assured of Christ's approval. I already cited the passage before:

> No doubt his fellow priests would condemn his act as sacrilege; but even if he was betraying them, he was not betraying his Lord. He loved him now in a different way from before. Every-

thing that had taken place until now had been necessary to bring him to this love. "Even now I am the last priest in this land. But Our Lord was not silent. Even if he had been silent, the priest's life until this day would have spoken of him."[14]

God kept quiet for Rodrigues's entire mission. Hence the title of the novel (*Silence*). Here, for the first time, we read that God has not kept silent. But neither is there any mention of speaking from God's side. So where did Rodrigues hear the "non-silence" of God? In the fact that he feels that God still loves him? Or, to be more precise, in the fact that he had to experience all of this, that he had to endure the stubborn silence of God, only to now realize that God loves him and what this means?

The novel seems to evoke something like this. But the suggestive phrases might also point to Rodrigues now hearing God's *silence* in the right way, only now realizing that God, of all beings, speaks in his silence. Because even if God had remained silent, "the priest's life until this day would have spoken of him." What does this mean? That he, through what he went through and experienced—also by what he is and does at this moment—testifies of God, of his telling silence. Then God speaks in the fact that Rodrigues illegally hears the confession of his traitor. Then Rodrigues's apostasy is the ultimate interpretation of what God has to say. God has always remained silent. Rodrigues has now heard this silence speak and gleans from it that his apostasy was vital to hear it, to hear God, to hear Him in the fact that his traitor asks him to hear his confession and that he does hear his confession. It is a secret confession; concealed at the moment it takes place and meant to remain concealed forever. But this concealment has Christ's approval, Rodrigues realizes. Therein God's silence speaks. Or, what comes down to the same thing: therein speaks God.

God Himself has become radically selfless here, and without falling into the trap the ruse of selflessness has laid for Him. At this point in time in Japan, the gesture with which God becomes selfless is not made to hide a subtle celebration of his Selfhood.

Here, the radical selflessness of God destroys Christianity to its last fiber. It radically excludes every testimony. Rodrigues might claim that his life still—also in the clandestine confession, also in his life as an apostate—bears witness to God, but this testimony is empty de facto. Nobody takes notice of the divine selflessness that Rodrigues assumes the testimony possesses. And as soon as this might be the case, the testimony is promptly nipped in the bud with an execution. Rodrigues's testimony is without testimony, if you will, without martyrdom, without the possibility of becoming a martyr. He is forever denied the "grace," the "mercy" of suffering for his testimony. The latter is from the outset nullified by the selflessness to which it wants to testify.

Perhaps it is still possible for Rodrigues, as an individual, to maintain some kind of Christian identity in this way—completely clandestinely and never recognized by any one as such, let alone acknowledged. But on this basis, a Christian identity *tout court*—Christianity as a religion, as a social institute, as a real organization—seems totally impossible. In its radicalism, selflessness cannot form the basis of a concretely developed, socially operational Christian "self." Can it be other than obvious?

And yet this does not prevent a fellow member of Rodrigues's order from contradicting the evidence a couple of centuries later. For Michel de Certeau, a Jesuit whose life's work concerned the mysticism of early modernity and who was extensively involved with the problem of self and selflessness in this tradition, Christianity's selflessness hides within itself a chance to provide this religion with its true basis again. Effacing the self is the core mission—and the only real "self"—of that religion, and to find a way out of its current crisis, it has to fully embrace that mission. The next chapter goes into a remarkable essay of Certeau's, in which he extensively develops this thesis.

8

As a Drop in the Ocean

Michel de Certeau's Selfless Christianity

Premodern man's relationship to the world was such that he was supposed to take part in it genuinely. The human spirit shared the Holy Spirit that holds together the divine and the human and guarantees man's contact with the origin of all that is: the creative God and his incarnate Son. Humans considered themselves to be as drops in the ocean of Creation. Yet, this ocean did not make them disappear. On the contrary, in the ocean was the Spirit, allowing the individual to have a relationship with both the ocean and all of his fellow human drops gathered in it.

As explained before,[1] this Spirit broke when modernity emerged. What is generally called "the death of God" is not so much his dying (immortals do not die that fast), but his withdrawal from our natural world. And once the triune God was locked up in heaven, the Spirit lost his job. Our self-understanding was no longer based on the supposition that we are borne by a divine Spirit that we share with everyone else and with the entire universe. Concerning our relationship to reality, our spirit became its own "support"—and so our new "subject." This is, in a nutshell, the Cartesian turn that founded modernity.

Spirituality is a modern term for a variety of things, but, among them, it undeniably also refers to the nostalgia for, as well as the survival of, the Holy Spirit. In spirituality, modern man is looking for a "support" or *subiectum* that is broader than the Cartesian one he is supposed to be based on. He suspects both the pretension and the narrowness of that Cartesian subject. He distrusts the idea of an all too self-assured and self-centered "self." That is why he looks for experiences that bring him

155

out of his "self," or at least deconstruct his ego, in order to feel again what it is to share life with life *as such*, to feel the primacy of life or of that "other" that both transcends and holds him at the same time. In medieval Christian culture, "spirituality" did the same, but it was not known by that name. It was simply called "religion." "Spirituality" became a proper concept only after the "death of the Spirit."[2]

Does spirituality, then, replace the bygone divine foundation of life and reality? Does it provide sense in a world where sense has lost self-evidence? This is a widespread definition of spirituality and it applies to many of its manifestations. What if, however, it is just the other way around? What if spirituality is not an attempt to find a new kind of sense in our modern, inherently senseless world, but on the contrary an acknowledgment of the loss of sense, as well as a way to lose oneself in the world that has become senseless? What if this is the real meaning of what a long-standing Christian tradition defines as becoming "a drop in the ocean"? And what if Christianity, in order to be faithful to its own mission, has to disappear as such a "drop" itself?

This is the basic question underlying Michel de Certeau's reflections on Christianity. As if Christianity, to remain faithful to its "spirituality," has to disappear in a kind of "spirituality for everyday life," in which the references to the Christian origin become imperceptible or, even, nonexistent. In this chapter, I analyze in detail an essay in which Certeau develops this provocative thesis.

Christianity, a New Mythology?

On May 22, 1973, a radio discussion was broadcasted between Michel de Certeau, known then as a Jesuit authority in the field of Christian mysticism, and Jean-Marie Domenach, the editor of the French journal *Esprit*. The radio program was entitled "Christianity, a new mythology?"[3] Yet, none of the speakers really answered the question. Instead, they could not stop dwelling "within" the question and did not succeed in leaving the phase of analyzing the crisis Christianity was in. Or did this crisis not in some way contain Christianity's very essence? The latter was the suggestion—which soon appeared to be the thesis—of Certeau's contribution. In the *éclatement*—in the breaking, the disintegration—of the Christian religion, he discovered the *éclat*—the radiance—of its very core. That core is not to be found in its doctrinal discourse nor in that of its "mythology." It is to be found in the moments its discourses break, where they lose control and get interrupted or haunted by something that is not discursive at all; which, with regard to its discourse, is marked by radical alterity or difference. Such is Certeau's main thesis in the 1973 radio discussion with Domenach.

To the written report of that discussion, he adds an essay entitled in its final, published version: "*Comme une goutte d'eau dans la mer*" (translated as "As a Drop in the Ocean").[4] It is a dense, at times somewhat abstruse and cryptic text. It does not really summarize the points made in the radio program, neither does it elaborate upon all of the issues raised there. In a way, Certeau's sole concern in the additional essay is the act itself of writing down the oral discussion. It is about the passage from oral dialog to the written report (as the original title of its draft version indicates: "From the Body to Writing"). The sole thing Certeau wants to make clear is that, in taking up his pen, writing down what was said and adding to it a proper essay, he is not willing to deny, repress, or change what occurred in the oral happening.

> In passing from the spoken to the written word, I am not attempting to "reinforce" the place I was speaking from, amass proofs, or block up the openings which an evening's talk may have left here. I would not want the written version to call to order—or forget—the "slips" which arise in discussion, all that escapes one's control in spoken language, as though it were necessary to subject the chance advent of desire, which has its source in the other, to the legality of writing.[5]

Writing is able to wipe out—to forget or to repress—the hesitations, misunderstandings, slips of the tongue, or whatever escapes the deliberate intentions of the speaking subject. It fixes both the uttered meanings and the place from where they are uttered; what one is saying and the locus from where this is said. This is why writing is rather blocking the truth than giving access to it, thus one of Certeau's main intuitions. According to him, truth is to be expected from what, in the very act of saying, escapes the said and resists written reports; not from what is held together by the discourse of an assured subject, but from what, in the very act of speaking, escapes the grip of the subject and the lines of its discourse. Truth is a matter of letting in a "desire" that "has its source in the other." It breaks through within a settled "text."[6] Truth is "other," "different," which is why writing *as such* represses or denies it.[7] Fixing the unfixable, it reduces the ungraspable and unknowable to the firm grip of knowledge.

However, the remedy for writing's faults is in its own hands. Writing itself is able to give the "desire of the other" a certain voice. It can *convert* itself and allow—instead of hide—otherness and (thus) truth. This is the explicit intention of Certeau's essay. In his act of writing, he wants to give room to the hesitations, misunderstandings, slips of the tongue, and other deficiencies of the broadcasted oral discussion. These deficiencies should be both the starting point and the main concern of his written essay.

> [T]hese glimpses allow writing to begin again. A certain work therefore introduces into established systems the mobility which the spoken word already betrays. It traces on our maps the longer voyages generated by the momentary "sallies" of conversation. Instead of moving from the written to the spoken, from an orthodoxy to its verbal illustration . . . the process starts from the mobility of speech, porous and tendered, more easily altered than writing by what is still only half expressed within it, and proceeds to produce a language which is reorganized by these first avowals, thus producing a shift in the ranks of knowledge or reason.[8]

Reintroducing in writing the slippery movements that are inherent to oral speaking: this is what Certeau intends to practice in his essay accompanying the discussion report. Deliberately giving a followed path all chances to deviate, as is the case in so many sixteenth- and seventeenth-century travel stories in which the presence and "desire of the other" still visibly disorients the point from where the traveler/author writes his report.[9] In his comments on the oral radio discussion about Christianity, Certeau opts for the same kind of disorientation and therefore follows the unusual way. Instead of going from Christianity's written doctrine to its oral illustration, he returns the doctrine to its oral origin—"oral" in the sense of nonfixed, a not fully known realm of potentialities, filled with "half-words" still able to tell different things than said in the doctrine appropriating the origin, "half-words" that therefore are able to modify, change, or alter the discourse of the reigning doctrine, to bring about "displacements" in its knowledge and its reason.

Christianity's *rupture instauratrice*

What, however, do these remarks about the relation between writing and speaking, between the scriptural and the oral, say about Christianity? Certeau's answer is uncannily simple. What is said in these remarks *is* the core of Christianity. Though dense, the passage that follows the one just quoted cannot be misunderstood: "Here, this process bears on Christianity: in fact, on the relation between a question of truth and my own position. Any analysis of this problem consequently puts in question the place from which I discuss it. There can be no textual work until the remarks I make on Christianity are unearthed from their silent opacity. It is the relation between these remarks and their site of production which is the real subject here."[10] The procedure of returning fixed writing to unfixed speaking expresses the core of what happens in sixteenth- and seventeenth-century Christian mysticism. Certeau had elaborated this insight in the lion's share of his publications during the two decades preceding the radio discussion with Domenach.[11] Already in pre- and early modernity, God's voice was no longer heard as speaking through his Creation, so Certeau had made clear. Not without adding, however, that in the mystical writings of the time, this kind of voice was still present, be it in a mute way. As if, in these texts, God's silence itself was given voice. And as if, for God, a speaking silence was a more adequate way to express Himself than all that was written down in the doctrine of religion and theology.[12]

Here, in his essay commenting on the radio talk he had with Domenach, he makes use of this thesis, though to typify not early modern mysticism but Christianity in general. The essence of Christian religion, so Certeau argues, is not to be found in what can be said *about* it ("*on* Christianity"), but in the *way* this is said or, more precisely, in the way in which what is said relates to the oral act of its saying. It is to be found in the primacy of the saying over the said. It is not a matter of evoking what is in the doctrine's texts, but of letting these texts work ("textual work"). It is a matter of digging out the texts' concealed postulates, that is, to re-find the level of their *production*, of the way in which an unfixed stream of thoughts has been set down in a fixed, *written* discourse. It is about finding, in the texts, traces of how the unstable act of utterance (*énonciation*) has been stabilized in a fixed "statement" (*énoncé*).

And, Certeau adds, this transition from the fixed to the unfixed must be seen in relation to the way in which someone is connected to the produced texts. For, as Certeau writes, the "site of production" is ultimately "my own position." What is revealed by exhuming the postulates of written discourses or doctrines, is the way in which I am their "subject." And this is to say that I am at the same time both *product* and *producer* of the discourse. I am made possible by the discourse; I only exist thanks to the fact that this discourse is readable as if it speaks about me as its subject/object. But at the same time, I am its subject in the sense that I actively intervene in it, independently, as its "agency."[13] All this is possible because my "proper" place in the text is precisely where it is not fixed, where it still lacks balance and coherence. In the locus of that lack, this balance and coherence are *actively produced*. They are made by "me." The lack on which the text is based allows me to fill it in as the text's subject, in both senses of the word: as the subject the text talks about and as the subject acting in, with, and through the text.

The locus of the lack, the place of the subject: this the place of (possible) truth as well. The question of truth is a matter of how I occupy my proper "position" in discourse, how I am its subject, its bearer or support. It is a matter of acknowledging that this position, though founding my identity, at the same time opens it up to a radical difference, an uncanny otherness whose voice I can allow into the text I "write." This is why I have to return what I *say* my identity is, to the *saying* as such. The *enunciated object* must be returned to the *subject of enunciation*.

But, again, how does this kind of advanced, typically twentieth-century theory of the subject tell something about Christianity's essence, about what it means to lend an ear to the *Glad Tidings* in our modern times? In his typically cryptic style, Certeau explains it in what follows:

> The movement which turns the object of the statement [*énoncé*] back toward the site of its utterance [*énonciation*] must moreover be situated in relation to a "way of proceeding" [*manière de faire*] specific for Christianity, if one is to take the latter not solely as on object of study but also as an operation. The whole evangelical tradition makes of such a movement the condition of a practice: "conversion" is that without which no "work" or "logos" of faith may be produced. If the site from which I speak were above suspicion, were placed beyond question, my analysis would cease to be evangelical, and would become the establishment of a "truth" with a religious content.[14]

Christianity is more than a doctrine to be examined as an "object of study." It is an "operation," a "practice," producing an "oeuvre," a "work" or a "logos of faith." And, Certeau adds, that oeuvre—as well as its operation—is based in a "conversion" that occurs in "the place from where I speak."

Does that mean that, producing Christianity on the "the site from which I speak," I *invent* it? That I create it out of nothing? Not at all. I do not invent it, I *convert* it. And I do so just as much as I am *converted by* it and *to* it. The discourse precedes me and offers me a place in its discursive world. It put me at a certain position. Yet, this is at the same time the position from which I convert and "displace" that discourse. It is the locus where I express my skepticism about it or put it into question. It is the locus of its displacement. And because that point of displacement is *my* place (the place where I am the discourse's subject), I make that discourse operative; I make it "work."

So, I—as locus of a "displacement"—am the point where the discourse *happens, occurs*. In the locus where I stand and displace that discourse, it contingently takes place. As a subject, I am the discourse's *incarnation*, giving body to it, being its contingent bearer. I convert the "infinity" of Christian doctrine into a finite reality, supported by a finite subject that, converted to that doctrine, at the same time converts that very doctrine. Although I am myself the product of this discourse, being its subject I made it contingent, working, productive.

Now we might see better how that theory of the subject as "displacement" expresses "the evangelical tradition," and in what sense the evangelical character of the analysis depends on the insight in the "displacing" activity of the subject. A few pages farther on in his essay, Certeau explains this as the core of what happens in the evangelic procedure, that is to say, in the attention and the response one has to the *Good News*'s call. "This 'model' refers to the New Testament combination of 'following [Jesus]' and 'conversion'—of *Nachfolge* and *metanoia*: the first term indicates a going beyond which the name of Jesus opens up, the other a corresponding transformation of consciousness and of conduct."[15] The subject's relation to the discourse is modeled on the believer's relation to Christ's call. Christ asks us to follow Him, but in order to do so, one has to change one's mind and behavior—one needs to *convert*. Yet, conversion seems not to be that simple. For Christ's call can only be heard *on the very basis of* someone's conversion. So, conversion in a way comes first, and makes Christ's call, if not possible, at least effective. It is in this sense that the conversion makes the call "productive." It is my conversion—or, as we read a few sentences further on, my "decision"—that decides what to do with the call coming from Christ or from the text reporting his call. A few lines farther, Certeau writes: "The call which is the principle of this relation cannot be known outside of the response which it receives."[16]

And what is one answering to, when responding to Christ's call? What does one become faithful to, once one says "Yes" to the Lord's injunction, "Follow me"? Neither to the content of Christ's discourse, nor to the fullness of his presence. What one follows by obeying Christ's commandment, is absent from that very commandment. Precisely this absence is followed. Christ's call comes from his *voice*, which, in his commandment, is wiped away by the response or even by the mass of responses and respondents, as Certeau declares a few lines farther on: "The 'follow me' comes from a voice which has been effaced, forever irrecuperable, vanished into the changes which echo it back, drowned in the throng of its respondents. It has nothing which is proper to it, no concrete place and no abstract expression. It is no longer anything except the tracing of a passage—made possible by it—a relation between an arrival (birth) and a departure (death), then between a return (resurrection) and a disappearance (ascension), indefinitely."[17] Obeying Jesus is obeying a "passage." It is obeying what is absent from the commandment that is issued. It is following only a name, a name without a proper place and indicating an unlocalizable absence. This absence has a place there *because of* my obedience and *thanks to* the performativity of my response, to the "practice" of my "conversion." Christ's commandment—or, more generally, Christianity's commandment—is a discourse, and my obedience, which converts me, "converts" that discourse as well: it opens that discourse up to its own absentee, to its own "excess,"[18] to the "other" haunting the identity that it performs.

> A signifying practice intervenes in received identities . . . and in contractual stabilities . . . as a break which institutes a relation which is not defined by conformity to a Law, but by conversion toward the other, no longer a "fidelity" but a "faith." Instead of secret "existence" [*être-là*] as principle and domain of just actions, there is the act of "coming" or "following," which makes for trust in the other, signals to him

and "makes truth" [qui *fait* confiance à l'autre, lui *fait* signe et '*fait*' la vérité']. But it functions in a necessary relation to institutions and received forms which in principle are maintained. The eruption of Jesus does not found a new site—a Testament, a religion—which would have a different content but the same form as the preceding one. It introduces the non-site of a difference into a system of sites [*Il introduit le non-lieu d'une différence dans un système de lieux*].[19]

Christianity is not simply a doctrine and an institution, it is a *practice* vis-à-vis that doctrine and institution. It interferes with the doctrine and the institute, it interrupts them, in order to convert them to the "other" whose absence they hide, an "other" who is their very origin. At its core, Christianity is an "instituting rupture," a "founding break" (*rupture instauratrice*).[20] Elsewhere in this essay, we read that the "Christian specificity can now be signaled only by a break in operative rationalities or social formations."[21]

Yet, taking up again the "founding break" does not *reconcile* Christianity with its origin or restore its originality. That origin is "'other," it is a "passage" that can never be appropriated. It can only be "practiced" in a moment of "break" or "rupture," a moment of interference with the ruling discourse or institution. And it can do this *only for a moment*, since this practice is not capable of fully appropriating the possibilities of the "rupture." This is why, according to Certeau, Christianity *as such* cannot be defined as "fidelity" to its doctrine. It is a "faith," which for him means having trust precisely in what is lacking in a doctrine. It is having trust in the openness to the doctrine's own subversive potentialities, to its own otherness. And this kind of faith can only be "practiced" in an "act of coming and following," "which makes for trust in the other, signals to him and 'makes truth.'"

A Subversive Drop of Water in the Sea

Certeau himself does not use the word *subversive* here, but that is exactly what characterizes his definition of the founding core of Christianity. For Christianity's autocritical gesture only "functions in a necessary relation to institutions and received forms which in principle are maintained," as said in the quote above. So, it is a matter of neither destroying[22] nor changing Christianity, but of celebrating its nonappropriable origin: "the ineffability of the subject, saying itself,"[23] or the always already disappeared "passage" it is based upon. This "passage" has always already been repressed, and it can only be celebrated as the inherently instantaneous "return of the repressed," as a repressed that, even in its return, refounds its repressed state.[24]

The founding "passage," "the irruption of Jesus," is strictly *subversive*, since (as Certeau writes in the quote above) it "does not found a new site—a Testament, a religion—which would have a different content but the same form as the preceding one." The entire history of the relationship between the "elect people and the one God" is characterized by "the caesura at work," Certeau writes in the next sentence.[25]

A "caesura at work": another name for the subversion that is the core of Christian and, even, monotheistic tradition; another name for faith, defined as "the relation that this caesura *inscribes* in the *place* where it has been produced (the one of the Covenant)."[26] "Believing is 'coming' or 'following' (a gesture marked by a separation), leaving one's place, being disarmed by this exile out of identity and contract, and thus renouncing possession and heritage so as to be delivered to the voice of the other and dependent on this coming or response."[27] Faith is the transfiguration "of the 'letter' of the Law into the 'poem' of difference"; "the conversion of the legality of the text . . . into the weakness of a fable."[28] So, faith makes Christianity's "instituting rupture" work. Faith is, Certeau writes, "the operation which is traced in the effective sites of our social belonging when these sites are put into relation with the break of which the condition of possibility is the evangelical fable, throughout its present and past versions."[29]

But what if, in our time, Christianity has lost its own "effective sites"? In previous times, it did have such "effective sites," indeed. Its religion reigned over the Western world and, in the eyes of Certeau, it lived its "essence" as a kind of "coherent strategy around its border-lines."[30] Together with the institution of the Church and its doctrinal power, these borderlines have faded away. As hegemonic power, "civil society has replaced the Church." So, Christianity's "de-centering" and "subversive" activity now concerns civil society, and no longer acts within a proper Christian space (the Church). Now, Christianity only exists in "anonymous" practices—practices Christians can no longer consider to be theirs.[31] Now, it is up to the individual believers and their contingent alliances to de-center and subvert (not so much the Church, its institution and its doctrine, as) the institutionalized secular culture that has replaced the Church.[32]

So, since Christianity is no longer itself a hegemonic social body, it has been reduced to its very essence and, in a way, "privatized." It is now up to private Christian initiatives to make the "transit" from "body" to "writing" (as the title of the longer version of Certeau's essay indicates: "From the Body to Writing, a Christian Transit").[33] "Writing," here, is to be understood in the active sense that Certeau gives to the term: allowing, within the boundaries of a written and fixed text, the voice of the other's *oral* call. "What survives this progressive collapse of the 'body'—a central problem for all present developments—is the formal relation between going beyond a situation and the decision to 'do' faith. . . . As the ecclesiastical 'body of sense' loses its effectivity, it is for Christians themselves to assure the articulation of this 'model' with actual situations."[34] It is up to individual Christians to take the decision to subvert social and cultural institutions by giving voice to the "other" who is calling through society's and culture's "ruptures." This decision, however, is not meant to create a new and proper identity. It can no longer be seen as the "homogeneous tactics" of an ecclesial body, of a church, or of any other visible Christian identity. That body or identity is gone; it can only survive as the return of the repressed, as something that even at the time of the Church was disappearing in its return. It can only survive in a "fable," in a story unable to fix its saying (*fari*) into an established discourse, doctrine, or *doxa*.

So, the returned of the Christian repressed is even more invisible and ungraspable now. Breaking with the notion of an *Ecclesia Aeterna*, Certeau ends his essay with the idea that Christian faith, fable, and practice are a kind of

> fragile and floating text, witness of itself alone, yet lost in the innumerable murmur of language, and hence perishable. But this fable heralds the joy of obliterating itself in what it figures, of returning to the anonymous work out of which it was born, of converting itself to this other which it is not. The writing of belief, in its weakness, appears on the ocean of language only to disappear, taken up into the work of uncovering, in other writings, the movement by which, ceaselessly, they "come" and "go." According to an expression of the mystics, it is a "drop in the ocean."[35]

These are the last words of Certeau's essay. At least of the version that appeared in Le christianisme éclaté. The original and longer version gives us one more paragraph to read.[36] There, the core of Christianity—the "'evangelical' mark"—is once more described as an opération passante et passagère (a fleeting and rapid operation). To explain this, Certeau refers to the "angel" with whom the patriarch Jacob fought in the night near the Yabboq when his name was changed into "Israel," as well as to the thief in the night about which the Gospel talks as being the way in which the Messiah will come (1 Tess. 5:2). And Certeau associates both figures to the idea of the uncanny—unheimlichkeit—that Freud ascribes to dreams. "It is a fleeting and rapid operation. Its 'evangelical' mark would be the wound which the angel at Yabbok (Genesis 32:23–32), the night-time thief of the parable, the uncanny familiarity of the dream produces by day in a territory or an activity."[37] And it is then that Certeau "signs" his text, saying that even his name hides the relationship with this "other" whom no identity, no "name" can appropriate. Which is to say that every identity or name ultimately originates in a call coming from the other. "Signing" his essay, Certeau writes that even a signature calls out to its "other":

> This text is in fact a stage in the itinerancy produced by the quest for the proper name; that is to say, the name which comes to us always from the other. 'Michel' is 'Who is like El?'—who is like the Unnameable, God? This word says the opposite of the proper. In the (fearful? respectful? retiring?) mode of the question, it calls for its erasure.[38]

To have one's name explained as "Who is like the nameless?" wipes out one's identity at the very moment it is named and fixed. As a drop in the ocean. According to Certeau, Christianity's essential mission is summarized in this wiping gesture that deconstructs the construction of every identity, including its own. The impossibility of his own name, of an own proper name as such: for Certeau, this is the marque évangélique; this is what Christian faith is about.

Frame of Reference: One Way

In the background of Certeau's theory of Christianity, one recognizes the influence of several theoretical frameworks that were dominant in his days. First of all, there is Michel Foucault. Certeau owes his method to Foucault: to analyze discourses dug up in the basements of unfrequented libraries as well as the ones heard in everyday life. But the way in which he handles this method is not exactly the same. For Certeau's aim is neither simply to lay bare the discourses that have formed—and changed—the different *epistemes* and their caesuras that constitute the genealogy of the *episteme* we live in today.[39] Nor is it simply to discover the *dispositives,* which in Foucault's conceptual apparatus are broader than epistemes since they include nondiscursive elements as well, such as practices, strategies, institutions.[40] Of course, like Foucault, Michel de Certeau is interested in the changes taking place in the *epistemes* and *dispositives* underlying our history and present identity, but, unlike Foucault, his interest goes beyond that.[41]

That certainly goes for his interest in the modern subject. For Foucault, the subject is the instance "subjected" to the modern discourse. This is why "man," once he has become a "subject"—in the sense of "object" of the human sciences—will disappear with these sciences as easily as "a face engraved in sand on a seashore."[42] If only for this reason, the discourse's subject is not Foucault's main point of interest. Just as little is his interest in himself as being the subject of his text. Asked where he is himself in his text, Foucault replied: "No I am not where you are lying in wait for me, but over here, laughing at you."[43] The subject of a discourse is never where one expects it to be, not even the subject of Foucault's own discourse. The subject is by definition "passing," vanishing, and one can even practice discourse analysis in order to write oneself "away." In the same passage from *The Archeology of Knowledge,* Foucault adds: "I am no doubt not the only one who writes in order to have no face. Do not ask who I am and do not ask me to remain the same."[44]

It is clear that Certeau cannot but fully approve this thesis. Real thought is not fixed on an identity: "Identity freezes the gesture of thinking. It pays homage to an order. To think, on the contrary, is to pass through; it is to question that order, to marvel that it exists, to wonder what made it possible, to seek, in passing over its landscape, traces of the movements that formed it, to discover in these histories supposedly laid to rest 'how and to what extent it would be possible to think otherwise.'"[45] Foucault's remark about identity matches the way Certeau ends the essay we studied in detail—at least in its original version as posthumously published in *La faiblesse de croire.* There, Certeau evokes his own proper name in its quality of, precisely, wiping away all "property" ("it calls for its erasure"). Here, the theoretical frame of reference is not so much Michel Foucault as Jacques Derrida, more exactly the way in which Derrida signs some of his essays, thus putting forward the radical "improper" nature of proper names.[46] Derridian deconstruction has shown that the inscription of the written trace always already spoils the unstained and full identity it intends to affirm. Even a signature, in its very act of confirming the authenticity of the subject of the enunciation (*le sujet de l'énonciation*), at the same time crosses out that authenticity. Performing the authentic author, a signature is supported by the unavoidable possibility of inauthenticity characterizing/deconstructing any authenticity. By presenting his own proper name as "the contrary of what is proper," Certeau is obviously referring to Derridian deconstruction.

Yet, what is definitely neither Foucauldian nor Derridian is Certeau's persistent emphasis on the subject. The subject is his main point of interest, however passing, disappearing, nonidentical, or nonoriginal it may be. In spite of its vanishing character, he nonetheless ascribes to its locus an active productivity and emancipatory force, and even an "evangelical hallmark."

Except for the latter attribution, the frame of reference here is Lacanian psychoanalytical theory, which is an explicit theory of the subject.[47] Certeau is very familiar with it. He was a member of the École Freudienne de Paris (Lacan's school) and a loyal participant in Lacan's weekly seminar, and he wrote several essays on Freudian and Lacanian theory.[48] Like so many French theories of the midst of the twentieth century, Lacanian theory is poststructural. Not without reserve, it embraces the paradigm of Lévi-Strauss's structuralism that affirms the relative autonomy of the "symbolic order," that is to say, the field of representations that people share with one another and that constitute their "culture."[49] This field is not to be understood on the basis of people's intentions, of the sense of life expressed in it for instance. Structured "symbolically" (i.e., as a linguistic field, a language), it functions in an autonomous way, independently from the meanings expressed in it. The field *precedes* the individual, who, contrary to what he thinks, is subjected to it. This symbolic structure, disconnected from the biological level and obedient to an autonomous logic, is the field where man lives his cultural life, including his subjective identity. In Lacan's interpretation, the libidinal logic Freud discovered—the polymorphously perverse logic obedient to the pleasure principle—is at work in that field, as far as it constitutes the unconscious of the individual. This is why, so Lacan argues, the field of the unconscious—*die andere Schauplatz*, as Freud calls it[50]—is not the private set of repressed wishes, but the public realm of the "symbolic order"—of the "signifiers" that people share with one another. Man's subjectivity is but an effect of that symbolic order. That order is the "material" of which the human identity is made. The individual subject is but a supposition, imagined thanks to the machinery of the symbolic order and enabling the individual to consider himself as being his own subject/bearer.

In a strictly structuralist view, the subject/support/bearer of man's identity is the symbolic order. If Lacan is a *post*-structuralist, it is because of his different view on the individual subject. For Lacan, this subject, however imaginary it may be, intervenes in the symbolic field in a specific way. It introduces a proper logic subverting the logic of that field. Its locus is the void that is inherent to the symbolic system. Being a realm of signifiers endlessly referring to other signifiers without ever arriving at the final "signified" or the "real" thing to which they refer, that order rests in a constitutive lack. That lack—i.e., the point in the system where it is about to come full circle without ever succeeding in it—is the subject's locus. That lack is the locus where the libidinal being constitutes itself as an unfulfillable longing for a "self," that is, as subject of desire.[51] Occupying the locus of that lack, the libidinal system acts *as if* it has a ground. And it is this "as if"—this radically fictitious subject—that intervenes in the logic of the symbolic order. Not as its creator, since it is a mere effect of that order. But as what is able to subvert its "normal" logic. So, although the subject consciously considers himself to be the fixed ground of a symbolic system, unconsciously, it is the place where the system is susceptible to changes, since the locus of that subject is the system's lack, its "non-ground," its lack of ground (which, precisely, is its only ground).

Even if the Lacanian system is not its direct source, Certeau's thought is so imbued with it that this reference is able to clarify many of the concepts he uses in the essay we read. The age of *writing* (i.e., of fixing the world in an objective, controllable, and manageable way, as Certeau defines it) coincides with a vehement denial of the real status of the subject, of the fact that the subject is a fictitious invention at the locus where that world (being a "symbolic universe") rests in its lack. The Cartesian subject supposes itself to relate to the world as if it is disconnected and free from it, as if that world is a blank sheet of paper on which it can limitlessly write what it wants—read: manipulate the world. According to Certeau, this supposition is built upon a denial.

Anything that escapes this written world, Certeau argues, cancels out that denial and gives truth a chance. And this truth says that the world is built upon a void, upon what Certeau calls an "instituting rupture," a *rupture instauratrice*: at the point where the world (symbolic order) is lacking, *there* is its foundation. In the locus of its "displacement," it has its "proper" place. That "proper" place is mere lack, mere difference, "the non-site of a difference in a system of sites."[52]

And where can I discover the world's "non-site"? Certeau's answer is thoroughly Lacanian: at "the place of its enunciation" ("the site of its utterance [*énonciation*]").[53] At the place where the discourse that constitutes the world (the symbolic order) is spoken. There, the subject has its "practice," there it "operates." There, we meet the unfixed "subject" of the world. There, the subject intervenes in the discourse by which it is at the same time constituted.

Which is not to say that, being a subject, I can create that discourse/world at will. The "site from where I speak" (*le lieu d'où je parle*)[54] cannot be appropriated, not even by me, but from that position I *can* affirm the lack upon which my discourse rests, thus allowing otherness and change. Subverting from within the discourse that constitutes me, I can open up its "site of production," the place where it is produced and, thus, is changeable.[55] Being subjected to that enunciated discourse, I can take the position of its "subject of the utterance" (*sujet de l'énonciation*), which is the way to open the "enunciated" toward its otherness, its active productivity, its changeability. It is the way to open it toward its truth, so Certeau argues. That is, to recall just one example, the way Certeau interprets the May 68 Revolt: it is a *prise de parole*, a "capture of speech."[56] In a closed world, this "capture of speech" rediscovers both the practice and the subject of enunciation, of speaking instead of writing, of displacing the written and opening it to alterity and change.

Frame of Reference: The Other Way Around

It is clear now that many of Certeau's concepts and schemes can be translated in Lacanian terms without betraying the core of his thought. In a modern world that has become a fixed and controlled system, Certeau's theory tries to affirm the world's unfixed ground: only there, its true subject/bearer is to be found. And only there, at the locus of this subject, one finds the truth as "different," "Other," *Autre*.

But once again the question arises: Where is Christianity in all of this? Certeau's answer is already known: this *is* Christianity. Christianity is that practice, returning the "'enunciated'"—its own, but, since this has lost social support, that of our post-Christian age as well—to the "subject of the enunciation" and, thus, opening it to alterity and truth, to wit, God. For, according to Certeau, God is not the rock of certainty giving our world its solid foundation. God is uncertain, and faith means to abandon oneself to uncertainty, to go away to a still unknown country, like Abraham leaving Ur in Chaldea. At its core, faith is skepticism. It is abandoning oneself to a questionable site, which is no other than the "site from where one speaks." As we read in a passage from Certeau's essay that has already been cited: "If the site from which I speak were above suspicion, were placed beyond question, my analysis [of Christianity and of current culture] would cease to be evangelical, and would become the establishment of a "truth" with a religious content."[57] Listening to Christ's call or subjecting myself to his doctrine implies a "conversion" that not only converts me (recognizing the void—the Other—from where I am speaking), but at the same time converts this doctrine and makes it open to changes. Saying "yes" to Christ is confronting Christian, or other, doctrines with their own subject as "passing," "vanishing," unstable, excessive—as "the non-site of a difference in a system of sites."[58] Being Christian implies breaking open its tradition and doctrine to reactivate its "founding break."

Yet, the question persists: Where is Christianity in all of this? If Christianity is to be defined in theoretical terms referring to Lacan and others, what then is still typically Christian about Christianity? And, another question directly linked to this one: Are the terms Certeau borrows from contemporary discourse theories not twisted to be made compatible with Christianity? Does Certeau not "Christianize" the concepts and schemes of the discourse theories of his time? In other words, are the discourse theories of his age really Certeau's theoretical frame of reference to explain Christianity, or does he, the other way around, use Christianity as a frame of reference to interpret these modern theories?

As long as Certeau analyzes the sixteenth- and seventeenth-century corpus of mystical texts, it is legitimate for him to notice that God's voice, become mute in the outside world, still is heard in the "interior castle" of the Christian mystic soul.[59] Since the "death of God," listening to the voice of an absent God has become the paradigm of modern Christian religiosity. But does it define the essence of Christianity *as such*, as Certeau states?

The crisis that Christianity was hit by at the end of the Middle Ages and the beginning of Modernity, is not only a crisis, but reveals at the same time its very essence, so Certeau argues. The mute voice that then speaks through the written word is not simply a voice that in medieval times spoke more loudly, being recognized by the then-established culture. That mute voice has *always* been Christianity's essence, also in those premodern times. According to Certeau, even in the fully Christian Middle Ages, the God who spoke through nature was not the God providing the world with its solid ground, but the God that broke—or, more exactly, subverted—such supposed ground. The core of the Christian message—Jesus's call—has always been an obedience, not so much to a Law as to what deconstructs and subverts that law. It has always been a "founding break," indeed, but not a break that "does . . . found a new site—a Testament, a religion—," but a "break" that "introduces the non-site of a difference in a system of sites."[60]

Certeau embraces the undermining by the twentieth century's critical and deconstructive thought of the entire tradition of Western metaphysics and the discrediting of every ontological foundation of reality. "That which we call reality is based on a lack," so he repeats a central Lacanian insight. The point from where we relate to reality—our *subiectum*—has no ground in that reality; it is a merely fictitious point of which we imagine that it escapes all doubt and fiction. Returning to that point (i.e., to what Certeau, with Lacan among others, calls *le sujet de l'énonciation*), one discovers a lack of ground, a non-site that wipes itself out, or, what amounts to the same thing, a "site" where one cannot "stand" but only "wander," "pass by."

All of these concepts and schemes are *negative*. They acknowledge the "destruction" of the foundations upon which the world was once built. Yet, for Certeau, they are positive, precisely because of their Christian value. How is this possible? Is it not precisely his Christian presupposition that allows Certeau to embrace these critical concepts and schemes? In advance, he already has faith in the grounding character of what lacks any ground, and it is on this basis that he appropriates modern critical theory that undermines all foundations of reality.

By so doing, is Certeau not neutralizing the critical theories he uses? If the world is experienced as lacking an ultimate ground, who then guarantees that this lack, as a kind of non-ground, is in fact something *positive*, something at our service, something good—as good as the Christian God claims to be? Why should we not consider it, too, as something bad, something evil, the source of radical evil, even? If things have no ground, if a "non-site" to wander in is our real home, if excess and transgression are genuine elements in our obedience to laws, can one not just as well conclude that we are living in a sadistic universe?

All of this implies that faith is the basic supposition underlying Certeau's affirmation of both Christianity and modernity. For him, Christianity is an affirmation of its own lack of ground, its own basic weakness. Yet, its "weakness of faith" (the title of *La faiblesse de croire*) can be read as "faith in weakness"—a faith in the power of weakness. If Christian faith is in crisis, that very crisis is an excellent context for it to rediscover itself; for, essentially, Christianity is a faith *in* that very crisis. If, "as a drop of water," Christianity is disappearing "in the ocean" of our post-Christian secular time, the most Christian attitude is to acknowledge and to approve it. The Holy Spirit is gone forever, but his revival in the broad variety of spiritual movements is genuinely Christian. Such is the conclusion one can draw from Certeau's essay we read on the "Christian Transit."[61]

What Is Spirituality?

So, what is spirituality according to Certeau? It is not so much a matter of having faith in a "sense" that persists in the modern senseless world. It is, on the contrary, rather a matter of having faith in the very absence of sense. Spirituality is about trusting our condition of being lost in a senseless world. It is not meant to fill in that lack of sense, but to live it as it is, as our positive human condition. We *are* ourselves that lack of sense and, therefore, we pass by ("like Jesus, this 'significant passer-by' ["*passant considerable*"]"), meeting the truth about our "self" in the moment it passes by and disappears.[62] As a drop in the ocean.

So, what then is spirituality? Is it the "exercise" (in the sense in which Ignatius of Loyola uses the word) of trying to get us to a point at which we are ready to disappear in the "ocean"? Or is it the exercise of remembering that disappearing as a drop in the ocean is not the aim but only a point of reference, a point at which our desire is directed, but in which it is not meant to *really* disappear? Is spirituality a way to lose ourselves in the lack of sense that characterizes our modern world, or is it a way to *relate to* our genuine *desire to* get lost in it? Is it wandering in order to find the lack we can disappear in? Or is it wandering even if we have found that lack, precisely in order *not* to disappear in it? To say it with another of Certeau's terms and in parallel with the way in which he treats mysticism: Is spirituality a "fable," or is it what the fable is *about*? Is it the fable telling *about* "the drop in the ocean," or is it the way to *become* this drop?

Let us return to the already cited last sentences of Certeau's essay accompanying the 1973 radio discussion. In light of his own theory, his thesis about Christianity applies to spirituality as well. It is, he writes, a

> fragile and floating text, witness of itself alone, yet lost in the innumerable murmur of language, and hence perishable. But this fable heralds the joy of obliterating itself in what it figures, of returning to the anonymous work out of which it was born, of converting itself to this other which it is not. The writing of belief, in its weakness, appears on the ocean of language only to disappear, taken up into the work of uncovering, in other writings, the movement by which, ceaselessly, they "come" and "go." According to an expression of the mystics, it is a "drop in the ocean."[63]

Christianity—and, by extension, spirituality—is not simply a fixed "written" tradition, it is at its core a "practice" subverting that *écriture*. It is a "writing" in the shape of a "fable" (i.e., allowing the *voice* of what is beyond writing). It is a "writing" and a "fable" announcing "the joy of obliterating itself in what it figures, [the joy] of returning to the anonymous work out of which it was born, of converting itself to this other which it is not."

Is Christianity/spirituality a matter of being wiped away and disappearing in the lack, the *rupture instauratrice* it rests upon? The quoted passage says something else. Christianity/spirituality is the "writing" *telling about* this; it is the "fable" announcing it. It is a fable that is aware of the fact that, by times, its subject both fades away in the lack upon which it rests and reappears again in that very place. Christianity/spirituality is the "movement" by which, in the universe of discourses, the ones of faith "ceaselessly 'come' and 'go.'" To which Certeau adds: "According to an expression of the mystics, it is 'a drop in the ocean.'"

So, what is like "a drop in the ocean" is not something (the subject, the voice beyond "writing") disappearing once and for all in the lack it is located in; it is what disappears *and* reappears in the *fable* telling about that very disappearing/reappearing. For Certeau, Christianity and spirituality are first of all *narrative* practices, *telling about* our condition of disappearing in the discourse that represents us. Within the realm of "writing," it says—remembers, considers—that what is repressed by "writing," what remains beyond "writing." But this kind of "writing" does not bring the repressed "beyond" to the surface once and for all, it does not turn it into reality, neither does it say that we *should* do so, which is to say that we should *actively* and *really* disappear before—and in—that "other that [we] are not."

The fable about the disappearance of the subject tells us about the human condition in which we are; it shows the void or absence that is our genuine support, our subject. But, unlike a widespread interpretation with a long tradition, it does not tell us that we *really* should vanish in it. The "fable" is not to be confused with a commandment or a law, telling us we should *become* "a drop in the ocean."

If Christianity and spirituality are fables, these fables also have to tell us about this kind of erroneous interpretation, which indeed belongs to the fable of the Christian tradition. "Spirituality" is also there in order to help us remember and keep us wary of this incorrect interpretation.

In this respect, it is regrettable that Certeau does not specify his references to the quote about the "drop." A reference to Fénelon would have been especially clarifying. To be faithful to God, so Fénelon states on so many pages in his voluminous oeuvre, one must be aware that one is nothing more than a drop in the ocean, and that, to be faithful to God and even to oneself, one has to do everything in order to become such a drop, which is to say that one has to exist in a way that is almost similar to disappearing. The one who really—or, as Fénélon says, *purely*—loves God, knows he is nothing and, consequently, has to do everything he can in order to really become nothing. Remember the passage we quoted from one of his *Lettres spirituelles*:

> Really be nothing, in everything and everywhere. . . . Suffer in peace, abandon yourself; go, like Abraham, without knowing where to. . . . Love the hand of God that beats and destroys us. The creature is only made to be destroyed as the one who has made it for Himself sees fit [*au bon plaisir*]. What a prosperous use of our substance! Our nothing glorifies the eternal Being and the entire God. . . . Let us be the holocaust which love's fire reduces to ashes.[64]

According to Certeau, Christianity/spirituality is about the modern sub-ject's repressed truth, a truth saying that it always already disappears in the "instituting rupture" of its discourse. But this is not an incitement to really disappear, as is the case in Fénélon's *pur amour*. In Fénelon, the reference to this "rupture" risks to turn into mere cruelty and even masochistic perversion.[65] In Certeau, Christianity/spirituality is not so much what its "fable" is about, it is that "fable" as such. It is a discursive praxis remembering a kind of disappearing as the basic condition of the human subject, a condition that holds human discourse open and makes man free. Yet, to this "fable," oeuvres such as Fénelon's belong as well. And of course, they are not to be remembered as an *example* to follow, but as an image showing us the dark side of the "instituting rupture" that at the same time renders openness and freedom.

For Certeau, spirituality is never simply a matter of experience. Of course, it is about experience, but in his view, experience is always already mediated by a discourse that, through experience (among other things) is turned into a "fable." This is why spirituality—even if it goes beyond Christian religion, even if it turns into a spirituality of everyday life—can never simply neglect the religious traditions from which it originates. For in these traditions, it meets the struggle with the kind of "founding break" or "rupture" that is at the heart of its own praxis. And remembering the bad, pernicious pages in the history of that struggle is as important as to remember the glorious ones. For the relationship to the "founding break" cannot allow a fixed position (the position of a "writing" subject, in the conceptual sense as defined by Certeau); it requires a "wandering," a "passing," in the sense that the subject never stops to pass by and to wander around "in" the locus of its disappearance. Which is why the subject does not *really* disappear, but keeps talking about its disappearance as about its "proper" but impossible condition.

Rodrigues Revisited

Does the position, implied in the thesis that Certeau defends here, not come close to the one of his fictitious predecessor whom we met in previous chapter, the Jesuit Rodrigues from Shūsaku Endō's novel *Silence*? Was Rodrigues, after his apostasy, not also absorbed by Japanese society, like a drop is absorbed by the ocean? Did he not relinquish, to the utmost, every form of "self," including his Christian "self"? And did he not recognize therein the ultimate grace that Christ's doctrine proclaimed? Rodrigues had become one with the pagan Japanese "ocean." He had resisted this "ocean" for so long that he wanted to convert that ocean, drop by drop, to the only, real truth, the Christian God. Until he realized in an ultimate moment that he himself, his ego, had always been the greatest obstacle, and that consequently he had to leave this Christian ego behind in order to reduce himself to just an openness making space for the Other whom his Christianity was all about. Ego-less, he would have to be the "site"—the completely *empty* site—where the Other could appear as Other. And where or how could he be this "empty site," this "mere openness"?

The novel suggests that Rodrigues only succeeded in one specific situation, namely the confession with which the story of his life ends. This confession in a certain sense sets up the ultimate point in Rodrigues's self-destructive transgression. As a former priest, he hears the confession of a Japanese man, an act of disobedience toward the Catholic authorities. Moreover, he does this as an official Japanese Buddhist and therefore knowing well that it will cost him his life as soon as it becomes known. This is also highly likely, since the sin he has to forgive is that of betrayal, the betrayal of which he was the victim at numerous times during his tragic existence—and this at the hand of the one unreliable Japanese person whom he is now, with this very confession, sacramentally forgiving for the umpteenth time. Rodrigues's act is in all respects a radically transgressive gesture with which he subverts himself—read: he causes every form of self that he still might have, to disappear.

It is, however, Rodrigues's act—his "practice"—that makes "the difference." His act brings the existing order back to the difference— the *break* or *rupture*—on which it is founded. And therefore this act of his sweeps away the ego that executes it, and even sweeps away the act itself. As it is being performed, the act renounces rigorously every possible effect. The drop immediately removes the difference it makes to the "ocean" and disappears into its endless waters.

And yet. Did Rodrigues's deed really make the difference? Did he really confront this ocean with the otherness, with the *rupture*, the fracture, the fissure in which it has its origin, its ever-expropriating source?

The selflessness of Rodrigues's gesture immediately smothered its effect. Could the same not be said about the task Certeau sees for Christianity? Is Christianity not also paralyzed in advance by its self-effacing? What might a Christianity that realizes itself in its own disappearance still mean? One should appreciate that it wants to make space for radical otherness in the supremacy of modernity's extreme self-culture. But can such a gesture allow any ego to be put out of the game? Does it benefit the engagement when the ego allows itself to be completely absorbed or pushed away by the envisaged otherness? Can Christianity fulfill its task to detect the crevices and openings in modernity's culture of the self in order to benefit the truth that is "other," when it allows itself to be wiped away and to have its own self destroyed?

And the problem has still another face as well. For effacing the self can easily be a hidden way to promote that very self. Remember Fénelon, of whom we learned that even the radical selflessness of the *pur amour* conceals a self-assured ego who decides itself to love God, radically independent from this God. Numerous are the ways in which we moderns intend to efface our "self" while in fact, they are hidden ways to promote it.

So here again is the question: How to give voice to the Other and avoid the ruse of, by doing so, promoting the self all the more? But even when this ruse is avoided, when the ego does not celebrate selflessness as an opportunity to affirm itself as bigger and more certain than ever, when it authentically succeeds in effacing itself, then the first question still remains. How to give the things that selflessness is all about (criticism of the false self, of the intolerable, dangerous pretentions of individuality) a chance when there is no self, no ego, no well-organized identity to take responsibility for them?

And, indeed, this problem is not limited to Christianity. In all its aspects, modernity demands a strongly profiled identity, a free and self-conscious ego that can affirm itself as an equal in a world of equals. But this modern ego is aware, at the same time, of the untenable pretensions inherent to holding up a fixed identity. Do we not realize that we only *desire* such a fixed identity because we do not have it and never will? Is this not a way to say that our ego basically lives from openness to the other? And this might be the reason as well why we remain fascinated by selflessness, including the selflessnes present in the Christian mystical tradition. On the one hand: desiring a fixed self, on the other, fascinated by selflessness: the modern Ego oscillates between the two, unable to make a definite choice. Self and selflessness are aspects of the same insoluble problem at the very heart of modernity.

In our multicultural world, everyone must be able to be him- or herself. Until recently we concluded from this that everyone should get the necessary chances to build his or her own identity. We now better comprehend that the many identities primarily have to realize that each of them is marked by otherness, that each of them is in an own, specific way not him- or herself.

Until recently, we held up the idea that, in a multicultural world, we have to tolerate and respect each other's identity—and thus each other's otherness. Not that this has lost its validity today, on the contrary, but more than before, we now see the boundaries of this tolerance policy. It binds everyone up too much in their own identity and obliges them to conservatively uphold the untenable pretension of a fixed self. What we have to learn to see and respect in each other is not so much someone's otherness over and against us, but especially also his or her *otherness over and against him- or herself*. Not that everyone does not have an identity of their own, but no one's identity is what it professes to be: that is the basis on which all people on our cosmopolitical, multicultural planet can find themselves equal to each other. That I myself am marked by a lack of self and therefore also have a sense of—and even a desire for— selflessness: that is what binds people of all races, nations, and cultures to each other; that is the basis for a *modern* society.

In Certeau's thought a renewed attempt can be found again and again at articulating modern culture from this point of view, convinced as he is that Christianity and its affirmation of otherness, too, can make a substantial contribution here. Whether giving up every self would be a constructive contribution, as Certeau suggests, nevertheless remains the question.

The fortunes of his fictitious predecessor, padre Rodrigues, seem to rather to suggest the opposite.

MYSTICISM IN A MODERN WORLD

9

Down with Religion, Long Live Mysticism

Reflections on Spirituality's Popularity

> But since today . . . this name [of "mysticism"] sounds bad to the
> ears of the people, why . . . not put in its place the name of "spi-
> ritual," more well-known, softer, and which could have the same
> effect . . . by, in addition, also opposing the true spiritual ones to
> the false spiritual ones, by fighting the false spirituality of the one
> with the true spirituality of the other?
>
> —Jean-Pierre de Caussade, *Bossuet, maître d'oraison*

Currently, religion does not receive a good press. While many turn their
back on it, others are so obsessed by it that, in its name, they attack
the foundations of modern free society. To the ears of many, even the
word religion sounds suspicious today.

None of this goes for "spirituality." Spirituality is the in thing.[1]
And yet, it is anything but easy to clearly distinguish it from religion
or religiosity, if only because the historical origin and background of
spirituality are undeniably religious. Perhaps this kind of ambiguity
belongs to spirituality's very definition. Many who declare themselves
antireligious are not reluctant to sit side by side with genuinely religious
people during all kinds of "spiritual" events. From a social perspective,
spirituality seems to succeed where traditional religions all too often fail.
And where religion tries to embrace or, if possible, appropriate spirituality,
it is often spirituality that wins at the expense of religion.

What then is "spirituality"? And why is it generally more appreciated than religion despite its obvious connotation with religion and religiosity? How did spirituality, contrary to religion, attain such good fame within the social?

Instead of approaching the question via a reflection on spirituality, this chapter takes a different, in some sense opposite, direction and approaches spirituality via the problem of "the social." What has happened to the social that it reacts positively to spirituality, and rather negatively to religion? What has happened to the social that has made it so difficult for traditional religion to find its place in it, while spirituality seems to feel more at home there?

Indeed, something has happened to the social. It has become *modern*. As is the case with nearly every aspect of modernity, religion is also highly involved in the development of the modern social, if only because modern sociality has distanced itself from the medieval, explicitly religious shape of the social. To distance oneself from it, however, does not mean to get rid of religion as such. A kind of "distance" belongs to the very heart of religion and religiosity. And, as I will explain, "spirituality" (i.e., the popular phenomenon we know) is not without a link to that kind of "distance."

The Emergence of Modernity and the Modern Social

Social is a *modern* term. Of course, premodern times were social as well, but people then did not use this word to indicate their living together. The term as we use it today was coined only during the seventeenth and eighteenth century. From then on, people in the West started to speak about their living together in terms that directly referred to the Latin *socius*, its plural *socii*, and its abstract form *societas*. Previously, the terms in Western languages constructed on the basis of these Latin words did not refer to a general way of living together. The words for that were *civis* and *civitas*—as they were already used in Augustine's famous *De civitate dei* (AD 410–430), and were still used in Thomas Hobbes's sociopolitical treatise: *De Cive* (AD 1642).[2] In the ages before modernity, *socius* and *societas* referred to a small, close community, where the participants were associates—where they were each other's mates and companions. Ignatius of Loyola, for instance, called the small group of followers of his mystical path a *societas*, a "society."

The words *society* and *social* in the *general*, everyday sense of the words as we use them today, date from the century in which modernity's paradigm started to be applied to political reality and that finally culminated in the American (AD 1776) and the French Revolution (AD 1789). For the revolutionaries of the time, the term still had its full meaning: *societas* meant an association of companions and mates, but—and this makes a huge difference—it now applied to everyone, to the *volonté générale,* to the "general will" of a nation in its totality (and, even, to the "general will" of all nations).³ Defining all men as "free, equal, and brother," as the major slogan of the French Revolution put forward, means declaring all men "social," members of a "society," of a virtually universal assembly of free and equal mates and companions.

To put it more abstractly: the *subject* of humanity—in its political shape—became humanity itself, humanity as it is equally realized in every individual. Together with the American Revolution, the French Revolution procured this change of the political subject. The political system was no longer grounded in God; power no longer lay with those who were God's substitutes: no longer with the clerical estate managing man's orientation toward eternal salvation, and no longer with the nobility's estate responsible for the profane, worldly dimension of human politics. From now on, political power over humans had its ground—its *subiectum*—in those humans themselves. People became their own political subject; they became the ground of the political power to which they were subjected.

As explained in previous chapters, this was only possible on the basis of a more general and profound change of the subject, which is at the basis of modernity as such.⁴ Modern man no longer understands himself on the basis of his being created by and grounded in God. He relates to reality on a basis that coincides with himself. Or, what amounts to the same thing, he considers himself as fundamentally free—even free vis-à-vis the foundation on which he is based. Of course, he remains depending on and based in being—and, for those who believe so, in being's Creator—but his *relationship to* being or to God is based solely in man himself. For this reason, Descartes had redefined man's (i.e., the *cogito*'s) kind of being as radically different from the kind of being of the world, from the being of what was considered to be the "object" (of the subject's knowledge). Man is free, which is to say: really and substantially disconnected from the (objective) world in (and by) which he lives.

But what is the basis of *that* freedom? What is the ground of the free subject? From a Cartesian perspective, this question seems senseless, given the fact that man himself is the subject/ground. However, since he is only the subject/ground of his *relationship to* reality, the question remains what the subject/ground of that subject is. Does it have its ground in reality? This does not seem to be so, since man's position is *vis-à-vis* reality. He can suppose God to be the basis of his free position vis-à-vis reality, but precisely his freedom presupposes himself, too, to be principally free with respect to God as well.

However legitimate the question of the ground of the Cartesian subject is, the latter is no longer in the position to answer or even sincerely put that very question, since the subject immediately puts itself forward precisely as the subject of that question—thus denying the real question, "What is the subject of the subject?" or, more specifically, "What is the real/ontological ground of the freedom on the basis of which we relate to reality?"

The Emergence of Spirituality

And where is spirituality in all of this?

It is hard to say, if only because the term *spirituality* is so difficult to define. But what is not difficult to see, is that all of this is *in* spirituality, and that the heart of spirituality beats to the rhythm of these thoroughly modern problems. The philosophical issues just mentioned—the huge questions that haunt the death of God and the rise of the modern subject—are absolutely *in* and *behind* the phenomenon that in the early modern age was for the first time baptized *spirituality*.

This is not to say that the phenomenon itself was new. Of course it was not. In premodern Western culture, there was a great tradition of what we now call spirituality: from the early ages of Christianity, via the variety of medieval "spiritual movements" inspired by mystics as different as Bernard of Clairvaux and Hildegard of Bingen, up to "spiritual" giants such as Ruusbroec, Eckhart, and Suso. The word *spiritualis* was not referring to a religious, devotional practice but indicated the state of the "clergy," or, more general, of the supra-natural order, over and against the natural, earthly order of laymen.[5]

The word *spirituality* started to be used in early seventeenth-century France as a general name indicating the long mystical tradition and the update it had received.[6] *Spirituality*, in the sense it has today, has its semantic origin in the word *spiritualité* used at that time to indicate "the mystical path" (*la voie mystique*) or "the inner life" (*la vie intérieure*).

And in the then-rising *spiritualité*, the profound, metaphysical problems that characterized early modernity were far from absent.

It is not a coincidence that, in the century when the modern subject is coined as the unique source of certainty beyond any possible doubt, a movement rises where precisely this self-assured subject is thoroughly put into question. For this is what happens in this first "modern" mystical wave—i.e., in the *spiritualité de la vie intérieure*, as one can find in authors such as Cardinal De Bérule,[7] François de Sales,[8] Jeanne de Chantal,[9] Marie de l'Incarnation,[10] Madame Guyon,[11] François de Fénélon,[12] François Lamy, and others.

All of these devout men and women were searching for God. And if their search was deliberately not theoretical, it was not because theory as such *is* incompatible with it, but because theory had *become* so. Herein lies the difference with the "spiritual" movements of earlier centuries. Of course, Ruusbroec and Eckhart also knew that theory is limited and that the ultimate union with God is beyond human rationality, but the limited condition of their rationality was considered to be itself rational: it indicated nothing less than that the *subject* of that rationality was God of whom man knew that He was—although beyond knowledge—knowledge's solid ground. Precisely the unknowable character of God guaranteed that He was the *subiectum* of both the world and the knowledge of that world. A millennium-long tradition of Neo-Platonic thinking—which went back to Pseudo-Dionysius (fifth century AD), whose impact on medieval Christianity is difficult to overestimate—made it possible to integrate the unknowable nature of the subject (of both the world and our knowledge of it) as its ultimate "theoretical" hallmark.

At the time of early modern *spiritualité*, this kind of unknowable *subiectum* in which all knowledge is grounded (i.e., God) finds itself in a process of losing its very function of *subiectum*. Following their "mystical path," the practitioners of the new *spiritualité* are in search of the "subject." For them, however, that path no longer leads directly to the subject that the medieval mystic was supposed to find, namely, the ontological God. Instead, the new "inner way" makes the searcher bump against the subject *he himself* is. And, what is more, he is bumping against the fact that, precisely because he is the subject of his relationship to God, he is himself an obstacle on his way to find the *real* subject, the subject of the real, the ontological *subiectum*.

In a way, the *spiritualité* of the early modern mystic takes a path that, though not theoretical, is nonetheless similar to the one Descartes takes. Descartes, too, is in search of the *subiectum*, of that which gives ground to the world and to our relationship to it. And in order to find it, he also takes a path "inward," investigating his own thinking.[13] In other words, he doubts, and realizes he must not give up this doubt until something *really* resists it. Only that which unambiguously resists doubt is worth to be considered as *subiectum*. And it turns out to be, instead of God, doubt itself, which is to say, the "self" as supposed—and revealed—by that very doubt.

What occurs on the path of early modern *spiritualité* is formally not so very different. The mystic is in search of God as the ground/ *subiectum* of his very search. And he starts his search with the premodern presumption that this is at the same time the ground/*subiectum* of being as such. But the *subiectum* he finds does not turn out to be God, but *himself*. Contrary to Descartes, however, the contemporary *homme spirituel* is far from satisfied with that outcome.[14] In his eyes, it marks the very failure of his search, or at least an obstacle. Confronted with his "self" as the *subiectum* of his relationship to God and the world, he realizes that this "self" is not the *subiectum* of reality, but is a *subiectum* blocking the access to the real *subiectum*. In order to reach the *real subiectum*, so he realizes, he has to overcome the unreal *subiectum* that he is himself. He has to destroy, deconstruct, sublimate, or neutralize it (the "spiritual" literature of the time offers a variety of ways for that) in order to find what he is really looking for: the real *subiectum*, the grounding ground of both man and reality, God.

So, what early modern spiritual man experiences is not without a link to the basic problem of early modernity, which anachronistically can be entitled "the split of the subject." Indeed, what his spiritual experience deals with is the split between, on the one hand, the subject as *subiectum* of reality and, on the other, the subject as *subiectum* of man's relationship to reality.

Descartes, in a way, simply represses that problem by inventing two realities, two different "beings": *res extensa* and *res cogitans*, mechanical objectivity and free subjectivity, determined matter and undetermined, free soul. Although the early modern mystics immediately integrate this difference in their discourse and opt for the soul against the body, the "split" that lies at the heart of their experience is the one between the subject as bearer of their relationship to God and the subject they are looking for: the subject of the real, God. What is an absolute certainty for Descartes (we are ourselves the *subiectum* of our relationship to reality) is put into question by the mystics whose experiences are steps in their search for the subject *of that subject*, the "grounding ground" of the "ground" one supposes one is standing upon when relating to reality. This abyss—this tension between the (human) subject and the subject of that subject—constitutes the core of the mystical experience of those who, in seventeenth-century France, follow the path of the *vie intérieure*. And even if they arrive at the real subject (God), the path that has brought them there is a long and patient "deconstructive analysis" of the modern subject that they are, the subject of their relationship to the real.

It is not a coincidence that, during the seventeenth century, the only place where something like a "science of the subject" is practiced, is precisely in the writings of the practitioners of *spiritualité*. For Descartes, a *science* of the subject is in principle impossible, not because the subject is too difficult to grasp, but precisely because it is too obvious. The moment that I doubt or think about the subject, I reinstall it as the subject of that very doubt and thinking and, consequently, of my relationship to reality in general. Thinking—a discursive inquiry into the subject that I am—is not necessary, because the slightest thinking about (read: doubting) it, immediately reveals it in its full substantial certainty. The mystics of Descartes's time, however, experienced this same subject as highly problematic, if only because it was the subject solely of their experience and not of the real that was experienced.[15] And in their attempts to overcome the obstacle of the Cartesian subject, they were the only ones really questioning the new subject and patiently studying it. In a way, every spiritual author of the century had his own "theory of the subject." In the new kind of science that established itself in the same century, however, theories questioning the subject were nearly absent.

Of course, Descartes wrote an essay on "the passions of the soul."[16] Yet, what the "spiritual" authors of his time wrote about passions is incomparably more elaborate and nuanced on what we nowadays call the "subjective" than Descartes's reflections on the soul. In a century where there was no such thing as the human sciences (i.e., the sciences of the human subject as an affective, passionate, willing, and thinking being), the "science" of the human as a subject could only be found in the (contemporary) "spiritual" writings. There we find a variety of attempts at a theory of desire, as well as profoundly elaborate inquiries into the human passions.

Spiritualité as Dispositive for the Modern Social

And where, then, is the social in all of this? Is the experience reported by seventeenth-century *spiritualité* not all too intimate, all too private to be social? Is it not thoroughly asocial? It is indeed, but its private character itself as well as the fact that it was widely appreciated by contemporaries is *as such* a social phenomenon. Taking a closer look, the intimacy of the mystical experience seems not to be without a link with the privatized situation that each individual in a modern society was in. In the intimate struggle that the mystical contemporary fought in the solitude of his cell, the early modern citizen could recognize the basic problem that he, too, had to deal with. Formally, the mystic's struggle was not different from the one that his contemporary citizen had to fight. And, as will become clear, that struggle with the subject can be put in "social" terms as well—or, more exactly, in terms that announce the emergence of the modern social.

In the Middle Ages, *subject* was basically a political term. Not in its abstract, metaphysical shape of *subiectum*, but in that of *subiectus* (with its synonym *subditus*), which means "subjected to."[17] A medieval man understood himself as *subiectus*, subjected to God—and this goes also for his political condition. Living together was conceived as an organized web of "subjection." The subjection to God was translated into the subjection of the lower to the higher: the peasants/serfs to the knights, the knights to the lords, the lords to the king, the king to God; or, for the *mundus spiritualis*: the parishioners to the priests, the priests to the bishops, the bishops to the archbishops, the archbishops to the pope, the pope to God. Everyone was subjected to someone higher and nearer to the One (God) to whom everyone was subjected. This is what Bossuet still has in mind when, at the end of the seventeenth century, he states: "All men are born subjects."[18]

So, what is at stake in the experience of early modern *spiritualité* is a deconstruction of *that* subject, a deconstruction that prepares its radical change, that is, the change from medieval to modern political subject—or, as Étienne Balibar puts it, from subject to citizen.[19] If the mystical experience of the early modern *homme spirituel* is "asocial," it is so first of all in comparison with the medieval "sociality" of subjection. He does not meet God so much in what he shares with his superiors, as he does in the intimacy of his own heart; not so much in the community life with his fellows, as in the lonely struggle with himself, in the loneliness of his own *vie intérieur*.

It is not a coincidence that, during the entire seventeenth century, the word *spiritualité* was always somewhat negatively loaded.[20] It was not until the late sixteenth century that the mystical tradition was introduced in France, not only from Spain, but for a substantial part also from Germany and the Low Countries, precisely the area where the "heresy" of Reformation came from. Did these men and women who promoted the new *spiritualité* not embrace the typically Protestant idea that one's relationship to God is first of all a matter of one's own heart and personal devotion, and not of the church, priests, sacraments, and other kinds of sacred mediation? For they advocated that if man is *subiectus*, he is so only and directly with respect to God, and not via the mediation of popes, bishops, and established ecclesiastical institutes.

In fact, one of the genuine battlefields of the sociopolitical struggle of the new subject occurred in the very heart of the modern mystic. For, contrary to what official power feared about them, the spiritual man or woman fully wanted to be *subiectus*: subjected to their superiors, because subjected to God. However, precisely their desire to be subjected to God confronted them with themselves in the position of *modern* subjects. Since the God for whom they were searching was losing his position as *subiectum*, it had become less evident to be *subiectus*, subjected to Him. Inevitably, the mystic experienced first of all that he was the (free) subject of a possible subjection (his being *subiectus*/citizen of God), and only on that basis could he work on his union with God, the divine *subiectum*. Put in "social" terms: in his intention to be absolutely loyal to the community of the church, he first had to come to terms with himself, with the (modern) subject he is, and therefore had to take his distance with respect to his authorities. Early modern mystical experience is always an experience of modern freedom as well, not as a triumph, but as an infinite problematic tension. That tension lies at the heart of the *spiritualité* experience—and it was precisely that which the official religious authorities feared in that experience.

Remember, for instance, one of the central issues in the *spiritualité* movement: the *pur amour*, and more precisely the way Fénelon defends it. To love God purely, I must overcome myself, more precisely my self-interest, so Fénelon stresses again and again. The ultimate phase in my attempt to fully love God, the *really* pure love, consists of the one love I have for God, even if hypothetically I were to know that He has condemned me to the eternal pains in hell.[21] To love God even then is to love Him without any trace of *amour-propre*: this is *pur amour*. Here, the mystic is radically *subiectus*, subjected to God. But where is his *subiectum* then? Is it with God, to whom he has radically delivered himself? It only *seems* to be like that. In fact, the subject—the ground or base of his love—is with himself, and *only* with himself. Whatever God does, even if He does not love me at all and has condemned me to eternal hell, I can still decide to love Him. In his love to God, the Fénelonian mystic clearly posits himself as a modern subject. Despite his intention to leave all he has, all his interests, all his "self" to God, and to recognize Him as *subiectum*, it is the mystic himself who turns out to be established as *subiectum*: as a free modern subject, keeping his distance from whatever he meets, even from God. His love for God is ultimately a matter of his human, all too human will, however problematic that will might be.[22]

"In, not of the world": this phrase summarizes the earliest paradigm of Christian sociality.[23] The Christian considered himself already living in the realm of the realized messianic promises, but since the Messiah had returned to the Father "for a while," that Messianic state was not yet generally implemented. For now, that state was only present in the Christian communities, which in that sense were "in, but not of the world." This dispositive was at the basis of the huge ascetic movement of the fourth and fifth centuries and of the age-long medieval monastic culture, which profoundly influenced our Western civilization.

In the age of *spiritualité*, this dispositive was lived in the mystical experience, although now in a *modern* way, thus preparing the paradigm of post-Christian, modern sociality. *L'homme spirituel* considered himself to live in a world he was not from. But, unlike before, this experience was lived as a conflict between the spiritual individual and his *own* religious community—an unsolvable, inherently problematic conflict hallmarking the core of his sociality. Of course the spiritual man wanted to obey his religious superiors and to be *subiectus*, as Christians had always been. And he did what he could to be so. But the mystical path he followed forced him to do this in the capacity of the (modern) *subiectum* that he was. And unlike the old real *subiectum* (God) for which he was searching, this new *subiectum* that he faced and that he had to overcome, first of all separated him from his fellows and community, and allowed him to join them only in a "second" instance, after he had first taken the decision to do so in complete, private freedom. In his search for the divine subject, the desire of the mystic is without doubt to be a loyal *subiectus*, but that search makes him a modern subject, a "citizen," one whose relationship to God is impossible without the affirmation of his own free will. Yet he has to destroy that very freedom by means of itself in order to become the desired *subiectus* of God and his divine Order.

The inner "social" conflict of the "spiritual man" sheds light on the inner conflict of the early modern political subject. Conscious of being *himself* the subject of his political condition, ready to take freedom as the basis of society, he in the same moment realizes that he must freely choose to become the *subiectus* of that new *subiectum,* of society becoming itself its own ground—or of the "mortal God" which is society, to say it with Hobbes.[24] The latter's early modern political philosophy illustrates this strikingly.

How to freely subject myself to a freedom-based society? This is the paradox that has haunted the modern political condition since its start in the seventeenth century—a condition that was often openly lived as a paradox during the numerous political and social revolutions of the last centuries, and that has not stopped haunting the sociopolitical condition of our day. Reading the mystical writings of the early modern spiritual authors provides insight into the intimate, subjective struggle that is still inherent to our late modern citizenship.

Spirituality and the Social

It is clear now that the central problem of the early modern "inner experience" lies in the fact that a Cartesian kind of subject (necessarily) discovered itself to be an obstacle on its way to the real, divine *subiectum.* This "inner experience," however, and the way in which the problem of the subject is involved in it, led to two opposite reactions.

The *first* manner to deal with the problematic (modern) subject consists in denying or neutralizing it, so that it becomes directly the *subiectus* of the divine *subiectum.* Putting aside himself as *subiectum,* the subject can subject himself to God who presents Himself in the shape of divine mediations such as religious rules, rituals, sacraments, and all other sacred components that constitute the life of the organized Church. In that case the "mystical" experience of the modern devout nullifies itself at the very moment it occurs. This experience opts immediately for a nonmystical way to relate to God, a way of "blind" obedience to and trust in God.

This is why those who were opposed to the *spiritualité* and its mysticism understood so well what they were about—which is also the reason why the disputes (the famous *Querelles,* like the one on "Quietism") were so profound and had such a social resonance as well. The

Jansenists, who were generally opposed to the wave of *spiritualité*, knew perfectly what it was about, for their position was in a way based on the same "inner experience." So was, for instance, the experience at the basis of Blaise Pascal's religiosity: it was the genuinely modern mystical experience of being *subjected* to God but not without being first subjected to oneself, that is, to be free with respect to any subjection to God.[25] This experience, however, led Pascal to strictly obedient subjection to the doctrine of Revelation and not to the exploration of his "inner life," that is, not to *spiritualité*.

Secondly, *spiritualité*, "inner life," the "mystical path" are names for the other reaction to the same modern "inner experience." Confronted with one's own subject as major obstacle to obtain access to the real divine *subiectum*, this reaction, instead of denying one's own subject, focuses on it—assured as it is that it is there the divine is to be found. The modern mystic, too, is led by nostalgia for that medieval *subiectum* (God), and in some sense, you can call him even less modern than the nonmystical fellow of his day in the sense that he believes that God is the *subiectum* of his own, private (modern) subject. For the modern mystic, God must be somewhere deep down in his inner "self," under-lying his own (modern) subject, even if that appears at first sight to be an obstacle. Only by facing and overcoming that obstacle, a modern experience gives way to the mystical. Here *l'homme spirituel* cannot cling to the traditional means of mediation—however loyal he remains to sacraments, priests, Church, and so on. He must take his distance from that mediation and tarry within that distance, namely, the distance he embodies himself as subject with respect to the divine *subiectum*. He must give way to his own subjectivity, not in order to simply trust it, but to examine it, to explore the dark ways it goes and to follow those ways, despite their darkness.

Spiritualité was so popular in the seventeenth century due to the fact that it responded to a focus on the freedom that characterizes the modern subject. Even while this subjectivity was seen as an obstacle, all spiritual men and women focused on it, made room for it, and took the liberty to discover the often dark, but always free paths of their inner life. Their inner experiences were in fact exercises in—and explorations of—a typically modern freedom.

It is this freedom that has made *spirituality* popular to the present day. It calls for free religiosity, for a religiosity that acknowledges man's subjective freedom. Indeed, it treats freedom—*modern* freedom—as the place where the old metaphysical God is to be found. But by doing so, it makes God change into a modern God. In this way, religiosity becomes all the more "spiritual" to the extent that it gives up the metaphysical pretention of its search. Instead of being the ontological ground of our freedom, God becomes an ultimate point of reference through which we can free ourselves from any ground. Remember, for instance (to quote only one example), what a late modern, twentieth-century mystic, Simone Weil, wrote in her famous *Gravity and Grace* (1947):

> The miser deprives himself of his treasure because of his desire for it. If we can let our whole good rest with something hidden in the ground, why not with God?
>
> But when God has become as full of significance as the treasure is for the miser, we have to tell ourselves insistently that he does not exist. We must experience the fact that we love him, even if he does not exist.
>
> It is he who, through the operation of the dark night, withdraws himself in order not to be loved like the treasure is by the miser.[26]

It is not that God does not exist for Weil. On the contrary, she sincerely believes in Him. But to do so, she realizes that she has to give up all metaphysical pretension concerning God, even the one ascertaining his existence. She remains in her Cartesian subjectivity, in the subjectivity that is an obstacle to the access to the real, divine *subiectum*. The modernity of her "spirituality" consists in *not* surpassing the obstacle of her own subjectivity, but only emptying it in order to make full room for her *desire for* God. If God is the answer to our questions as well as to the question we *are*, it is an answer that does not "close" these questions. That *God* is the answer means that the questions remain open, and that the way in which God demands us to live these questions is a way to *keep* them open. It is in this sense that the quote from Weil is a striking illustration of *modern* spirituality.

And this spirituality is not without its link to the "modern social," that is, to the problematic, radically "questionable" way in which modern people live together. It is not merely a coincidence that the mystical Weil had been a radically social militant—in a variety of shapes: from bolshevist, via revolutionary syndicalist, to liberal reformist.[27] The experience that made her join the workers who suffered under the hard labor conditions of early-twentieth-century capitalism, and that brought her to Barcelona in 1936 to support the republicans against the fascists,[28] is not radically different from her mystical experience. And this goes also for someone like Titus Brandsma, whose "inner life" obliged him to defend educational and press freedom against the fascist regime of his day.[29]

This is not to say, however, that the modern mystic is social *because of* his ideas. Of course, he has social ideas, but his spirituality itself is social, not necessarily because he realizes those ideas, but because his spirituality shares the kind of openness and freedom that lies at the basis of the social as well. Operating in the difficult and even abysmal, limitless field of his free soul, the modern mystic has an immediate feeling for the abysmally free ground of modern sociality. Titus Brandsma had specific ideas about the political, but what his spirituality obliged him to defend about the political was, in the end, the ability of having free ideas as such. Simone Weil participated in various kinds of social movements and even took up arms in an antifascist war; yet, according to herself, she was never busy realizing a sociopolitical program. Despite her many essays on social and political issues, her specifically spiritual or mystical writings contain numerous negative passages on the social and the political, passages in which "the social" is put forward as a false aim in one's life, as what she calls "the Great Beast," namely, the false idol that misleads the true aim of human desire.[30] It is not her ideas about or preoccupations with society and politics that make her profoundly social; it is her spirituality. It is there she meets the open space that is shared by both the "inner experience" of the mystic and the ground of the modern social: freedom. It is her spirituality that, in 1942, during the last months of her life, made her long to be honored by the Resistance in London with a mission in occupied France in order to be able to contribute personally to the war against the Nazis.[31]

All of this is not to say that the social engagement of the mystic is per se morally good. He shares the modern condition that puts him in the position of free subject—free also from the ontological Good assumed by previous times—obliging him ultimately to choose/decide for himself what is good.[32] Seventeenth-century France gives an example of a bad moral and sociopolitical use of *spiritualité*. Remember, for instance, François Leclaire du Tremblay, better known as the Père Joseph, the "Gray Eminence."[33] He built up a great reputation as a spiritual man and leader, being at the origin of many spiritual congregations of his time. Soon, however, this became the "night-side" of his activities. During the day, he was the political advisor and righthand man of Richelieu (during the *Régence* and the early years of Louis XIII). Wearing his monk's habit at the Louvre Palace, keeping strictly his monastic vows, including the one of poverty, he developed himself as the most perfidious politician of his time. His Machiavellian political tactics and intrigues are part of the origin of the most disastrous conflict of his time, the infamous Thirty Years' War. Although in a morally negative way, this too is an example of the direct link between modern spirituality and the modern social, that is to say, the abysmal space of modern freedom. However intimately private it seems, spirituality shares with the political the same ground and therefore is always also political, social.

Spirituality, in all the shapes it takes in today's culture, must be aware of the common ground it shares with the modern social. This is only one of the reasons spirituality should be deliberately "pensive." Although often describing itself as beyond rationality, it should not stop *thinking,* certainly not about itself, about its theories or anti-theories, and its practices. For even if spirituality operates beyond the limits of rationality, this beyond is not without connection to it. It is no longer the connection that Neoplatonism put forward, the beyond as substantial subject of being. But operating within the space of the modern subject, spirituality makes possible the experience of the limits of rationality and, more precisely, of the fact that the subject, free as it is (even free from rationality), is situated at the limits of rationality, and not afraid to operate beyond them as well. Today's spirituality must be pensive, if only in order to share its experience of these limits and the beyond with all modern subjects.

10

Selflessly Powerful

On Pseudo-Dionysius, Agamben, and Lefort

It was indeed necessary to be able to speak in order to allow the
question "How to avoid speaking?"

—Jacques Derrida, *Psyche*

The exception is to positive law what negative theology is to positive theology.

—Giorgio Agamben, *Homo sacer*

Failing Words

Words fail. At the very moment they profess to express reality as it
is, they appear to be themselves the greatest obstacle to what they are
intending to say. Only words able to admit *this*, have a shot at illuminating some truth.

This statement cannot readily be called young. Maybe it is as old
as philosophy itself. It can be found in numerous texts from antiquity,
the Middle Ages, and the Renaissance, and it marks many a modern
and late-modern discourse. It can be found in subtle mystics such as
Eckhart, Ruusbroec, and Simone Weil, but also in crude positivists such
as Wittgenstein.[1]

No one pushed this statement to the fore with such far-reaching
consequences as the early Christian author who portrayed his texts as if

they were penned by Dionysius the Areopagite, an Athenian convert of the apostle Paul.[2] This fifth-century author, who was actually schooled in Neoplatonism and is hereafter called Pseudo-Dionysius, applied this thesis to a global theory of reality, or more precisely, to that which lends reality its "self," that is, the ground of its existence. At the end of the fifth and the beginning of the sixth century, this ground was commonly identified with the Christian, creative, and redeeming God. The self of all things—and even more so the self of all selves collected—escapes the words that have been forged for it, including the word *self*. Even that very word refers to a selflessness that escapes the term, just as it escapes the other term that is used for it: God.

As is evident from every page of Pseudo-Dionysius's oeuvre, we have but words to speak about God but none of them is able to capture Him. And in all the words that we use to speak about God, this insight, in particular, must resound: that they are mere words, words that are only possible thanks to the One about whom they speak but who can never fully be expressed through these words. The words we came up with for the truth—even the word that claims that truth "is"—do not say what they say, even if they are anything but untrue for this reason. In one of Pseudo-Dionysius's treatises, we read that "truth is in no way like the things that have being, and we have no knowledge at all of its incomprehensible and ineffable transcendence and invisibility."[3] The names we use for this truth—and thus for God—are all "divine names" (which is the title of Pseudo-Dionysius's longest treatise)[4] because these names too, like everything that is, ultimately come from Him. But none of these words can bring us to what we would like to express with them. Their claim edges closest to the truth where they admit that their truth claim fails, that these claims get stuck in their words. Only then are these words worthy of the divinity that they name. Divine words require that those who pronounce them allow for the failing of their words to resonate. This failure, this negativity, is indispensable in truly speaking about God.

This is "negative theology" to its core. And, certainly in "non-theological" times, when God is no longer seen as the source and ground of reality, a similarly negative way of speaking formally remains fashionable. Definitely in post-Kantian times, in which we know all too well that "things themselves" are unknowable, the *via negativa* offers a wonderful grammar and rhetoric to point out the limitedness that marks the pretensions of human thought. And, in these times, speaking *about*

God is possibly marked even more strongly by this negative theological condition. If there is one thing where words fail, so say believers and nonbelievers alike, it is in speaking about God.

But unlike nonbelievers, who consider the matter sorted out and religion bereft of its ground, believers often cite this statement with jubilation. In an era in which God has been declared dead, this is where they find a way to cling to God. Concerning Him, every word falls short, they argue, also the word that declares Him dead. The modern person may thus bury the "God issue" and believe it to be "solved," but this rhetorical violence does not affect God at all. In our late-modern, post-Christian times, negative theology seems to be *the* way out for everyone who still wants to speak about and believe in God, in other words: for theology in both the narrow and broad sense of the word.

Yet even so, the question arises as to what exactly happens when you confirm God's existence by saying that no word is fitting to talk about God. More abstractly: What happens when you say that that which you say cannot be said? For then you have said it, after all. You might have said that you cannot say it, you expressly declared it "unsayable," but in this way your speaking helped you get a strong grip on this unspeakable thing. You speak on the basis of a truth that neither you nor anyone else knows or can know. Who, then, would still dare contradict you?

In this way, a power is incorporated in the powerlessness of speaking that nothing and no one can withstand. Nobody can express God, no word can get a grip on Him, but precisely by saying this, one bestows upon one's own speaking the majesty of the unsayable, a majesty against which no one has any defense.

It is evident on every page of Pseudo-Dionysius's oeuvre. God is not this and not that, but not because He is nothing of the sort, but because He is *more,* because He is *beyond*—*hyper* in Greek—nothing and everything. Even whether He *is* or not, is not to be determined, not because He does not exist at all, but because He is *beyond* (*hyper*) this dichotomy, because He is *more* than whoever or whatever exists, even more than existence itself. Every "not" in the discourse about Him, every negative predicate invariably points *upward* and says that He is "above" being and not-being, that He needs nothing, not even being, to be who He is, and that for this very reason He is God and—accordingly—eludes every word. His escape route from the hold of language knows but one direction: upward. One who embraces this insight embraces an *absolutum*—in the literal sense of the word: something that withdraws from the all-too-mundane difference between being and not-being. In this way, especially one's own speaking in saying exactly this is afforded an absolute character.

Saying that nothing can be said about God can provide a discourse with a truth claim unmatched by any mortal power. This is not only evident from the texts of Pseudo-Dionysius, but primarily also from the way in which these texts were read and implemented by the Christian authorities of the following centuries. This is to say that Pseudo-Diony-sius's oeuvre is also, and above all, about *power*, including *political* power.

Power

Is Pseudo-Dionysius not, ultimately, the author of a text entitled *Peri tès ouranias hierarchias*: "about the celestial hierarchy"? He is indeed, but the question is whether the Late Antique Greek word *hierarchia* in the title has the connotation of power, as the word *hierarchy* does today. This does not seem to be the case. *Hierarchia* means "divine principle," and has no direct conceptual connotation of power. That is already clear in the definition Pseudo-Dionysius explicitly presents to his reader: "In my opinion a hierarchy is a sacred place in an order, a state of understanding and an activity approximating as closely as possible to the divine. And it is uplifted to the imitation of God in proportion to the enlightenments divinely given to it. . . . The goal of a hierarchy then, is to enable beings to be as like as possible to God and to be at one with him."[5] The semantic field to which *hierarchy* belongs here is not primarily that of "power," "force," "ability," "energy," and the like. It is a *topological* term that stands for a "sacred *place*," a place within an order. If it functions as an "authority," it is because it is looked up to. In Pseudo-Dionysius's Neoplatonic universe, hierarchical principles are "points" or "platforms" within the multilayered cosmos, where, at several places, the emanation of the One has, as it were, contracted to a single "point." The unity of the One is manifested and reflected in concentrated fashion in such a "point." Therefore, a hierarchical principle forms a beacon or authoritative example according to which the whole of the cosmos, which emanates from the One, can orient itself in its return to the One. In that sense, that principle is a center of "understanding" and at the same time the effect of "enlightenments." The hierarchical principles contain a knowledge (they are "spirits") that points the multitude of beings in the direction of their identity, their unity, namely, the One. *Hierarchical principles* is the conceptual term for beings such as "seraphs," "archangels," and "angels": celestial beings in whom mortal human beings can mirror themselves and to whom they can become equal in the long run, when they open *their* knowledge and activity to the former's knowledge and activity.

The "celestial hierarchy," however, is not without implications for the earthly human hierarchy:

> The source of spiritual perfection provided us with perceptible images of these heavenly minds. He did so out of concern for us and because he wanted us to be made godlike. He made the heavenly hierarchies known to us. He made our own hierarchy a ministerial colleague of these divine hierarchies by an assimilation, to the extent that is humanly feasible, to their godlike priesthood.[6]

The "heavenly hierarchies" are so kind as to lead us, mortals, into the mystery, by providing us with "perceptible images." This implies that the celestial principles shape our own *mortal* "hierarchy," because the latter is (or should be) the collaborator of the former. And what, then, are our "own hierarchical principles" actually? They are those who lead our community and hold positions of power in it. Priests and those who hold higher offices within the church are invested with "hierarchy"—with the "divine principle." In the earthly world of confusing multiplicity, they radiate the light that comes from the One who is God, and subsequently hold the place that they are assigned in the community of the Church that is on its way to holiness. In fact, they also do so in the united human community *in general*, because ultimately, in the Christian eyes of Pseudo-Dionysius, all of humanity is moving to the moment at which it can partake of the perfect community of saints and angels.

And no, the "divine hierarchy" to which bishops and priests owe their position is not considered a talent or an ability to exercise power. We are, in other words, far removed from Aristotle, who thinks about political power in terms of "ability," "talent," "potency" to lead and empower the community of citizens. According to him, it is society's ontological "energy"—i.e., its very "essence"—that legitimizes politics and its authorities. An *archon* partakes in the *archè*, in the immanent, "physical" essence of the sociopolitical community. This is clearly not the way in which Pseudo-Dionysius thinks political power.

But is his thinking not about power at all? It is true that Pseudo-Dionysius does not think it in terms referring to Aristotle's "dynamic" and "energetic" model, but he still does have his own ideas about it. For him, political power is invested with and founded in a hierarchical principle. The (true) power in a (true) society is a derivative of the divine One— that is to say, of an instance exalted beyond being and not-being to such an extent that, in order to be what it is, it does not even need to exert power. This, however, is not to say that Pseudo-Dionysius's model does not consider social and political power as ontologically founded. For him, too, power is based on being, even if this ontological ground withdraws into the inaccessible domain of a mystery that can only be expressed in negative theological terms. And for that very reason, he reflects upon earthly political power in negative theological terms.

The question now is if, by considering the ground of power as "beyond being," one does not actually pave the way for a hegemonic or, even, an absolutist political power. Do politics and politicians not become more powerful when their ontological foundation is considered to be a separate entity that withdraws from any human grip?

Aristotle considered the foundation of being as its "first cause." The Christian reception of his oeuvre understood this "first cause" as a *separate, transcendent* entity, as a being disconnected from and situated *above* all beings. *First cause* was used as the philosophical term for the biblical creating God. As first principle, as *archè*, God exists on his own, and He existed before "being" was created. All that is, owes its existence to God's power. It is what it is, only to the extent that it partakes in the divine power that is beyond being and not-being. Formed as a Neoplatonist scholar in the line of Plotinus and Proclus, Pseudo-Dionysius accepts this interpretation, amplifies it, and integrates it in a complex and subtle, negative theological system.

This system also covers political governance. When we consider the latter within Pseudo-Dionysius's paradigm, we end up with a political power that ultimately remains "ineffable," "unspeakable."[7] So, ultimately, such power does not need to "speak," which in this case implies that it always has the possibility to disregard any call for accountability for its policy. Power over human beings is rooted in the Word of God, a Word expressing the "ineffable" mystery that underlies all beings, both nonhuman and human. So, when push comes to shove, such political power can keep divinely silent when it is asked for explanations concerning its governance. Strictly speaking, power is right precisely because it *cannot* explain why it is in the right. Here, we meet a rejection of democracy (which can be found already in Eusebius)[8] and, instead, a perfect dispositive for absolute power. So, it is no wonder that absolutist and other kinds of extreme power politics are far from absent from the history of Christianity.

Government

Even though the Italian philosopher Giorgio Agamben agrees with this analysis in general, in *Il Regno e la Gloria* (*The Kingdom and the Glory*), he puts some things in a slightly more nuanced way.[9] In this 2007 study on the Christian dispositives underlying Western politics, the author explains at length that, historically, power only very seldom expressed itself *purely* as power. Neither was governance—i.e., organizing, controlling, managing public and social affairs—ever just the practical side of a sovereign, closed, and mysterious power. If, in the Christian history of the West, politics referred to sovereign power for more than a thousand years, as it certainly did, it rarely did so *directly*. For power, in Christianity, was never simply a matter of sovereignty that ruled from on high; it was above all a matter of governance from down under, of management treating the facts of society in an "economical" way in order to optimize that society's potentials. Based on Christian principles, politics was actually "governance," "management," "economy." And that also applies to the highest form of power: God. Although sovereign, God's being, too, was characterized by "management" and "economy."

This is the central thesis of Agamben's book. Whoever wants to write a history of Western politics and expose the diverse schemes that legitimized its exercise of power should not, as far as the Christian part of it is concerned, necessarily consult the specific political texts from that tradition, texts that directly discuss political power. According to Agamben, one should rather study "purely" theological treatises: discourses (*logos*) that deal directly with God (*theos*). For Christianity does not simply describe God as a sovereign power, withdrawn behind the curtain of his mystery. The Christian God also stands for "governance." *Oikonomia* is the word the Greek Fathers use here: "economy" or, more literally, housekeeping, management of the *oikos* (house).[10] For these Early Christian authors, the term is semantically far removed from the idea of a top-down exercise of power.

God Himself should be thought of as a "household," an "economy." The term characterizes one of the most central elements of Christian doctrine: the Trinity.[11] In other words, God has a household, or more precisely, He *is* one. It coincides with the interrelationship between the Father, the Son, and the Spirit, a relationship thought to be perfect, even so perfect that there is not the slightest hierarchy (in our sense of the term) among the participants. It is a relationship of complete but no less lively and active unity. God is what He is *as* "relationship," *as* "economy." Here, God's *being* and God's *doing* (his *action*) perfectly coincide. That God is who and what He *is*, fully coincides with what He *does*; that is: with the household (economy) of His interpersonal community.

Oikonomia, however, does not only stand for God's household *at "home"* (with Father, Son, and Spirit). The term also refers to God's "household" relationship to his creation in general, and to mankind in particular. The term *oikonomia* is aways also understood in the sense of "economy of salvation." Here, the term exceeds even the exclusively male household of the Trinity and includes the other sex. In *that* "economy," the Son is born of a woman, incarnated in her by the Spirit, in order to bring salvation and redemption in the world that has drifted away from the Father.

God is the fullness of being, a fullness so full that it is beyond being and not-being. But God does not merely dwell in his hyper-ontological *being*, He also *acts*. He stands for *action* as well, both within the sphere of His own household and within that of the world external to Him. More precisely: He gives existence to His creation and, more so, brings salvation and redemption to it, now that that creation has been driven away from Him.

God's being and God's action: according to Agamben, this is a crucial distinction within Christian theology, not so much because it keeps the two neatly separate from each other, but because in and through that separation, they connect with each other in a complex and somehow tricky way.

It is the "hierarchy" of "angelic beings" who take care of this connection. They represent the well-ordered "bureaucracy" of celestial beings, situated between the Supreme Deity and His earthly creation: from Seraphs, Cherubs, and Thrones, who are closest to God, via Dominions, Forces, and Powers, who form a kind of celestial midfield, to Monarchs, Archangels, and Angels who—in that order—are closest to human beings. This hierarchy in itself points to the fact that we are not dealing here with pure institutions of power, but rather with an administration and management apparatus. Angels organize and manage the domain where God's externally oriented actions operate. They organize the "order" in the celestial domain, in the sense that they keep the whole of the cosmos vertically, transcendentally oriented. And this also applies to humanity, to whom messages of divine origin are transmitted—messages that have to go through the whole hierarchically structured apparatus of celestial officials before they are filtered in such a way that human beings are able to infer them from the epiphany of an Angel (who is ranked lowest in that hierarchy).

The actions of angels bear witness to the actions of God. But their testimony is most evident when they no longer partake in God's actions but only sing His praises. Besides the angelic beings that function as officials in the celestial administration of God's externally oriented actions, there are those who only sing God's praises and, in that sense, bear witness, not to His actions, but to His pure being—angels that only exist to reflect God's glory back in the direction of God, who is praised not for what He *does*, but purely for what He *is*: a power that, to be who or what it is, does not even have to act in relation to us.

That praise is, moreover, something we humans aim for as well, also in our politics. Politics comprises the management of the human community. In this capacity, however, it is part of—and mirrors—the celestial government. In that sense, human politics is indeed ultimately oriented toward a collective and uninterrupted liturgy of God. The imperative of *labora* (work), which in a certain sense also applies to politics, is ultimately oriented toward that of *ora*, the imperative to pray and praise, and to make human life a permanent liturgy venerating God's holy majesty. But in the meantime, in order to achieve this aim, there is work to be done and there are actions to be taken—actions through which we partake in God's actions and through which we are ordered and managed by way of a political apparatus that mirrors the well-ordered administration apparatus of celestial officials, from the Angels all the way up to the Seraphs.

The Empty Seat of Power from the Neoplatonic Perspective

But where, within the sphere of these political administrations—the celestial as well as the earthly one—does the sovereign power of God

Figure 10.1. *God's empty throne*; fourth–ninth century.

manifest itself? Where does it come to the fore *as such*? As sovereign as power might consider itself, it is hardly manifested anywhere. It remains hidden behind its administration, behind its governing apparatus. The place where power *as such* could/should appear, remains empty (Figure 10.1).[12] De facto, power is only manifested in management. Only there is it tangibly present, but not without clarifying that it does not quite, and, in fact, not even at all, coincide with that management, but that it is *more* than this management and infinitely above—and beyond—it.

In Pseudo-Dionysius-inspired Christian political thought, power is seen as sovereign, as grounded in God who needs nothing, not even being, to be who He is. This negative theological prerogative makes this God thoroughly absolute. However, it also exposes the highly problematic character of God's position here, which—as we will see—has direct effect on political power.

After all, if God in His omnipotence does not even have to act to be who He is, why then did He act at all? If God, to be who He is, really needs nothing, not even being, why then did He create something outside of Himself? The theory of the Trinity can, according to Agamben, be considered an attempt at facing this problem.[13]

After all, the idea of a triune God allows the action to not only come from God's sovereign being but to situate it *within* the deity itself, where being and acting seamlessly coincide. God *is*; He is the over-fullness of being (transcending the dichotomy of being and not-being). Yet, according to Pseudo-Dionysius, this *being* of God is at the same time *acting* as well. It is simultaneously "relationship," "household," "economy." This makes conceivable that creation did not just *coincidentally* slip from God—"despite" Himself, if you will—but that, from the nature of His *being*, God proceeded to the *act* of creation. He always already is economy in Himself. He therefore spontaneously has an "economic" relation with what He creates. Pseudo-Dionysius's Neoplatonism offers a nuanced grammar to consider this. Reality is not a product that slipped from God despite His fullness, it is a "logical" (read: "*more*-than-logical") emanation, an externalization of an economy that already determines the intimate life of the divine triune household.

This line of reasoning, however, barely conceals that it basically serves to keep the problem hidden. The triune God is, above all, a mystery—and functions in that way. This is why earthly power does not take example so much from God's celestial *power* as from the celestial *hierarchy*. It does not identify with God's sovereignty that is above being and not-being, but takes example from how He *works* and *acts* in relation to His creatures. Political power, in other words, is modeled after the celestial administration, the "economic actions of angels" with their strict order and perfect functioning. Put differently, power functions as a matter of "good governance." It is clear to Agamben that our contemporary practice of that name already had its equivalent in the Christian doctrine of power as described in Pseudo-Dionysius's treatise *The Celestial Hierarchy*.

But if, in politics, sovereign divine power never *directly* serves as model, what role does it play in that practice? Does it function as the foundation of human governance? This is how the theoretical narrative of Pseudo-Dionysius indeed puts it. God is the foundation, the true "self" of political power, while power in its concrete execution never completely reaches this "self," but only keeps on "managing" things in that direction. But what, then, exactly is this true "self"?

De facto, this "self" functions as selfless or, in Agamben's terms, as a *state of exception*. It is the central thesis that Agamben defends in all his political analyses and that, here, he observes as being at work behind Pseudo-Dionysius's argumentation.

Power is never fully itself; it rarely rules directly on the basis of its essence, its sovereignty. It rather prefers to rely on the logic of governing and sociopolitical management. This provides an "order" with fixed rules and keeps the sociopolitical machine lubricated. But when, then, does sovereign power come up *as such*? Only at the moment when the management of the sociopolitical machine fails, when governance no longer delivers the expected results. Then power is called in in a way that cannot be considered as anything but a state of exception. In contrast to power's own discourse, that power should not be seen as the ground and principle of governance but as that which escapes governance, as that which does *not* adhere to its rules, but makes its decisions sovereignly: without rules, without reason, without accountability.

Or, which amounts to the same thing, the "ground" of political power—its "self"—only reveals itself in (and as) a state of exception, in (and as) the specific condition in which it surrenders its proclaimed "self," becomes "selfless" and permits itself to make no matter what decision.[14] Here, it becomes clear what sovereignty means: that decisions can be made without grounds, without reason, without accountability. The self of power is that place where power is no longer bound to something, not even to its own "self."

In other essays, Agamben often refers to the same hidden logic that underlies the paradigm of modern Western politics. With Foucault, he calls it the "biopolitical" paradigm. It dates from the midst of the eighteenth century. Only then is *bios* (life)—i.e., the preservation of and care for the life of a nation's population—invoked as a ground for politics and political power. Before, the paradigm of political power was "sovereignty," defined as "the right to kill," the power to deprive someone of his or her life.[15] However, so Agamben states, the elements that enable the biopolitical logic are already to be found in classical antiquity, in Aristotle, for instance in the distinction he draws, at the beginning of his *Politeia*, between *bios* and *zoè*, between life as it plays out in society and natural, "bare life," *la vita nuda*, life "itself."[16] And that distinction does not only contain the elements of the biological paradigm, but at the same time hides the structure of sovereign power. Behind the biopolitical paradigm, the one of sovereignty is still at work—thus Agamben's central thesis.

But what does "bare life," "life itself," precisely mean? Its meaning emerges more clearly in a number of political-legal practices than in the philosophical systems of the time. Agamben refers to Roman law, more specifically to one of the most severe penalties stipulated therein, the sentence of *sacer esto,* which makes the convicted person *homo sacer.*[17] This verdict stems from the most ancient of times, and the term *sacer,* then, apparently does not refer to a "dedication to the divine," but to damnation and exclusion from all of society's domains, including that of the sacred and the divine. Declaring someone *homo sacer* banishes the condemned from *all* spheres of sociopolitical (including religious) life. A *homo sacer* is someone "who *may be killed and yet not sacrificed,*" Agamben writes.[18] Life nor death of a *homo sacer* have any right to existence anywhere, neither in the domain of the profane nor in that of the sacred. So, it is a radical form of being outlawed, in which even the customary "religious" way to still give death its meaning and func-tion, is excluded.[19]

Where do we find something like "life *itself*"? Not in the full and normal life of the citizen. On the contrary, according to Agamben; it is with the *homo sacer.* It is life in as far as it is at the mercy of radical arbitrariness, life that for the very same reason can just as easily be either spared or taken. In a philosophical argument, "life itself" stands for life that has the fullness of self-grounding. In reality (and for Agamben reality is always first and foremost sociopolitical), "life itself" is life in as far as it has been *ex*cluded from society and, being excluded, is nevertheless *in*cluded since it remains subjected to that society. Life "itself" is therefore to be defined as "inclusive exclusion," to use a typically Agambenian expression.[20] With respect to life "itself" ("bare life"), politics and its laws operate within a "zone of indistinction."[21] In this zone, the supporting differences (between good and evil, true and false, high and low) upon which society and its laws rest, are no longer valid. There, arbitrariness rules and allows sovereign decisions to be made about someone's life and death.

It is in this "selfless" *zone of indistinction* that the true "self" of a legal order is manifested. A modern society, founded on a constitution and on the Universal Declaration of Human Rights, shows its ultimate "self" where people are locked up in camps, stripped of their rights and subjected to sovereign, that is, random decisions. Legitimizing itself "biopolitically" as the guardian of its subjects, modern society displays its "real" power where it reduces people to "bare life" and announces verdicts on their life and death in brutal arbitrariness. Behind civil- and human-rights-based societal governance, a sovereign power hides that only reveals itself in the state of exception, where that power suspends and replaces the laws of government with sovereign randomness.

This is what the ineffable mystery of power is all about, Agamben states. In this unspeakable mystery, he does not perceive its so-called mystical ground, but rather the lack of ground or, more precisely, the ability of power not to have to stick to its own ground and logic in order to be what it is. Sovereign power formally occupies the same place as the *homo sacer*, the included excluded one, with this difference, that power is sovereign and, in this capacity, able to reduce each of its citizens to *homo sacer*. In principle, power is basically an exception that is not only confirmed by the rule but can also at the same time ignore it—and that, in the case of an actual state of exception, does ignore it.

Now we understand why sovereign power hardly ever expresses itself *as such* and likes to leave the place on the basis of which it functions empty. It leaves power to the administration, to the economy through which a society is kept on track by its own laws. But the true paradigm of governance does not lie with governance itself but with the state of exception through which that governance is suspended—not to finally make society coincide with itself, but to surrender it to the complete arbitrariness of a sovereign power.

Pseudo-Dionysius's treatise about celestial hierarchical principles offers a ground and a model for the earthly hierarchies and holds the mirror of a well-ordered administration up to those in power. But where that administration reverts back to its original principle and unites the chaotic multiplicity of society into a collective hymn to the One who is God, there, it goes beyond its own logic and becomes sovereign, purely arbitrary power. Where administration fully realizes its goal, it de facto overshoots that goal and becomes whimsical, sovereign power. That is, according to Agamben, what actually lies behind the unsayable mystery of the God who is supposed to bring unity: an anarchist zone in which prevailing distinctions have been erased and where, when push comes to shove, administrators can do what they want, despite all rules imposed by their administrative economy and management logic.

The Empty Seat of Power from the Modern Perspective

No wonder, then, that the kind of politics that came into effect with the Christianization of our culture in the fourth and fifth centuries gave way to an authoritarian politics that dominated European history for almost a millennium and a half in various forms, from feudality to absolutism. In any case, the democratic tendency that unquestionably characterized Greek and Roman antiquity and that was not easily crushed, not even under the Roman Principate, was turned in the opposite direction by Christianity. The practice of shielding the emperor from the citizens (by a sacred aura, a palace, and a court) only became common in the middle of the third century and received an initial "boost" with Diocletian at the end of that century.[22] This trend was further confirmed under the Christian emperors of the next two centuries. Pseudo-Dionysius's negative theology—with its treatises on celestial and ecclesiastical hierarchical principles—gave this political practice a strong theoretical foundation. It contributed to similar ways of legitimizing and shaping power until the dawn of modernity in the seventeenth century. It is precisely the inexpressibility of God and the empty place that He occupies in government and its political discourses that made it possible for power to take the form of an administrative "political economy" with even greater sovereignty (and associated arbitrariness).

However, can only negative things be said about the negative theological tradition with respect to politics? That the ultimate foundation of power withdraws from every discourse, that political government ultimately stems from a mystically justified power: does this idea necessarily lead to authoritarian politics? Is the ultimate ground of political power not really something that eludes our grasp *anyway*, and is it not on that very basis we have to organize concrete politics?

Let us zoom in on modern democracy and the way in which it deals with power. The ground of political power being beyond the grip of society: Is this not eminently applicable to a democratic system? Of course, the will of the people—*ours*, in other words—forms the basis of a democratic power. But what do the people want? And also: *Who* are the people, who are "we"? Does this "we" ever succeed in expressing what it really wants? Does this not also withdraw from the "sayable"? Is who we are as a "people" or a social identity not ultimately equally inexpressible as the God of Pseudo-Dionysius? And if this is the case, can we indeed consider this ineffability as a marginal phenomenon in our political system? Is it not absolutely necessary to bear in mind that we, as the basis of our political order, ultimately do not really know who that "we" is who we are. Does something ineffable not form the basis of our democratic self-government?

The French political philosopher Claude Lefort would willingly go along with the suggestion that lies behind these questions.[23] For him, democracy as a political system in which power is based on the will of the people, is supported by a logic that is everything but at odds with that of negative theology. For Lefort, too, the "self" of the people is not immediately within the reach of that people. How would it be? Everyone is free to want what he or she wants, and the will of everyone together is a momentary and colorful collection of decrees that are not able to bring the people to unity, let alone to one act of will. The will and the self of the people lie beyond what the people can grasp and say. They are literally unspeakable. But unlike what is the case within a negative theological logic, a democratic people can and may never speak *in the name of* the unspeakable.

And this is not just a detail. Because it means that the unspeakable, which undoubtedly takes a central position here, does not ask to finally cease speaking. On the contrary, here the unspeakable explicitly calls for never ceasing to speak. In a democracy the power lies with the people themselves, but that this "self" remains unspeakable at long last expresses, above all, that everyone must continuously enter into discussion with everyone in order to politically shape the democratic governance of their community. Democracy is the culture of unceasing discussion, of organized *dissensus*, where, it is true, the seat of power is occupied by members of the community, but never forever, never because that place would "naturally" belong to them.[24] In principle, that place remains empty and is never occupied more than temporarily by the representatives the people have elected—the people who do not vote as a close-knit social unity but as a fragmented political body, each for themself in the intimacy of a voting booth. On the day when all positions of power are declared vacant, the people "themselves" do rule, but indeed as an infinitely divided and splintered voice, from among whose splinters a new representation is chosen to occupy the seats of power. And these representatives have to tolerate the irrevocable temporality of their seats, just as they should take the never-ending discussions among their subjects for granted and even stimulate them—a discussion that manifests itself in parliament, the press, the media, labor unions, action and other groups, to which they as rulers have to answer time and again.

Here, too, the formal structure of a negative theological logic can be recognized. The ultimate power in a democracy is a *negativum*, an impossibility of the people to fully be with themselves and to realize that "self." In the entire democratic political system, this *negativum* remains the ultimate point of reference. But unlike that of Pseudo-Dionysius, this *negativum* does not lend itself to an absolute power but to a never-ending and repetitively organized blockade of every inclination toward it. If the "self" that rules in a democracy is unspeakable, then this given prohibits us from stopping speaking and requires the conversation to be taken up again and again. This conversation gives voice, not to the unity of the people, but to their constant, more-or-less chaotic plurality.

Coda

That words fall short when we speak about God can bring us to the point of distrusting all words and ultimately to fall silent in a wordless panegyric before His throne. This insight constitutes the heart of Pseudo-Dionysius's thought.

But the same scenario might just as well bring us to the insight that, if we want to speak about the unsayable God, the only thing that we are left with is precisely to speak, and only to speak. The fact that God escapes every word can just as well lead to the conclusion that we can only rely on words, no matter how crooked, clumsy, and limited they might appear, and that we should cherish words precisely because they, like everything, come from God.

The latter is far from Pseudo-Dionysius's thought. It is more in line with, for instance, Jewish religiosity. God made Himself known in the Word, but unlike in Christianity, that Word has not become flesh. It has remained what it is, namely, the material letter that reached us from God without assuring us that we would grasp the letter's "spirit" and be able to come to Him through His Words. Words, letters: they are the only thing of His that we have, and we should cherish them to infinity. No "economy" is to be developed with these Words, and these Words themselves are far from "economical." The Word that we have received from God throws us back on ourselves and compels us to honor that Word in an endless verbal and written cult, even at the level of its material letters. And instead of honoring God *beyond* the Word (as angels do), the Jewish cult means honoring the Word itself for what it is: something we mortals share and that allows us to enter into a discussion with each other. The unknowable God is subsequently not the object of angelic worship *beyond* mortal language, but the object of discussion among mortals here and now, who endlessly continue to explore the divinity of the names of God, without ever speaking *in* the name of this divinity or, beyond every spoken word, claiming His power.

You can say nothing about the unspeakable.

You can only speak about the unspeakable.

Two different conclusions based on an identical negative theological fact. I believe modernity is urging us to opt for the latter.

11

Selflessness and Science

On Mysticism, Materialism, and Psychoanalysis

The greatest obstacle on the path that a mystic walks is the self. The first chapter has sufficiently thematized that. It has also become clear why this obstacle was less problematic for a *premodern* mystic. Beyond his personal self lies a bigger, truer Self, ground and source of everything that is: the divine *subiectum*. Premodern mystics spontaneously understood themselves on the basis of this divine subject. Emptying out their own individual self brought them closer to the true Self of which they knew they—and everything else that exists—were a part.

For early modern mystics, however, the confrontation with their own self as an obstacle on their mystical path turned out to be a more difficult and painful matter. Since the outside world bears less testimony to God, to find Him the mystic is now more reliant than ever on the intimacy of his inner path toward God. The interior of the human soul is the only place left to find God. This is why the mystic needs first of all to expel the local "controller" from this interior. The true, divine Self that he seeks is to be found *beyond* his individual self. As firmly as their medieval predecessors, the early modern mystic still believes that man's true self is not located in himself but in God. But unlike his predecessors, he can no longer spontaneously understand himself on the basis of the divine Self, on the basis of being "given" by God. A modern believer is free *in* and *with respect to* the reality of all that is, God included. If he believes the divine Self to be the ground of all that is, he has *freely chosen* to do so. His choice implies an initial freedom—and consequently a free human self—with respect to the divine Self. It is this free self that the modern mystic has to overcome. He has to annihilate it in order to reach his true ground, God. A mystic needs to "kill" the self that is only his, but, as mentioned before, the only one who can do this is precisely that "self" of his.

This is the paradoxical task the mystic faces. It requires method and perseverance on a journey that runs through his own deepest and darkest interior. A profound exploration of his *vie intérieure* forces him to submit himself to an extensive and patient self-examination. He needs to trace his "interior life" along the countless erratic roads it wanders, including the roads of its hedonistic self-love in which human passions make it linger. These passions bind him to a mortal and vain Ego and forbid his interior from becoming the empty space that is open to God only. One of the early modern spiritual authors, Louis Lallemant, writes in his *Doctrine spirituelle*:

> There is in us a very depth of malice, which we do not per-
> ceive, because we never seriously examine our own interior.
> If we did, we should find therein a multitude of desires and
> irregular appetites for the honours, the pleasures, and the
> comforts of the world unceasingly fermenting in our heart.[1]

The annihilation of such "appetites" implies the annihilation of the "self." This is why the mystic needs to familiarize himself with these appetites and passions and their most secret of twists. No wonder that so many early modern spiritual treatises read like studies of the human passions, of the cluttered array of moods and drives that inspire the inner life.

Is this one of the reasons why the spiritual literature of the time was so hugely popular and successful? Where else could the reader of the day find extensive accounts of human cravings and other feelings that stir his soul? These could definitely not be found in contemporary science. Scientific discourses on the inner life of the human soul were, if existent at all, extremely meager.

Mysticism-less Self-Knowledge

That such discourses were meager was due to a radical change that took place in the field of "science." At the beginning of the seventeenth century, science had completely reinvented itself, including its principle and ground. Descartes had localized that ground in the human *cogito*, the thinking subject. By doing so, he had provided a radical new theoretical basis for what then was known as the "soul." Had he also provided a new "science of the "soul"? Not exactly. How could he have? Is the subject—and all the typical forms of "subjectivity" that go back to it—not something that has no need of science at all? Not because it eludes any scientific grip, but because it has always already been supposed (and, consequently, known) by science—since science has its "bearer," its *subiectum* in that *cogito*, in that "thinking subject." As soon as one starts to think about—read: to doubt—the subject, that subject reveals itself as that which escapes every doubt and is instantly known. One does not need to examine the thinking instance: it appears in complete, unassailable lucidity at the first attempt at thinking, even where thinking reduces itself to ruthless doubt. The same applies to anxiety, to joy, to sadness, and to all other kinds of feeling: they do not reveal themselves *at the end* of a discursive path of examination; they reveal themselves at once, and in the same stroke their ground and foundation as well: the *cogito*, the subject.

And yet Descartes *did* set up a scientific examination of the passions—an examination that he likely would have taken to the next level had it not been aborted by his sudden death.[2] The reason for this research, however, was not so much a clarification of the passions *as such*. An understanding of the latter was first of all meant to explain the relationship between soul and body. This was indeed the delicate issue he faced, once he had promoted the *cogito* as the new subject of scientific knowledge. This *cogito* was conceived as being free—free in the sense that, in principle, it has nothing in common with the world it is thinking (doubting) about. That world is the mechanical realm of lifeless bodies, the *res extensa*, a realm determined by physical laws and lacking any kind of self-determination or freedom. Doubting whether the *cogito* is subject to such laws immediately makes clear that it is not. The *cogito* is precisely what escapes both doubt and lawfulness: it is immediate, full "presence to itself." This is the reason why Descartes concludes that the *cogito* is ontologically different from the determined, "objective" *res extensa*. The *res cogitans*, the subject of knowledge, is self-determining. It is free, *radically* free.

But what about us, human beings, who are both *res cogitans* and *res extensa*—spirit and matter, soul and body? How should one understand the relationship between soul and body? Though these two seem intrinsically connected to one another, they are two different kinds of being, the one radically free, the other entirely determined. That the spirit—in Latin: *anima*—"animates" the body, as on the basis of Aristotelean theory had always been thought before, is obviously no option for Descartes. After all, the spirit (*cogito*) had been discovered to be independent through the realization that it has nothing in common with the world it thinks about/doubts. Unlike what Aristotle taught, matter is not "animated." For Descartes, the *anima* (the soul or spirit) is a self-conscious skeptic within a world full of "un-animated," "dead," "geometric" bodies. The human body, too, is to be considered this way. The human soul, on the other hand, is something completely different, even if it seems to be at home in the human body. The soul is radical self-animation, freedom.

But how, then, do body and soul work together in that same human "home"? Descartes's rational explanation does not get much farther than to speculate about the "glande pineal," the pineal gland in the center between the two halves of the brain. There he "physically" localizes the interaction between soul and body.[3] The Cartesian-inspired solutions that came after him remained insufficient too; they were at least not perceived as sufficient and did not influence the further history of modern science. Nor did "occasionalism," the philosophical system of Malebranche that was highly successful at the time and provided a whole new theory on God's intervention in a world divided into bodies and souls.[4] None of these systems succeeded in presenting a convincing theory on the passions. A Cartesian-based science of the passions—and of the subjective, in general—never took off, in fact.

Yet, all the while, in nonscientific circles, more precisely in religious milieus where *spiritualité* was practiced, the study of the soul and its variety of passions topped the agenda, albeit to combat these passions, to neutralize or annihilate them, or to ensure indifference to them.

A *scientific* study of the passions, and of the subjective in general, only became possible when the problematic dualism of body and soul was solved. That solution came in the middle of the eighteenth century, with so-called materialism. The solution was drastic and severe. One of the two elements was simply declared nonexistent. La Mettrie's 1747 philosophical pamphlet, *L'homme machine* (*Machine Man*), summarizes clearly the point made by the majority of Enlightenment philosophers of the day.[5] La Mettrie's basic premise is that everything we used to attribute to the spirit, to what Descartes defines as *res cogitans*—passions, affects, expressions of will, activities of the mind—should in fact entirely be attributed to the body, to the human *res extensa*. At the moment, La Mettrie adds, our knowledge of the latter is still insufficient, but science is progressing by leaps and bounds, and soon the knowledge of our corporeal machine will be so far advanced that anxiety, joy, and all other emotions and passions will be completely understood as bodily, neural processes. And the same applies to "free will" and to "free thinking," including that of science. They are all as determined and subjected to physical laws as Newton's apple is to the law of gravity. Feeling, will, and thought are finally open to objective, scientific study, La Mettrie concludes with undisguised euphoria.

This euphoria, however, cannot conceal that the arguments upon which the author bases his statement all lie in the future: science, *once* it will have developed further, *will* prove that the subjective returns to the objective corporeal. It goes without saying that the future tense of the argument reduces its evidential value to nil. Yet, the fact remains that La Mettrie's argument was historically successful, that materialism did provide the scientific paradigm for the "sciences of the human" that arose afterward. Human sciences—in other words, the sciences studying the *res* of the subjective—have become fully *objective* sciences.

The idea that everything we feel, want, and think can be examined and controlled as neural processes in our brain is today more alive than ever. This also applies to the "self" and everything we attribute to it. We may "think" that everything emanates from our "self," that we are the self who feels, wants, and thinks, but like all subjective activities, the "self," too, is the effect of objective, material, bodily processes. Knowledge of what we used to attribute to an independent self is in fact knowledge of processes that do not need an ego or "self" to be explained and clarified. Today's human sciences claim to have an objective understanding of feelings, passions, expressions of will, and thinking activities as they function; and that understanding is I-less, self-less.

Selfless Mysticism, Selfless Self-Knowledge

However, does this scientific materialism not deprive phenomena such as mysticism and *spiritualité* of all meaning and, even, *raison d'être*? How to still walk the inner path of "spiritual" life when no spirit or interior exists, when everything is a matter of "superficial," "dead" *res extensa*?

Why continue fighting the passions that tie me to my own self-interest when these passions themselves, including their logic of self-interest, are embedded in egoless, selfless laws of nature?

These are legitimate questions, and for the materialist *philosophe* of the eighteenth century, the answer is clear: neither God nor ego exists. So how could mysticism and the *vie intérieure* still have a right to exist?

However, does the *philosophe*'s negative response not conceal an unexpected connection with mysticism? If, for example, self-interest is merely the exponent of a natural process, then it is a self-interest *without self*, without an instance that claims this interest for itself. In other words: it is something entirely selfless. And was selflessness not the mental state awaiting the mystic at the end of his spiritual path? Was that not what the mystic strived for: that it is no longer he who lives, but the divine in him? According to materialism, the divine is indeed nonexistent, but this does not prevent a materialist from living without any self and living on the basis of something else, something selfless. For the materialist, it thus comes down to understanding that things such as self and self-consciousness no longer matter—that consciousness, too, is not what it pretends to be, but only an ephemeral byproduct of a purely material process. Not entirely unlike mysticism, science turns out to be a manner to unmask the false pretensions of the ego and the self, and to teach us how we can reconcile ourselves to the fact that it is not "we" who feel, think, and want, but something else in us. Before, that "something else" was called God, and now it is called Nature. This is what Paul-Henri Thiry, baron d'Holbach, one of the icons of eighteenth-century materialism, says in his famous *Système de la nature* (1770)—to provide just one example: "Man, in his origin, is an imperceptible point, a speck, of which the parts are without form; of which the mobility, the life, escapes his sense; in short, in which he does not perceive any sign of those qualities called *sentiment, feeling, thought, intelligence, force, reason,* &c."[6] A few lines farther on we read: "and man, an infinitely small portion of the globe, which is itself but an imperceptible point in the immensity of space, vainly believes it is for himself this universe is made; foolishly imagines he ought to be the confidant of nature; confidently flatters himself he is eternal and calls himself KING OF THE UNIVERSE!! O man! wilt thou never conceive that thou art but an ephemeron?"[7] Whether it is God or indeed Nature that must be acknowledged as the true ground (*subiectum*) of the individual self does not formally matter much to the ego. It comes down to becoming "egoless" or, even better, to accepting the selflessness one has always been.

But what could this mean: accepting selflessness? It is easier said than done. Just think of the paradox the second chapter of this book extensively explored: Who else but myself must accept my selflessness? This kind of *kenosis* of the self demands *my* best effort—an effort presuming precisely the strong self that I want to shrug off. Those who choose the spiritual path must subject the intimacy of their ego to the strongest kind of self-examination. This is only possible if they trace their passions and observe how these are seduced by *amour-propre*. And this again presumes an ego that resists these passions and is able to be indifferent to all of this seduction. This paradox generates an ego that remains indifferent even with respect to the eternal bliss that God promises—as has become clear with Fénelon's *pur amour*.

Such an attitude, however, does not formally distinguish itself that much from an attitude that deliberately seeks seduction and unrestrainedly embraces sinful passions. In that case, bathing in evil indicates that even this does not taint the egoless purity of one's love for God. So, it is not surprising that a certain kind of *pur amour* spirituality was able to recognize the purity of someone's love for God—and especially the indifference that this love requires—in one's willingness to deliberately embrace vice and sin.

In the accounts of the ecclesiastical court of Dijon, there is, for example, a case from 1699 ("peak year" of the *Querelle du quiétisme*) where priests were berated for what, at the time, was called "spiritual incest." They accompanied women followers—"Sisters of the Heart"—in their prayers and led them to a "passive state in which the soul is forbidden to 'demand anything from God, because doing so would be self-interested.'"[8] A witness claimed that during prayer meetings, one of the accused, Philibert Peultier, expected each of the women "penitents" present to spend some time alone with him. Charly Coleman's description is as sober as it is accurate:

> The women were made to loosen their clothing and press their bodies tightly against Peultier as he kissed them on the mouth. Then he would recite a formula adapted from the Song of Songs, such as "My beloved is entirely mine, and I am entirely hers," before sighing a breath that sent them into an ecstasy during which "they were so forcefully transported

by the pleasure that they no longer knew themselves." Peultier taught that these rituals induced an "illuminative and unitive" state. Mutual self-loss of priest and penitent thus reflected the more fundamental submission required by God.[9]

The loss of every form of self—the condition for a pure love for God— expressly seeks an environment of sinful passions and seduction. Here, the required holy indifference can show itself most clearly because, as is being shown, there is no more indication of any ego or self-love. At the mercy of sin, the penitent, liberated of her ego, appears to be immune to it. There no longer is something like a selfish ego that could be affected by it. In Coleman's version of this kind of quietist "doctrine," it sounds like this:

> How can God come to replace the self in this world? . . . How does one demonstrate pure passivity without negating it? Is it possible to indicate loss of will without willing it? In response, the Quietists of Dijon purportedly staged ceremonies that required the bodies of both director and penitent to register their abandon to each other and to God.[10]

Resisting sinful passions in this case coincides with totally abandoning the self to them. It is no wonder that the authorities intervened here—although the capital sentences that were passed rightly disturb our modern sensitivity.

But it is no wonder either that something comparable appears a few decades later in a literary genre that tells a similar story, while replacing "sin" by "nature," without taking anything away from the atmosphere of "self-surrender" and "self-loss." And it even makes explicit reference to "mysticism."

In 1748, a novel entitled *Thérèse philosophe* appeared.[11] In the first few lines, the main character, Thérèse, addresses a duke and emphasizes her strong hesitation to tell him her story. "What, sir, seriously, you want me to write my story? You want me to tell you of the mystic scenes of Mlle Éradice with the Reverend Father Dirrag, that I inform you of the adventures of Madame C *** with the Abbé T ***?"[12] The "mystical scenes" that follow in the first chapter of the novel are nothing less than overtly perverse sexual descriptions of the young Éradice being sexually abused by Father Dirrag, to which Thérèse, at first unwillingly but soon voluntarily, bears witness—scenes that all result in a frank ode to unbridled libertinism. *Thérèse philosophe*, which was published anonymously and is attributed to Jean-Baptiste de Boyer, Marquis d'Argens, can be seen as the first in a wave of libertine novels that are eminently characteristic of the French cultural landscape of the eighteenth century.

The reference to mysticism in the novel's opening passage is, in the first place, anecdotal. The novel recounts the story of the excessive sexual behavior a quietist priest, the Jesuit Jean-Baptiste Girard, engages in with the young Cathérine Cadière, a "penitent" who had come to him seeking spiritual guidance. At least, that is what the young woman accused her spiritual mentor of, after she had traded him for another, a Jansenist.[13] The incident became a public scandal that continued to linger long after 1731, the year the case went to trial—which, by the way, resulted in an acquittal for the accused priest.[14] Éradice and Dirrag are anagrams of the names of the ones involved in the real scandal. And Thérèse, the main character, also clearly refers to the famous mystic from sixteenth-century Ávila.

The novel's author also refers to mysticism on the level of its contents. Only a few lines after the opening sentence, at the moment when Thérèse falls for the duke and declares that she wants to tell her story after all, the author allows himself, via his protagonist, to issue a direct reminder to his reader that is completely in keeping with the kind of appeals against self-centeredness so typical of the mystical tradition. But instead of warning readers against the evils of the passions, the author actually encourages them to embrace all passions and completely abandon themselves to them, all in the name of a radical selflessness.

> Stupid mortals! You think yourselves masters of the passions that Nature has placed in you. They are the work of God. You want to destroy them, these passions, restrain them within certain limits. Mad men! You claim then to be second creators, more powerful than the first? Do you never see that everything is as it should be, and that all is well; that all comes from God, nothing from you, and it is as difficult to create a thought as to create an arm or an eye?[15]

Like so many erotic novels from the eighteenth century, this one displays a world in which the protagonists are free from the laws and norms imposed by religion. The state in which they are allows them to become one, not with God (as in the religious, mystical tradition), but with nature: nature, defined as a purely material, autonomously functioning *res extensa*—as a complex composition of mechanical gears, all of which, even the very smallest parts, heed a totally comprehensive pattern. The realm of the passions, which in the heyday of *spiritualité* was mapped as the source of sinful self-love, has a central place here as well, albeit no longer to shun those passions, but to unreservedly confirm and assume them. The pleasure they afford us keeps us in the realm of our finite human condition, which is as it should be. What should not be, however, is for us to manipulate or resist this pleasure, to consider ourselves above it and able to withdraw from it. What should not be is an Ego that allows itself to be distanced from these lusts and their impact on human behavior. The ode to pleasure performed in all keys by these libertine novels breaks with all ethical and social norms but never with those of nature. The pleasure the protagonists display indexes their profound naturalness.

The extreme attitude to God previously displayed by the most eccentric among the mystics now concerns Nature (often written with a capital *N* in those days). The libertine kind of abandonment to natural passions is, in a way, similar in its selflessness to the mystical battle against the same passions. Libertine freedom toward God, religion, or whatever institution coincides with an intended unification with Nature, and here, too, the own ego seems to be the biggest obstacle to such unification.

Self, Selflessness, and Excess

Today, libertine novels such as *Hélène Philosophe* come across as dated, to say the least. No one still reads a foreshadowing of our true natural state in the sexual escapades that are dished up in these novels, and we certainly do not feel inclined to surrender ourselves—and definitely not our "self"—to such practices in the hopes of finding our ultimate destination therein. Not that these kinds of desires would be completely out of place today or that our uninhibited dreams might not sometimes go this way, but if they do, we are indeed well aware that such escapades are fully excessive, also in the sense that they are hardly ever real, because they are all too momentary and fleeting. By no means do they portray the ultimate "value" that would indicate the fulfillment of everything else that we value. We are familiar with novels such as *Histoire d'O* and watch films such as *Fifty Shades of Grey* (Sam Taylor-Johnson, 2015), but public opinion generally refers to them as a somewhat insane pathological fantasy.[16]

And yet the question remains: Why are we at all interested in scenes showing us nothing but unrealistic and pathological excesses? For that is what we are. Given our contemporary visual culture, the term *interest* might even be an understatement. Perhaps we should rather use *fascination* or even *obsession*. Scenarios in which characters consciously seek out situations in which they put their ego at stake and dance on the edge of self-loss are all over the place in movies, games, and other forms of visual culture. In the erotic adventures that these offer, the desire to lose oneself in the sexual act, where one can be gloriously, unscrupulously selfless, is omnipresent. And, of course, everything is okay at the end of the film, and the threatened ego has just become stronger in the process. No matter how close the protagonist came to the precipice where there was a real threat of losing himself in the arms of the deadly *femme fatale* who crossed his path, for instance, he is invariably restored to the position of a powerful self, of an ego that appears to have emerged unscathed from the bath of evil in which it had been drowning. But meanwhile, we have been enjoying this bath and the constant threat of self-loss and selflessness of which the film was full. We know it is only film and fantasy, that it is pathological, and that everyday reality is completely different. But why is it precisely this self-loss and selflessness that lies at the very heart of what is able to entertain and relax us? Why are we so fascinated by overt displays of selflessness? Why does 95 percent of every single Hollywood movie's ode to the self effectively concern impending selflessness? As if the strong ego to which our culture compels us is strongly attracted to selflessness.

This question is not unrelated to a similar conclusion that can be drawn about the scientific discourses on the human and on human culture (or, more abstractly, on the subject and the subjective). Science must be value-free, every intervention of the subject is out of the question, even in the human sciences. As noted earlier, this kind of scientific discourse, too, honors the paradigm of objectivity. It studies the domain of human subjectivity, but does not presume any separate "subject," any "agent," "soul" or "self." What we typically indicate with the term *self*—the active agent on the basis of which one deliberately thinks what one thinks and wants what one wants—is, in the eyes of science, not such a self at all but the effect of a physical process that is analyzed in terms of its laws. Materialism owed its success in the eighteenth century to this understanding. And today's brain studies, too, still owe their prestige, both within the domain of the human sciences and in public opinion, to this understanding.

The so-called humanities and human sciences have become an endangered species. Spirit, soul, self: it is all a matter of the brain, and thus of neuroscience. The latter is momentarily considered as having the potential to remove the old distinction between *natural* sciences and *human* sciences (including *cultural* sciences). Only the study of nature—of the brain or other physical functions—is able to provide an understanding of "cultural" phenomena and of how what has until recently been called "spirit" functions within these phenomena.

But how do neuro- and other objective human sciences see themselves? Do they consider themselves capable of objectively approaching "themselves," that is to say, their *own* subject, the point *from which*—and on *the basis of which*—they practice science? This point was discovered by Descartes and conceptualized as the new subject of a therefore new—now objective—normativity of science. Objective science, however, only conquered history after it had set aside the Cartesian *cogito* as nonexistent. All reality, including the human being, is solely "body," "matter," "object," so La Mettrie stated, supported in this by the sciences to this day. Consequently, a separate science of the "subject" *as such* no longer makes sense.

But did the subject really disappear with the emergence of materialism and objective science? It is true that it has been divested of its substance. But has it also been deprived of its *place*? Has its *place* disappeared? Has everything become objective, even the *point* from which objective science organizes its empirical observation? Here we touch on the blind—and necessarily blind—spot of each objective science: the point from which it operates necessarily escapes the object it concerns—and thus its objective approach. This point can only find itself *outside* of the object, unequivocally separated from this object. This is the *conditio sine qua non* for modern science. This is what it is all about when the scientific point of view is described as "objective": that point itself does *not* belong to the object. This is what makes science "value-free" and "neutral."

This is the reason why, despite the crushing criticism leveled at Descartes by materialists and other philosophers, modern science can still be called Cartesian. Science only exists by the grace of the unbridgeable separation between subject and object. But, contrary to what Descartes stated, science is not concerned with two different kinds of being or *res*, because indeed only one *res* remains, that of the objective, the extent: the *res extensa*. But the point from which this extent is observed remains radically withdrawn from it. This is where the "self"—the ego, the subject—of science finds itself: the formal ground without which it cannot be what it is.

As such, this subject positions itself "excessively" with respect to the objective. The point from which a scientific object is observed cannot be objectively observed. All geniality of brain images notwithstanding, no image can be made of this point. By definition, science cannot be given a scientific *selfie* in which the scientific subject observes "what" precisely is observing.[17] Its "self" or "subject" is, in this sense, literally a *subiectum* or "supposition": an *imaginary* supposition, a *positio sub*—underlying—its observation. It is a premise that one cannot but assume. One can never "prove" it. And yet, this "excessive," imaginary "subject" is nonetheless the indispensable ground for every modern objective science.

Modern science has unlearned to see as problematic the fact that its own subject escapes its own scientific grip. It has rejected Descartes's foundation on the basis of an argument that is unsustainable, because it is situated in the future. But it maintains the idea that it is based on a problem-free starting point—a point defined for the first time by Descartes. Here, we meet the denial on which modern science, after all, is built: its subject/ground only works because and in so far as that science does *not* reflect upon its groundlessness.

Of course, it is hardly surprising that the motive and the desire underlying this denial is not scientifically reflected upon, either. But the question of what this motive might be does not thereby lose its legitimacy just yet. What motivates science to keep its own starting point, its "self," outside of its own attention? Or, what comes down to the same thing, why does science want to see everything, including itself, as *selfless*? What is so attractive about this selflessness?

More clearly, this question springs to mind when we consider the nonscientific discourse about the human, that of culture, literature, film, and games, for instance. The desire for selflessness is more sharply, more prominently present there. It is displayed there in all possible ways, even if at the end of the story it always needs to make space for a blatant apotheosis of the self.

Are not both the scientific and the nonscientific discourses about the human about the same desire to get rid of the ego, the self, the subject? And all of this notwithstanding the fact that both discourses continue to promote an independent ego, a self that is its own and its world's master and commander.

How should both desire for selflessness and desire for self-affirmation be considered as going together without being misled by their logical contradiction? In a certain sense, the history of early modernity invites us to consider this question. The path leading to selflessness that was central to mysticism and spiritual life, necessarily also accompanied the rise of an increasingly affirmative ego that moved itself forward as (Cartesian) subject (ground and starting point) of a new, in this instance modern, relationship to reality. This paradox was also revealed in contemporary mysticism itself: only selflessness gives access to God, but this selflessness presumes an indescribably strong self: a self that, for the love of God, is able to embrace gracefully the eternal pains of hell (as Fénelon phrased it). And what is more: the intention to completely eliminate the self makes the mystical way a science of the self and of its almost bottomless pit of hidden desires and passions. This paradox is present as well in the dominant movement in early modernity that completely distanced itself from mysticism. Enlightened materialists profiled themselves on the basis of a liberated, independent, and self-conscious ego, but this did not prohibit them from regarding the human being as a selfless machine in which ego and soul were ephemeral fantasies, "ghosts in the machine," in a way.

The problematic entanglement of self and selflessness has hardly been taken up by the human sciences since then. Where in exceptional circumstances this did happen, it resulted in the "selfless self"—the subject—of this science coming under attack. It is interesting to take a closer look at such an "exception" and to see how this "science" ended up meeting the challenge. Even if its solutions were contestable, it at least raised the problem. In light of the scientific developments of the last hundred and fifty years, that in itself is already an achievement.

In the following section, I will shortly discuss psychoanalysis as one of the few "human sciences" that explicitly shed some light on the enigmatic relationship between selflessness and self-affirmation that is so typical of our modernity. It may not be surprising that this science has developed its own interesting vision of what is at play in mysticism and spiritual life.

Psychoanalysis as Selfless Science . . .

In the twentieth century, psychoanalysis was perceived as a modern form of "logos of the psyche," "science of the soul." In this guise, psychoanalysis was welcomed in the psychology faculties of many American universities during the thirties and forties of the previous century. It was meant to balance the dominance of behaviorism. The latter is based on a radical denial of the soul or psyche and reduces everything ascribed to our "subjective" life to objective, empirically observable behavior. Anxiety only makes itself scientifically known in the way in which the body reacts to certain stimuli or impulses. Freud's "depth psychology" was seen as countering behaviorism, for it still allowed space for a psychical, "inner" life.

This is perhaps the main reason for the massive success that psychoanalysis enjoyed up until the 1970s. That reason, however, was wrong. On closer inspection, it is unjustified to regard psychoanalysis as a science acknowledging the existence of a "psyche" or "soul." Just as it was for eighteenth-century materialism, such thing as a soul or a *psyche* is nonexistent for psychoanalysis too. If psychoanalysis is grouped under "psychology," that is because the latter is a human science with a completely modern basis that embraces the materialist paradigm, stating that the "psyche" is not a proper "object." Psychoanalysis, too, reduces our so-called psychic life to physical reaction-formations, operating according to the paradigm of the stimulus/response theory that has formed the basis of modern biology since the nineteenth century.

Freudianism is more specifically to be understood as a particular type of cognition theory, a "psychology" that departs, in its theory about the way the human body reacts to stimuli, from the primacy of representations, of memory traces. Think of the manuscript that Freud added to one of his letters to Wilhelm Fliess and that is known under the title *Project for a Scientific Psychology* (1895).[18] When a stimulus enters into the "psychic apparatus" (that is not localized somewhere "deep inside" us, but is a surface structure),[19] it is first led through the "unconscious," which means: through a "system" in which memory traces are connected to earlier stimuli and stimuli responses. Here, the incoming stimulus is led to a similar one stored in the memory that previously evoked a positive response Only *thereafter* can the incoming stimulus be answered with an adequate response (a *spezifische Aktion*).[20]

For Freud, what is commonly called the *psyche* is the "apparatus" that controls someone's entire stimulus/reaction economy (or, in nontechnical terms: his "psychical life"). Antonio Negri's dictum "*Spirit* is brain" also applies to psychoanalysis.[21] It is fundamentally neuropsychoanalysis.[22] If psychoanalysis is currently still given credit somewhere, it is often on this basis.

It gets much less credit, however, where the principle it ascribes to the functioning of the stimulus/response apparatus is concerned. What controls the link between stimulus and response is of the order of the "wish." The neuronal system is an unconscious "wishing machine." It responds as it *wishes* to respond, and it is at the level of "wishing" that "neurotic" traumas, and psychic functioning in general, should be situated.

If this is true, it means that the organism, in the stimulus/response function, is subjected not only to the self-preservation principle (as applied in biology, including neurology) but also to a "wish" principle at the same time. *Lustprinzip*, "pleasure principle," Freud calls it.[23] He argues that the self-preservation principle of the organism intersects with—and is "perverted" by—the pleasure principle. Pleasure is a *formal* principle that implies a "distortion" (a "subversion" or "perversion") of the biological response functions.

The principle of biological functioning is self-preservation. Pleasure is what makes that functioning turn on itself, on its own functioning, disconnected from the direct purpose of that function. Then, the function operates more for the sake of the pleasure it yields than for the sake of the vital goal to which it is oriented. The child continues to suckle its mother's breast even after its hunger has been stilled. It *primordially* suckles, according to Freud, for the pleasure of the suckling activity itself; it spins around in (the pleasure it experiences in) the response.

In principle, the organism can experience pleasure in anything, even in matters that do not benefit self-preservation. Smoking, eating to the point of indigestion (bulimia), or preferring stubbornly to eat almost nothing (anorexia nervosa) are but a few of the many examples. According to the Freudian intuition, we do not live "naturally," but we "enjoy" nature (i.e., we "pervert" the natural life-functions on the basis of the pleasure principle).

. . . of the Self . . .

Just like the other modern human sciences, psychoanalytical theory is formally selfless in the double sense that has already been discussed: it does not consider the human being as a predetermined, substantial self (a soul or psyche), and it equally does not consider its own theory as based in such a predetermined self (as Descartes still did). The "self" with which its theory and practice are concerned is considered to be a construction built on pleasure and desire, and the basis of its theory cannot claim to be more than a presupposition—a "hypothetical idea," as Kant calls it. In this sense, it is in line with the materialism of the modern sciences.

This selfless materialism does, however, not restrain psychoanalysis to take seriously the *desire for* a self. Even if the self is only an illusionary construct of desire, this illusion is indispensable for our "libidinal life" (for our "pleasure economy," as Freud calls it). Underpinned only by a principle of pleasure and desire, illusions have proper reality value. Being libidinal, we can but suppose all our desires and feelings to go back to the same instance, the "self," and that they are directed from there. When we have serious mental problems, when we are like having lost control over our life, we are basically in trouble with this "supposition," namely, our "self." That the "self" entangling us is fundamentally an imaginary construct does not diminish the extent of the problem. And that problem cannot just be traced back to the laws of physical stimulus/reaction formations. It requires an approach that takes the imaginary character of the problem *as such* seriously. Among the sciences, psychoanalysis seems to go the farthest in the attempt to acknowledge and to lay bare the idiosyncratic logic of the imaginary. Only an understanding of the logic of the imaginary can take seriously the desire on which the "self" is based and, consequently, the mental problems one can have with one's "self."[24]

It is not only important to take seriously the desire for a "self," but also to understand why a libidinal being is at the same time capable of desiring to get rid of its "self." If desire precedes the self, it can equally desire something beyond the self. This is why Freud forged the concept of the death drive: if pleasure is the principle that leads the stimulus/response system, satisfying pleasure does not need to coincide with the preservation of life: satisfaction can also lead to the death of the satisfied organism.[25]

For Freud, the fact that people put their lives at stake in pursuit of pleasure, and can do so with fatal outcome, is not a counterargument against his concept of the pleasure principle. Such people, too, show that we live primordially from the primacy of desire and that desire precedes the "self." Basically selfless, the desiring self can try to rejoin this "base," which means: to annihilate itself. The ideological discourses and doctrines with which we give ourselves and our life meaning operate at the same time as a means to repress the dark, self-destructive tendency of our desire. Yet, these tales and doctrine can also activate such tendencies. Suicidal attacks in the name of celestial salvation or more earthly utopias make clear how human desire is not by definition bound to self-preservation.

Selfless and yet a self. That other authority in the psychoanalytic tradition, Jacques Lacan, deals with this (only apparent) contradiction in his concept of "alienation." Of course, there is such a thing as a "self," but then only as "phantasmatic" object of desire. As libidinal beings, we coincide with an originally selfless desire. It is on this basis that we identify ourselves with others in order to become "someone." Originally selfless, we construct an identity or self only after identification with others. To put it in a different way, we desire ourselves just as we desire another, another who is always farther away, who is always other—always different from the other with whom we identify de facto. In this sense, we are the "subject" (in the sense of "bearer") of a desire that is never totally ours and never reaches the real "self" for which it longs.

Remember that this desire does not operate on the real, biological level, but on the libidinal level, on the level where we are "desire machines." Freud defines this level as the realm of representations (*Vorstellungen*), the "matter" in (and with) which the "psychic apparatus" works. Lacan considers it a linguistic realm, a field of "signifiers," organized as a language. These signifiers do not only situate themselves on the inside of the individual's psychical apparatus, but also and especially outside of it, in the cultural field that this individual shares with others. It is via these signifiers that the libidinal being can identify with others and subsequently form an identity of his own. For Lacan, the "self" of the libidinal being is a *social* creature through and through, and its desire dances, so to say, from one signifier to the next—signifiers that it always adopts from others, from the social environment it is in. This "dance" endlessly drives human desire without ever being able to express the ultimate meaning that it pursues, nor the "real self" that it is after.

This is the structure of what Lacan calls "alienation." Yearning and only ever yearning, we are always alienated (from our "self") in a linguistic universe where we only exist in as far as a word represents us to another word, ad infinitum.[26] That is why humans are such "talking beings." Somewhere, Lacan describes them with a French neologism: *parlêtres*, speaking-beings.[27] Not that we would not live biologically (how would we not?). But "psychically"—or, what comes down to the same thing for Lacan, "libidinally"—we live on the language that represents us and *never stops* representing us, because it never reaches the outside of language (i.e., the beyond of desire). We live our existence *as* desire, and this is why we are at home only within the language (or, more broadly, the culture) that expresses us. In this language, we are "ourselves," though in a way in which we fundamentally remain estranged from ourselves. In that sense, we are ourselves while at the same time we ultimately remain selfless.

For Lacan, the fact that religion so obstinately persists in postreligious times goes back structurally to this fact. Religion gives shape and culture to the alienated condition of the human beings we are, to the insatiable desire with which we coincide. Of course, religion promises that our desire will be fulfilled, but this fulfilment is postponed to the afterlife, by way of which that religion actually expresses in language the unfulfilled, alienated condition of human desire. One day, at a time when time will no longer rule, we will totally be the self that we desire to be, so many religions claim. But here and now, in this world, human existence is characterized by lack, sin, and death, in brief: by unfulfilled desire. The self that realizes itself in the mundane continues to be characterized by the inability to be its real, true self. It remains, if you like, characterized by selflessness.

Self, yet selfless: religion is a way to give this human condition a fitting culture. Psychoanalytical theory and practice do not do something radically different: they, too, provide language and form for the dialectics between self and selflessness. Unlike religion, however, psychoanalysis acknowledges the irreducibly selfless condition of every self.

. . . and Its Pleasure

Many religions claim that the ultimate fulfillment of human desire lies in the hereafter, yet at the same time they indicate that, in exceptional circumstances, this fulfillment can also be experienced in the "here and now." Mortal, finite humans longing for God can have such moments without having to enter the afterlife. This happens in what is usually called a "mystical experience."

At first sight, these experiences seem irreconcilable with the Lacanian statement about the unfulfillable condition of human desire.

Lacan, however, developed a proper interpretation of what takes place in these kinds of experiences. If we *are* desire, its ultimate satisfaction implies that we are no longer desire and, consequently, that we *are* no longer, that we no longer exist. Desire's ultimate satisfaction implies the annihilation of ourselves as ground (subject) of that desire, and (which amounts to the same thing) the annihilation of ourselves—thus, the conclusion Lacan draws.

This kind of annihilation, however, does not have to imply a *real* death. Here, we meet what makes the satisfaction of a subject's desire conceivable within Lacanian theory. Lacan coined a concept for it: *jouissance*, enjoyment.[28] In the experience of enjoyment, Lacan argues, the subject's desire is indeed fully satisfied, and the libidinal being is no longer marked by lack and desire. Despite the fact that lack and (unfulfilled) desire are essential and constitutive for the human being, enjoyment is possible, because the lack has not *really* disappeared. Where the subject is usually the "bearer" of lack and desire, in enjoyment the subject itself *coincides* with that lack. In its function as "bearer," the subject is suspended for a moment; it temporarily "fades away," while its libidinal economy continues to float around on a "scenario of signifiers" (conceptualized by Lacan as a "phantasm").

When the subject finally takes unto him the ultimate object of its desire, it does not take it *into possession*, but rather *loses* itself in it. At the point where the longing subject has left all lack and desire behind and finally has "everything" it wants, there is no more "having," as there is no more subject. In this sense, the enjoying subject *has* or *possesses* nothing, because, at this moment, it *is* not(hing). It has lost every feeling of self, and it is this very selflessness that is enjoying then. This is, according to Lacan, the structure of satisfied desire, of *jouissance*.

The experience of the "little death" (*la petite mort*) as described in a innumerable ways in love poetry, accurately illustrates this.[29] When the poet describes the sublime enjoyment of the union with the beloved, an indefinable, somewhat bitter feeling resounds in his poetic description. Astonished at the sublime joy the beloved gave him, the poet realizes that at the very moment of enjoyment, he was not present. He realizes he lost himself in a timeless moment of enjoyment. In that moment, he had no awareness, neither of himself nor of the beloved, nor of their love, nor of their joy. As if enjoyment cannot stand any conscious presence. As if the abandonment that accompanies it also throws their "selves" overboard. The lover gives himself to the beloved, and vice versa, but in this gift, both lover and beloved disappear as points of reference, and the *moment suprême* only provides self-loss. Longing for the beloved, the lover cannot interpret the moment of enjoyment in terms of "conquest" or "acquisition," but only of "loss"—the loss not only of the desired "object," but of the longing subject as well.

According to Lacan, fulfillment of human desire should thus no longer be understood in terms of profit, acquisition, or self-realization, but in those of loss and self-surrender. Yet, it does not constitute a *real* but only a *phantasmatic* surrender of the self. Longing for the ultimate object, we experience its acquisition so intensely that we are not *really* with it, which is to say that we live it as if there is no longer a "we" who is with it. We are there as those who lose ourselves in it. *Real* enjoyment is impossible. Enjoyment is by definition "imaginary," "phantasmatic."

For the mystic, too, the satisfaction of his desire for God coincides with a loss of his "self." According to Lacanian theory, this holds little mystery. It much rather offers a fitting illustration of the concept of *jouissance*, enjoyment. In their descriptions of the last stage of the spiritual path, mystical texts describe in countless ways how the devout subject loses himself in the enjoyment of being lost in God, but how, at the same time, that enjoyment somehow fails, if only because it might be reported in the very text describing it. For Lacan, it is clear that it is this very failure that makes enjoyment possible. In a certain sense, mystics enjoy precisely this failure. Even in the moment when unity with God is experienced, the mystic does not fully know whether real unity might not actually be realized only in the next phase. Yet, at the same time, the mystic realizes that it does not really matter. Because his unity with God is a matter of enjoyment, the distinction no longer matters.

John of the Cross describes the spiritual path as the ascension of Mount Carmel and illustrates this complex process with a graphic sketch. At the top of the Mount—metaphor for the *unio mystica* with God—he writes "nada, nada, nada, nada, nada, nada y nada."[30] Seven times nothing, to emphasize that there really is nothing: that he, too, is nothing, and that even God is nothing. At least, such is one of the possible readings of this sevenfold *nada*. However, it is not to be found in so many words in John of the Cross's writings. In his own explanation, he will rather express himself by saying that God "is not something," that in the state of divine ecstasy, there is no longer any distinction for the mystic between the self and God, between the God seeker and the sought God, and that this is the experience of the divine Self, the experience of a God beyond self and not-self. John of the Cross interprets this not-something in the Neoplatonic sense. The loss of his mortal self makes it lose itself in God's selfless Self that is the source of the entire Creation.

Lacan endorses the downfall of this Neoplatonic—and, more broadly, Christian—way of thinking, caused by the emergence of modernity. The loss of the self in the *modern* mystical experience does not give access to a selfless Self that is exalted above being and not-being. According to Lacan, the latter is a phantasm. In his eyes, the loss of the self is a "phantasmic" event. The *nada* of John of the Cross does not describe something ontologically real; it describes a moment of *jouissance*.

Notes

Introduction

1. See also the pages on this painting in Smyth, *The Age of Correggio and the Carracci*, 484–86. For the life of the painter (1582–1647), see Giovan Pietro Bellori's *Vite de' pintori, scultori et architetti moderni* (1672); Bellori, *Lives of the Modern Painters*, 281–92.

2. Jacobus da Voragine's *Legenda aurea*, compiled around 1259–1266, is known in English as *The Golden Legend*. For the story of Mary Magdalene, see Jacobus da Voragine, *Golden Legend*, 374–83. For the story of her "translation," see p. 380.

3. Jacobus da Voragine, *Golden Legend*, 380.

4. See, for instance, Duperray, *Marie Madeleine*; Craymer, "Margery Kempe's Imitation."

5. Weinhart and Hollein, ~~Ich~~; for the work by Zaugg, see p. 49; for an overview of (and comment upon) Zaugg's entire oeuvre, see Mack, *Rémy Zaugg*.

6. Indeed "antireligious." Following Karl Barth, Miskotte considers "religion" a "commerce with God" and consequently a mockery of monotheism.

7. In 2017, Martin Scorsese directed *Silence*, a film based on Endō's novel.

Chapter 1. Love's Intimate Violence

Epigraph, original text: "En somme le bon plaisir de Dieu est le souverain objet de l'âme. . . . si [elle] savait que sa condamnation fût un peu plus agréable à Dieu que sa salvation, [elle] quitterait sa salvation et courrait à sa damnation"; translation MDK.

1. "Dear friends, let us love one another, for love comes from God. Everyone who loves has been born of God and knows God. Whoever does not love does not know God, because God is love" (1 John 4:7–8; New International Version).

2. "If I speak in the tongues of men or of angels, but do not have love, I am only a resounding gong or a clanging cymbal. . . . Love is patient, love is kind. It does not envy, it does not boast, it is not proud. It does not dishonor others, it is not self-seeking, it is not easily angered, it keeps no record of wrongs. Love does not delight in evil but rejoices with the truth. It always protects, always trusts, always hopes, always perseveres" (vv. 1–7 [NIV]).

3. This is what Jan Assmann calls *die mosaische Unterscheidung* (the Mosaic criterion), the criterion that distinguished the Jewish monotheistic religion from any other religion in the Ancient Near East. In short, it says that our relationship with the divine is subject to a double criterion: (1) only the one true God may be worshiped and (2) worshiping God means installing righteousness ("justice") among people. See especially the first two chapters in Assmann, *Price of Monotheism*, 8–55. See also De Kesel, *Goden breken [Breaking Gods]*, 31–46.

4. De Kesel, *Auschwitz mon amour*, 119–22.

5. *Eschaton* is the Greek term for the end of time; *apocalypse* for revelation. God has revealed Himself in the Law, but since we apparently failed to live in accordance with the Law, God is supposed to reveal Himself once again, now in a definite way: this is "apocalypse."

6. "After he said this, he was taken up before their very eyes, and a cloud hid him from their sight" (Acts 1:9 [NIV]).

7. "Jesus went on to say, 'In a little while you will see me no more, and then after a little while you will see me'" (John 16:16 [NIV]).

8. Acts 5:1–11 (NIV).

9. Some make the connection with the oath procedure as practiced in the cultures surrounding Palestine in the first centuries AD (Harril, "Divine Judgment").

10. This is the structure of what Jacques Lacan calls "perversion," the term for the way the "lack" marking (and founding) human desire is, by the same gesture, acknowledged *and* denied. Acknowledged by transferring the lack to the other—as for instance the sadist does by literally marking that "lack" (i.e., pain, suffering, fear, et cetera) on the victim's body; denied as, to continue with the same example, the sadist does by denying the "lack" (pain, suffering . . .) inflicted on the other while experiencing this as proof that pain and lack do not exist, that everything is perfect, and consequently that his own enjoyment is perfect. See chapter 10 in Lacan, *Éthique de psychanalyse*, 225–39; *Ethics of Psychoanalysis*, 191–203. See also: De Kesel, *Eros and Ethics*, 131–39.

11. Baslez, *Comment notre monde*, 72–94 (ch. 2).

12. Dating back to the first half of the second century, the *Letter to Diognetus* makes clear that Christians had integrated themselves particularly well into existing society. See Ehrman, *Apostolic Fathers*, 2:139–41. For a discussion, see De Kesel, "In, Not Of the World."

13. Nygren, *Agapè and Eros*. This famous book draws a sharp distinction between both types of love and appeals for *agape* as the hallmark of true Christian love.

14. "You awake us to delight in your praise; for You made us for Yourself, and our hearts are restless until they rest in You" (Augustine, *Confessions*, 3).

15. Fénelon, *Œuvres 1*, 999–1095; *Selected Writings*, 207–97.

16. "Soyez un vrai rien en tout et partout, mais il ne faut rien ajouter à ce pur rien. C'est sur le rien qu'il n'y a aucune prise. Il ne peut rien perdre. Le vrai rien ne résiste jamais, et il n'a point un moi dont il s'occupe. Soyez donc rien, et rien au-delà, et vous serez tout sans songer à l'être. Souffrez en paix, abandonnez-vous; allez, comme Abraham, sans savoir où. Recevez des hommes le soulagement que Dieu vous donnera par eux. Ce n'est pas d'eux, mais de lui par eux, qu'il faut le recevoir. Ne mêlez rien à l'abandon, non plus qu'au rien. Un tel vin doit être bu tout pur et sans mélange, une goutte d'eau lui ôte toute sa vertu. On perd infiniment à vouloir retenir la moindre ressource propre. Nulle réserve, je vous conjure. Il faut aimer la main de Dieu qui nous frappe et qui nous détruit. La créature n'a été faite que pour être détruite au on plaisir de celui qui ne l'a faite que pour lui. O heureux usage de notre substance ! Notre rien glorifie l'Être éternel et le tout Dieu. Périsse donc ce que l'amour-propre voudrait tant conserver ! Soyons l'holocauste que le feu de l'amour réduit en cendres. Le trouble ne vient jamais que de l'amour-propre, l'amour divin n'est que paix et abandon. Il n'y a qu'à souffrir, qu'à laisser tomber, qu'à perdre, qu'à retenir rien, qu'à n'arrêter jamais un seul moment la main crucifiante. Cette non-résistance est horrible à la nature, mais Dieu la donne]." Fénelon, *Œuvres de Fénelon*, 156–57; trans. MDK.

17. The idea expressed in this "supposition" is not originally Fénelon's. Fénelon draws on the spiritual tradition of his century. We already find it with François de Sales (1567–1622), as can be seen in the epigraph of this chapter. For an elaborated study of *pur amour* in all its radicality, see, e.g., Terestchenko, *Amour et désespoir*; "Querelle du pur amour"; and Le Brun, *Pur amour*, 117–211. For a more elaborate textual analysis of that "supposition," see chapter 2, pp. 62–63.

18. Fénelon, *Œuvres 1*, 610; translation MDK. It is significant that, toward the end of her biography of Fénelon, Sabine Melchior-Bonnet describes his oeuvre as a "mysticism of the will" (Melchior-Bonnet, *Fénelon*, 433).

19. See for instance: Schultess, "S'oublier soi-même"; Veillard-Baron, "Âme et l'amour"; Gorday, *François Fénelon*, 191.

20. The text by Lamy (1636–1711) that provoked Malebranche's criticism is *De la connaissance de soi-même* [*On the Knowledge of Oneself*, five volumes published between 1694 and 1698], and, more precisely, the last chapter of Volume III. It is included in the edition of Malebranche's most important text against

Lamy's *pur amour* theory: *Traité de l'amour de Dieu* (1697); see Malebranche, *Œuvres de Malebranche*, 122–31.

21. "Aimer comme souverain bien la cause qui nous rend capables d'aimer [love as sovereign good the cause that enables us to love]," so we read in *Traité sur l'amour de Dieu* (Malebranche, *Œuvres II*, 1060; translation MDK).

22. Malebranche, *Œuvres II*, 1066; translation MDK.

23. *Traité de la nature et de la grâce* (1680) was put on the *Index* in 1690; *De la recherche de la vérité*, Malebranche's first *magnum opus* (1674–75), in 1709.

24. "God necessarily [*invinciblement*] loves his substance, because He is well-pleased [*complaisance*] with Himself," so we read in one of the first sentences in *Traité de l'amour de Dieu*; Malebranche, *Œuvres II*, 1049; translation MDK.

25. Malebranche, *Œuvres II*, 1049–50.

26. "[U]n homme juste doit et peut accepter son anéantissement, supposé que Dieu le voulût" (Malebranche, *Œuvres II*, 1066; translation MDK).

27. For this last aspect of love, in which the feeling of selflessness goes hand in hand with that of enjoyment, see further chapter 11 (pp. 236–237).

28. "Let me become / the shadow of your shadow / the shadow of your hand / the shadow of your dog" (Jacques Brel, "Ne me quitte pas," English translation by Zafiris Gourgouliatos, accessed November 1, 2021, http://www.zafiris.net/articles/Ne_me_quitte_pas.htm.

29. Lacan, *Éthique de psychanalyse*, 304; *Ethics of Psychoanalysis*, 262.

30. This is one of the meanings of Jacques Lacan's formula: "man's desire is the Other's desire" (Lacan, *Écrits*, 628; *Écrits in English*, 525).

31. John of the Cross, *Collected Works*; Jean de Saint-Samson, *Pratique essentielle*; *Épithalame*.

32. Cited in Žižek, *Did Somebody Say*, 102–103.

Chapter 2. Selfless

Epigraph, original text: "Après encore dis je que, se il povoit estre que je retournasse a nient, auis comme je fins de nient, affin qu'il fust vengé de moy; il luy plaisoit, ce seroit ma plaisance"; Porete, *Mirouer des simples ames*, 107; translation MDK. See also: Porete, *Miroir des simples âmes*, 250; Spearing, *Medieval Writings*, 141.

1. Eckhart, *Essential Sermons*, 8–15; *Complete Works*, 420–26.

2. Eckhart, *Complete Works*, 420.

3. The original Middle High German text is cited from: Eckhart, *Werke I*, 552.

4. Eckhart, *Complete Works*, 421.

5. Eckhart, *Complete Works*, 421.

6. Eckhart, *Complete Works*, 421.

7. Eckhart, *Complete Works*, 420.

8. Eckhart, *Complete Works*, 420.

9. Eckhart, *Complete Works*, 421.

10. See the lemma "Sujet," by Étienne Balibar, Barbara Cassin, and Alain de Libera, in Cassin, *Vocabulaire européen*, 1233–53.

11. Eckhart, *Complete Works*, 422; *Werke I*, 554.

12. Eckhart, *Complete Works*, 422; *Werke I*, 554.

13. Eckhart, *Complete Works*, 422; *Werke I*, 554.

14. Eckhart, *Complete Works*, 422; *Werke I*, 554.

15. This definition of modernity that specifically emphasizes its break with medieval self-understanding (i.e., the change from God to man concerning the *subject*, i.e., the commonly supposed locus from where we relate to reality) fuels the line of argument of many of the chapters in this book and is strongly inspired by the work of Alexandre Koyré; see for instance Koyré, *Closed World*. See also Gillespie, *Theological Origins of Modernity*, 1–18. See also Gillespie, *The Theological Origins of Modernity*, 19–43; Shapin, *The Scientific Revolution*; De Libera, *L'invention du sujet moderne*. Needless to say, this modernity thesis is still the object of scholarly debate. Time and space, however, lack here to go in discussion with that debate, since such discussion would require a book in itself. For a brief overview, see Eisenstadt, *Multiple Modernities*.

16. Theoretically, both the Reformation and the change from medieval to modern self-understanding were prepared by the fourteenth- and fifteenth-century debates between the "realists" and the "nominalists" or, in the terms of the time, between the "via antiqua" and the "via moderna"; see, for instance: Hoenen, *Via Antiqua and Via Moderna in the Fifteenth Century*.

17. Montaigne, *Complete Essays*.

18. Sánches, *Daß nichts gewußt wird*; *That Nothing Is Known*.

19. Kant's philosophy amounts to a legitimization of Newtonian physics where, like with Descartes, the physical is a *res extensa*, a soulless, mechanical universe that purely follows external laws. But unlike Descartes, Kant argues that our knowledge of reality is not based on a stand-alone, substantial subject (Descartes's *cogito*) but on empirical observation and the way in which it is processed through the "knowledge apparatus." *Cogito* (in Kant's terms, the *Ich denke*) is a function in this apparatus that bundles observations. It stands for the "*ursprünglich-synthetischen Einheit der Apperzeption*," as he formulates it in *Kritik der reiner Vernunft* (Transzendentale Elementallehre, § 16).

20. This is to say that this is not the case in *all* of his texts. I only will read passages in which Fénelon himself focuses on the violent and paradoxical dimension of the self-loss. Needless to say that in the majority of his texts that emphasis is not there. See for instance Chrétien, *The Arch of Speech*: 54–55, where the author discusses Fénelon's idea of the "loving dimension" of man's "silence of listening" to God.

21. Terestchenko, *Amour et désespoir*; Le Brun, *Pur amour*.

22. Catalogued by Jacques Le Brun among the "Lettres et opuscules spirituelles" as number XIII, see: Fénelon, *Œuvres 1*, 613–23.

23. This is at least what Jacques Le Brun claims in Fénelon, *Œuvres 1*, 1434. Madame de Maintenon was the "morganatic" (or "left-handed") wife of Louis XIV, which implies that she did not have the title of queen, could not inherit from the king, and neither could the children she had with the king. See Maintenon, *Dialogues and Addresses*, 5.

24. Fénelon and Guyon, *Spiritual Progress*, 61–63; Fénelon, *Œuvres 1*, 613–14.

25. Fénelon and Guyon, *Spiritual Progress*, 64; Fénelon, *Œuvres 1*, 615; emphasis added. Fénelon's letter to Madame de Maintenon was also an answer to her question about what it means to renounce the self. The first sentence notably rings: "Si vous voulez, Madame, bien comprendre ce que c'est que se renoncer à soi-même . . ." (*Œuvres 1*, 613).

26. See the first lines of Augustine's *Confessiones* (Augustine, *Confessions*, 3).

27. Fénelon and Guyon, *Spiritual Progress*, 66; Fénelon, *Œuvres 1*, 616.

28. "Vous direz peut-être, Madame, que vous voudriez savoir d'une manière plus sensible et plus en détail ce que c'est que se renoncer: je vais tâcher de vous satisfaire" (*Œuvres 1*, 617).

29. Fénelon cites from the passage in which Christ demands his disciples to break with the world, including their own family. "Whoever comes to me and does not hate father and mother, wife and children, brothers and sisters, yes, and even life itself, cannot be my disciple. . . . So therefore, none of you can become my disciple if you do not give up all your possessions" (Luke 14: 26–27; 33; New Revised Standard Version). Fénelon cites again from the passage a few lines further.

30. Fénelon and Guyon, *Spiritual Progress*, 68; Fénelon, *Œuvres 1*, 618; emphasis added.

31. Fénelon and Guyon, *Spiritual Progress*, 68–69; Fénelon, *Œuvres 1*, 618.

32. Fénelon, *Œuvres 1*, 619.

33. Fénelon and Guyon, *Spiritual Progress*, 70; Fénelon, *Œuvres 1*, 619.

34. Fénelon and Guyon, *Spiritual Progress*, 70–71; Fénelon, *Œuvres 1*, 619–20.

35. Fénelon and Guyon, *Spiritual Progress*, 89–95; Fénelon, *Œuvres 1*, 589–603. In the English edition of 1853, this "letter" is entitled "On the Inward Teaching of the Spirit of God." For this *opuscule*, reference was mostly made to a letter to Madame de Maintenon from January 1690; see Fénelon, *Correspondence II*, 141–48.

36. Fénelon and Guyon, *Spiritual Progress*, 89; Fénelon, *Œuvres 1*, 589, 590.

37. *Œuvres 1*, 595: "alors il nous arrache le *moi* qui était au centre de notre amour"; "En cet état, Dieu prend soin de tout ce qui est nécessaire pour détacher cette personne d'elle-même"; translation MDK. These citations are

taken from the part of the "letter" that is not included in the English edition of 1853.

38. Fénelon and Guyon, *Spiritual Progress*, 121; Fénelon, *Œuvres 1*, 595.

39. Fénelon and Guyon, *Spiritual Progress*, 121–22; Fénelon, *Œuvres 1*, 595.

40. Fénelon and Guyon, *Spiritual Progress*, 128–29; Fénelon, *Œuvres 1*, 600.

41. Fénelon and Guyon, *Spiritual Progress*, 128–29; Fénelon, *Œuvres 1*, 600–601.

42. So, the last sentence of that *opuscule*; Fénelon and Guyon, *Spiritual Progress*, 133; Fénelon, *Œuvres 1*, 603.

43. Morgan, *On Becoming God*.

44. Fénelon and Guyon, *Spiritual Progress*, 132; Fénelon, *Œuvres 1*, 603.

45. "Love the hand of God that beats and destroys us. The creature is only made to be destroyed as the one who has made it for himself sees fit [*au bon plaisir*]. What a prosperous use of our substance! [*O heureux usage de notre substance!*] Our nothing glorifies the eternal Being and the entire God. May that which our *amour-propre* likes to preserve get lost. Let us be the holocaust [*Soyons l'holocauste*] that love's fire reduces to ashes." Fénelon, *Correspondance*, 572–73; translation MDK; I referred to the passage also on pp. 24, 71, 175.

46. *Œuvres 1*, 656–71.

47. *Œuvres 1*, 1445.

48. Fénelon has the Vulgate translation in mind ("universa propter semet ipsum operatus est Dominus"), which allows for this interpretation of the scripture. In fact, it says that God has given everything a purpose, that He, in other words, imposed a principle of purposeful order on His creation.

49. Fénelon, *Christian Perfection*; *Œuvres 1*, 659.

50. Fénelon, *Christian Perfection*; *Œuvres 1*, 661.

51. Fénelon, *Christian Perfection*; *Œuvres 1*, 661.

52. Fénelon, *Christian Perfection*; *Œuvres 1*, 662.

53. This is, incidentally, a constant in mystical literature: the end to which mystical desire aspires does not extinguish this yearning when it is reached. On the contrary, it stokes it even more. It can already be found in one of the founding fathers of Christian mysticism, Gregory of Nyssa (fourth century): "This truly is the vision of God: never to be satisfied in the desire to see him? . . . Thus, no limit would interrupt growth in the ascent to God, since no limit to the Good can be found nor is the increasing of desire for the Good brought to an end because it is satisfied" (Gregory of Nyssa, *The Live of Moses*: 115 [II, 239]).

54. Eckhart, *Complete Works*, 96.

55. As with each sermon, this one, too, is a comment on a verse from the Bible, this time from the gospel of John (4: 23): "Woman a time shall come and now is, when the true worshipers will worship the Father in spirit and in truth, and such the Father seeks." Eckhart, *Complete Works*, 95.

56. Eckhart, *Complete Works*, 96.

57. Eckhart, *Complete Works*, 96.

58. In another sermon we read: "Here God's ground is my ground and my ground is God's ground. Here I live from my own as God lives from His own. For the man who has once for an instant looked into this ground, a thousand marks of red minted gold are the same as a brass farthing. Out of this inmost ground, all your works should be wrought without Why. I say truly, as long as you do works for the sake of heaven or God or eternal bliss, from without, you are at fault. . . . If a man asked life for a thousand years, 'Why do you live?' if it could answer it would only say, 'I live because I live.' That is because life lives from its own ground, and gushes forth from its own. Therefore it lives without Why, because it lives for itself. And so, if you were to ask a genuine man who acted from his own ground, 'Why do you act?' if he were to answer properly he would simply say, 'I act because I act'" (Eckhart, *Complete Works*, 109–10).

Chapter 3. Love Thy Neighbor Purely

1. "All the believers were one in heart and mind. No one claimed that any of their possessions was their own, but they shared everything they had. With great power the apostles continued to testify to the resurrection of the Lord Jesus. And God's grace was so powerfully at work in them all that there were no needy persons among them. For from time to time those who owned land or houses sold them, brought the money from the sales and put it at the apostles' feet, and it was distributed to anyone who had need" (Acts 4:32–35; New International Version).

2. See for instance Matter, *Voice of my Beloved*; Astell and Cavadini, "Song of Songs."

3. See chapter 1, p. 24.

4. Fénelon, *Œuvres de Fénelon*, 156; my translation.

5. Hence, Fénelon's conclusion that "really, God would not charge us with the responsibility of others" (Fénelon, *Œuvres I*, 1041; my translation); see also Zini, "Peut on être indifferent?," 259.

6. Schmitt Maass, Stockhorst, and Ahn, *Fénelon in the Enlightenment*, 14.

7. The document was first published by d'Alembert in the second half of the eighteenth century and then by Renouard in 1825; see: Renouard, *Lettre de Fénelon à Louis XIV*, 5–8. For the most recent publication of the *Lettre*, see: Fénelon, *Œuvres I*, 541–51; *Selected Writings*, 198–205.

8. This is at least the conclusion drawn by Jean Orcibal and approved by Jacques Le Brun: Fénelon, *Œuvres I*, 1410–11.

9. It was "the most read literary work in eighteenth century France (after the Bible), cherished and praised by Rousseau, it was first translated into English in the very year of its publication." Thus Patrick Riley in his introduction to the English translation: Fénelon, *Telemachus*, xvi. See also Hillenaar, *Le secret de Télémaque*, 5 ff.

10. Fénelon, *Telemachus*, xvii.

11. In *Télémaque* we read: "He [the king] can do anything to the people, but the laws can do anything to him. He has the absolute power in doing good, but his hands are tied from doing wrong. The care of the people, the most important of all trusts, is committed to him by the laws, on condition that he be the father of his subjects." Fénelon, *Telemachus*, 60.

12. Fénelon, *Telemachus*, xvii.

13. See for instance Fénelon's *Examen de conscience sur les devoirs de la royauté*, in Fénelon, *Œuvres II*, 971–1009. For an extract in English, see: Rowen, *From Absolutism to Revolution*, 68–73.

14. Fénelon, *Œuvres I*, 668; my translation.

15. Fénelon, *Selected Writings*, 198. For the French text, see: Fénelon, *Œuvres I*, 543.

16. Fénelon, *Selected Writings*, 198; *Œuvres I*, 543.

17. Fénelon, *Selected Writings*, 203; *Œuvres I*, 548–49.

18. See the *Lettre spirituelle* with the title *Sur la fréquente communion*; Fénelon, *Œuvres*, 92.

19. "When you have the State in mind, you work for yourself: the good of one makes the glory of the other," quoted in Cherel, *Fénelon ou la religion*, 157; my translation.

20. According to Hobbes, the power ruling society is based on a "social contract" by which every participant has freely rendered his natural "rights" (which are absolutely free and therefore the cause of a "war of everyone against everyone") for a "law" attributed to the sovereign. So the sovereign delivers society from its natural violence (symbolized by the biblical figure of the Leviathan), transforming this violence into the power of the order of law.

21. See the famous formulation of the Hobbesian "social contract" in the seventeenth chapter of the *Leviathan*: "as if every man should say to every man, *I Authorise and give up my Right of Governing myself, to this Man, or to this Assemble of men* [i.e., the sovereign], *on this condition, that thou give up thy Right to him, and Authorise all his Actions in like manner.* This done, the Multitude so united in one Person, is called Common Wealth, in Latin Civitas. This is the generation of that great Leviathan, or rather (to speak more reverently) of that *Mortal God*, to which we owe under the *immortal God*, our peace and defence." Thomas Hobbes, *Leviathan*, 120 (Hobbes's italics, capitals, and orthography).

22. See chapter 1, pp. 25–26.

Chapter 4. Nothing Writes

1. See pp. 62–63.

2. Guyon, *Œuvres mystiques*, 709; this translation and all others from this volume are by me, MDK.

3. Sales, Œuvres, 770; *Treatise on the Love of God*, 375; translation modified, MDK.

4. Guyon, Œuvres mystiques, 709.

5. Guyon, Œuvres mystiques, 705.

6. Farther on, she speaks of "that stupid indifference"; Guyon, Œuvres mystiques, 708.

7. Guyon, Œuvres mystiques, 711–12.

8. Fénelon, Œuvres I, 610; see above, chapter 1, p. 26.

9. Guyon and Fénelon, *Correspondance secrète*,113; this and all further translations from this volume are mine, MDK.

10. Guyon, Œuvres mystiques, 712.

11. Guyon and Fénelon, *Correspondance secrète*, 311.

12. Guyon and Fénelon, *Correspondance secrète*, 312.

13. Guyon, Œuvres mystiques, 139–263; *Torrents et Commentaire*, 69–190.

14. Guyon, Œuvres mystiques, 150; *Torrents et Commentaires*, 71.

15. Guyon, Œuvres mystiques, 239–40; *Torrents et Commentaires*, 141–42.

16. Guyon, Œuvres mystiques, 227.

17. "Long live Jesus, Mary, Joseph! It is in their name and to obey Your Reverence, that I will begin to write what I do not know myself, trying as much as I can to let my mind and my pen lead to the movement of God, making no other movement than the one of my hand." Guyon, Œuvres mystiques, 150; *Torrents et Commentaires*, 71. The confessor who asked Guyon to write her book is François Lacombe; see Guyon, *La Vie par elle-même*, 517–18.

18. Trémolières, "Donner à lire Mme Guyon," 549.

19. Guyon, *Selected Writings*, 248–49; *La Vie par elle-même*, 602–603.

20. Guyon, *Selected Writings*, 249; *La Vie par elle-même*, 603.

21. Guyon, *Selected Writings*, 249–50; *La Vie par elle-même*, 604.

22. Guyon, *La Vie par elle-même*, 517; my translation. In this passage, Guyon describes how she came to write *Les torrents*.

23. Guyon, *La Vie par elle-même*, 517–18.

24. Guyon, *Selected Writings*, 250; *La Vie par elle-même*, 605.

25. Guyon, Œuvres mystiques, 240–41; *Torrents et Commentaires*, 142–43.

26. Guyon, Œuvres mystiques, 241; *Torrents et Commentaires*, 143.

27. Guyon, Œuvres mystiques, 241; *Torrents et Commentaires*, 143.

28. Guyon quotes Romans 6:5.

29. Guyon quotes John 8:36.

30. Guyon, Œuvres mystiques, 241–42; *Torrents et Commentaires*, 143–44.

31. Galatians 5: 1: "It is for freedom that Christ has set us free. Stand firm, then, and do not let yourselves be burdened again by a yoke of slavery"; 5, 13: "You, my brothers and sisters, were called to be free. But do not use your freedom to indulge the flesh; rather, serve one another humbly in love" (New International Version). See also Romans 8:21.

32. See pp. 16–18.
33. Guyon, Œuvres mystiques, 247.
34. Gaddis, There Is No Crime.
35. Guyon, Œuvres mystiques, 247–48.
36. Guyon, Œuvres mystiques, 248.
37. The author himself provides such an overview in, for instance, his collection of essays, entitled Le livre à Venire (translated as The Book to Come).
38. Blanchot, The Space of Literature, 20; L'espace littéraire, 10.
39. Blanchot, The Space of Literature, 21–22; L'espace littéraire, 11–12.
40. In the same context, Blanchot writes: "He whose life depends upon the work, either because he is a writer or because he is a reader, belongs to the solitude of that which expresses nothing except the word being: the word which language shelters by hiding it, or causes to appear when language itself disappears into the silent void of the work . . . whoever reads it enters into the affirmation of the work's solitude, just as he who writes it belongs to the risk of this solitude" (Blanchot, The Space of Literature, 21; L'espace littéraire, 11).
41. Blanchot, The Space of Literature, 22; L'espace littéraire, 12.
42. Blanchot, The Space of Literature, 25–26; L'espace littéraire, 17.
43. Pessoa, A Little Larger, 314.

Chapter 5. The Power to Say I

1. Koyré, Closed World; see also De Kesel, Eros and Ethics, 59–60.
2. Cottingham, Stoothoff, and Murdoch, Philosophical Writings of Descartes, volume 2: 16.
3. See the first chapter of Gravity and Grace, 1–4; French original: La pesanteur et la grâce, 1–5.
4. Gravity and Grace, 26; La pesanteur et la grâce, 29. For the note as edited in the Œuvres complètes, see Weil, Œuvres complètes VI/2, 461. For a comment, see for instance Vetö, Métaphysique religieuse, 35.
5. Thibon, editor of Gravity and Grace, has intervened in Weil's text here and dropped a part of the sentence. In the French édition of the Cahiers we read: "Destruction du je. Nous ne possédons rien au monde sinon le pouvoir de dire je, parce que toute autre chose au monde, même notre caractère, notre intelligence, nos amours et nos haines, peut nous être enlevé par la fortune, mais non le pouvoir de dire je." Weil, Œuvres complètes VI/2, 461.
6. Weil, Gravity and Grace, 26–27; La pesanteur et la grâce, 29; original text: Weil, Œuvres complètes VI/2, 461.
7. For an extended explanation on how Weil sees the political, see: Moulakis, Simone Weil and the Politics of Self-Denial.

8. Weil, *Gravity and Grace*, 26; *La pesanteur et la grâce*, 29; original text: Weil, *Œuvres complètes VI/2*, 461–62.

9. Weil, *Gravity and Grace*, 27; *La pesanteur et la grâce*, 30; original text: Weil, *Œuvres complètes VI/2*, 461.

10. "some months of labor in a factory, between December 1934 and August 1935," so Florence de Lussy writes, adding in a footnote: "Some weeks, should we say, if one does not count . . . the sick leaves"; Weil, *Œuvres*, 21.

11. Weil, *Waiting for God* (1951 ed.), 66; *Attente de Dieu*, 51.

12. Weil, *Waiting for God* (1951 ed.), 66–67; *Attente de Dieu*, 52.

13. Weil, *Waiting for God* (1951 ed.), 124–25; *Attente de Dieu*, 115–16.

14. While the "gaze" does not change the outside world, it has not to change man's inner life either. See for instance the following note: "One should not try to change as such or efface desires and aversions, pleasures and pains. You should undergo them in a passive way like sensations of colours and without giving them more credit. . . . Accepting in that way, and in no other, desires and aversions, pleasures and pains in all of the kinds they are present in me. All comes from God as it comes from the totally blind fate. (Is this what Spinoza understood as the salvation of knowledge?)" Weil, *Œuvres complètes VI/3*, 110–11; my translation.

15. Weil, *L'iliade*, 71–115. See also Gold, "Simone Weil."

16. Weil, *Waiting for God* (1951 ed.), 67; *Attente de Dieu*, 52–53.

17. Weil, *Waiting for God* (1951 ed.), 68; *Attente de Dieu*, 53.

18. "The greatness of Christianity is that it does not seek a cure for suffering, but a supernatural use of suffering." Weil, *Œuvres complètes VI/3*, 64; my translation.

19. See, for instance: " 'My God, my God, why hast thou forsaken me?' There we have the real proof that Christianity is something divine." Weil, *Gravity and Grace*, 87, 186; *La pesanteur et la grâce*, 102.

20. Weil, *Gravity and Grace*, 27; *La pesanteur et la grâce*, 30.

21. Weil, *Gravity and Grace*, 27; *La pesanteur et la grâce*, 30.

22. "This world as utterly empty of God is God himself. . . . This is why all consolation in misfortune leads away from love and from truth." Weil, *Gravity and Grace*, 110.

23. Weil, *Gravity and Grace*, 41–42; *La pesanteur et la grâce*, 47–48. See also *Œuvres complètes VI/3*, 60: "That I disappear, so that these things that I see become, because they will no longer be things that I see, perfectly beautiful." See also: "Our disappearing self must become a hole through which God and creation look at each other." Weil, *Œuvres complètes VI/4*, 316; my translation.

24. Weil, *Gravity and Grace*, 91; *La pesanteur et la grâce*, 107.

25. Weil, *Gravity and Grace*, 143; *La pesanteur et la grâce*, 163.

26. "The object of science is the beautiful (that is to say order, proportion, harmony) in so far as it is suprasensible and necessary." Weil, *Gravity and Grace*, 148; translation modified; *La pesanteur et la grâce*, 170.

27. *Gravity and Grace*, 56; *La pesanteur et la grâce*, 64.

28. See for instance: Morgan, *Weaving the World: Simone Weil on Science, Mathematics, and Love*.

Chapter 6. Contra-Religious Religion

Note: Since there is no English translation of the books by Miskotte referred to here, all translations are by MDK.

1. Miskotte, . . . *als een die dient*, 259–60; emphases by Miskotte. Cited in: Liagre Böhl, *Miskotte*, 59–60.

2. *Experiential pietism*: this is how we translate the Dutch term *bevindelijkheid*, which is used in traditional Dutch (Calvinist) Protestantism for a state of lived experience of God's grace. The preoccupation with "experiential pietism" has its origin in the Further Reformation (*Nadere Reformatie*), a reform movement in seventeenth-century Dutch Calvinism.

3. Liagre Böhl, *Theoloog in de branding*, 60; translation Joey Kok (JK) and MDK.

4. *Van verborgen Omgang* [*On Hidden Communion*] is the title Miskotte gives to the series of contemplations of his intimate wrestling with God and faith that was published from December 5, 1924, to February 7, 1925, in eight consecutive issues of his *Church Newsletter*. The passage cited above is almost the whole second part (title: *On Hidden Communion. 1b. A Testimony*). As is customary in the Protestant tradition, their title seems to indicate that he presents this series of considerations as a commentary on a verse from the Bible, in this case the opening of the seventh verse of Psalm 25 in the so-called Dutch "Metrical psalter of 1773" (assessed October 20, 2021, http://www.psalmboek.nl/zingen.php?psID=25&psvID=7); "To find God's hidden communion [Gods *verborgen* omgang vinden]."

5. Miskotte refers to this term of Bonhoeffer's in *When the Gods are Silent*, published in Dutch (under the title *Als de goden zwijgen*) in 1956. The English translation by John W. Doberstein appeared in 1967; see Miskotte, *When the Gods are Silent*, 79.

6. See chapter 2 ("Theoclasme") in De Kesel, *Goden breken* [*Breaking Gods*], 31–47.

7. In his diary entry of May 12, 1921, Miskotte allows himself the following provocative statement: "Like a soup of rat's tails, that is what all edifying literature is to me" (Miskotte, Uit de dagboeken, 176; note of 12 May 1921; cited in Liagre-Böhl, *Miskotte*, 40; translation JK and MDK).

8. In his *Church Newsletter* of January 24, 1925, still in the series *On Hidden Communion*, Miskotte cites, by way of illustrating the kind of experience he describes here, an entire passage from Ruusbroec's *The Spiritual Espousals*. What is remarkable is that he cites it on January 24 without any reference to source or author. He only reveals these in the next issue, of February 7, immediately adding: "It has been in the library of the hall for years without anyone noticing." See Miskotte, . . . *als een die dient*, 293–94, 299.

9. Parmenides, Fragment 5 (6DK): "It is necessary to assert and conceive that this is Being. For it is for being, but Nothing is not" (χρὴ τὸ λέγειν τε νοεῖν τ' ἐὸν ἔμμεναι, ἔστι γὰρ εἶναι, μηδὲν δ' οὐκ ἔστιν ·). Coxon, *Fragments of Parmenides*, 58–59.

10. In his dialogue *The Republic*, Plato does not stage the myth of the cave to explain the relation between Ideas (being) and *mimesis* (not-being, imitation, shadow, illusion). For this, he does not need *mythos*; it can easily be explained on the basis of *logos*. But why is there *mimesis* at all; why, besides being, is there something like "not-being"? *Logos* cannot provide an explanation. For this, it needs to call on a *mythos* that is able to explain that being, even if it is only what it is, basically also generates more than itself, that it is an inexhaustibly giving goodness. This is the Idea of the Good, an Idea that can only be expressed with a story, a *mythos*.

11. Miskotte, . . . *als een die dient*, 254.

12. Miskotte, . . . *als een die dient*, 254–55. Miskotte plays with the Dutch word for "answer," *antwoord*, whose etymology can literally be read as "counter-word," a word that comes from the other side, a word that answers us. The English word *answer* has a similar etymology, being derived from *and-* ("against") and *swaru* ("a speaking, affirmation, oath").

13. Miskotte, . . . *als een die dient*, 255; emphases by Miskotte.

14. Miskotte, . . . *als een die dient*, 272. Later, in the *Church Newsletter* of December 27, we read: "Oh, *therein* 'believers' and 'non-believers' are so united, that the life of God is a mystery for them both. With this difference, that for the latter it is a mystery that they *face* and for the former a mystery in which they are *included*" (. . . *als een die dient*, 271; emphases by Miskotte).

15. This is the first line of the *Church Newsletter* of January 10, 1925 (Miskotte, . . . *als een die dient*, 277). Thereby Miskotte repeats the last sentence of his piece *On Hidden Communion* from the previous newsletter (December 27, 1924), . . . *als een die dient*, 273.

16. Miskotte, . . . *als een die dient*, 255.

17. Miskotte, . . . *als een die dient*, 255; emphases by Miskotte.

18. Miskotte, . . . *als een die dient*, 260; I underline the sentence fragments that Liagre Böhl omitted.

19. Miskotte, . . . *als een die dient*, 259.

20. Heidegger, *End of Philosophy*. Furthermore, Miskotte's reference to Heidegger is generally negative because he perceives in his philosophy of being

a modern form of "paganism," meaning a "veneration of the fundamental powers and primal forms of Being, which may indeed and fully be called religious" (Miskotte, *Als de goden zwijgen*, 43).

21. See Karl Barth's *Kirchliche Dogmatik I*, 2, § 17; Barth, *Church Dogmatics*, 297–324.

22. Assmann, *Price of Monotheism*.

23. *Religio* is a Latin term that has no equivalent in the other languages of classical Antiquity. Only the Romans had a separate word describing the thought, texts, and actions that comprise the relationship of humankind to the divine. See, among others, Sachot, *Quand le christianisme*, 62ff.

24. For an archaic religious consciousness, unlike for our "philosophical," "scientific" mind, death does not equal not-being. For an archaic mind, death *is* there: it is the name for the "sacral" domain where (profane) life comes from, but where the constituent differences (life versus death, good versus evil, true versus false, and the like) controlling profane life are not valid.

25. And this not by treating Him with gifts. Whereas the gods—in order to assert themselves as such—depended on sacrifices and the praises of mortals, the monotheistic God, as Truth, does not depend on anything. Not that monotheism plainly prohibits us from making sacrifices to or praising God, but every sacrifice and accolade must at the same time confess that God does not live from sacrifices, accolades, or other gifts; moreover, that these gifts *to* Him also come *from* Him, and that only that tribute and that sacrifice is true that concedes, strictly speaking, to being superfluous in God's eyes.

26. See chapter 2 in De Kesel, *Goden breken [Breaking Gods]*.

27. The paradigm of the gift, as I use it here, refers to the gift theory of Marcel Mauss's well-known *The Gift*; Mauss, *Sociologie et anthropologie*, 161–64; *The Gift*, 16–18.

28. Plato, *Symposium* 189A–193D.

29. Plato, *Politeia* 509B.

30. Miskotte, . . . *als een die dient*, 255; emphases by Miskotte.

31. Miskotte, . . . *als een die dient*, 255.

32. Miskotte, *Uit de dagboeken*, 261.

Chapter 7. The Path of Mercy Means Simply that You Abandon Self

1. Endō, *Silence*, 156. Shūsaku Endō is Japanese, *Silence* is set in Japan, but the storyline and theme are inherently Christian. Endō belongs to the small Christian minority in Japan, and his oeuvre mainly touches on issues concerning Christianity.

2. Endō, *Silence*, 156.

3. "It's called the pit. You've probably heard about it. They bind you in such a way that you can move neither hands nor feet; and then they hang you upside down in a pit." . . . "These little openings are made behind the ears so that you won't die immediately. The blood trickles out drop by drop." Endō, *Silence*, 156.

4. Endō, *Silence*, 181.

5. Endō, *Silence*, 183.

6. Endō, *Silence*, 203–204.

7. "Righteousness will be his belt and faithfulness the sash around his waist. The wolf will live with the lamb, the leopard will lie with the goat, the calf and the lion and the yearling together; and a little child will lead them" (Isaiah 11, 5–6; New International Version). "He will judge between many peoples and will settle disputes for strong nations far and wide. They will beat their swords into plowshares and their spears into pruning hooks. Nation will not take up sword against nation, nor will they train for war anymore" (Micah 4:3; New International Version).

8. See, for instance, Luke 9:23; 14:26–27.

9. Holte, "Logos Spermatikos."

10. Also see chapter 1, p. 18.

11. Yamamoto-Wilson, *Pain, Pleasure, and Perversity*.

12. Endō, *Silence*, 180.

13. Fénelon, *Œuvres de Fénelon*, 156–57; translation MDK.

14. Endō, *Silence*, 203–204.

Chapter 8. As a Drop in the Ocean

1. See chapter 2, pp. 47–50.

2. For a history of the originally French term spiritualité, see Tinsley, *French Expressions*, 226–43.

3. "Le Christianisme, une nouvelle mythologie?," in Certeau and Domenach, *Christianisme éclaté*, 7. The page numbers in this chapter all refer to this edition.

4. This is, more precisely, the title of the version that appeared in *Le christianisme éclaté*. Thanks to Luce Giard, we have access to the original, much longer version, which she included in the posthumous collection from 1987, *La faiblesse de croire*, under the title: "Du corps à l'écriture: un transit chrétien"; in: Certeau, *Faiblesse de croire*, 267–305; English translation: "The Weakness of Believing. From the Body to Writing, a Christian Transit," in Certeau, *Certeau Reader*, 214–43. For the publication of the radio discussion, Certeau was asked to shorten this text, in order to keep the balance with Domenach's essay. Since it develops systematically (although sometimes cryptically as well) the main points

of Certeau's theory on Christianity, my comment focuses on the "official" version. For a "first" comment on that text as well as for its biographical context, see Dosse, *Michel de Certeau*, 203–206.

5. Certeau, *Certeau Reader*, 214, *Faiblesse de croire*, 267; Certeau and Domenach, *Christianisme éclaté*, 79.

6. In a later essay, describing sixteenth- and seventeenth-century mysticism, Certeau writes about this "desire of the other": "How will the desire in search of a *you* cross the language which deceives him [the longing mystic] by bringing to the recipient another message or by substituting the enunciation [*énonciation*] itself of an I by the enunciated [*énoncé*] of an idea" (Certeau, "*L'énonciation mystique*," 196–97; my translation).

7. On Certeau's concept of "writing" (*écriture*), see for instance Carrard, "History as a Kind of Writing"; Highmore, *Michel de Certeau* (especially ch. 2).

8. Certeau, *Certeau Reader*, 167; *Faiblesse de croire*, 267; Certeau and Domenach, *Christianisme éclaté*, 79–80.

9. See for instance Certeau's essay on Jean de Léry's 1578 book *Histoire d'un voyage faict en la terre du Bresil*, "Ethno graphie—L'oralité, ou l'espace de l'autre," in his *L'écriture de l'histoire*, 215–48 (English translation in *Certeau Reader*, 129–49) or his essay on Jean François Lafitau's *Mœurs des souvages amériquains conparées aux mœurs des premier temps* from 1724 ("Histoire et anthropologie chez Lafitau," in Certeau, *Lieu de l'autre*, 89–111).

10. Certeau, *Certeau Reader*, 214–15; *Faiblesse de croire*, 267–68; Certeau and Domenach, *Christianisme éclaté*, 80.

11. See, among other publications, Surin, *Guide spirituel; Correspondance*; several "early" essays in the posthumous Certeau, *Lieu de l'autre*.

12. For a more general explanation of Certeau's concept of the "voice," see for instance Highmore, *Michel de Certeau*, 74ff.

13. Or, as he puts it in "L'énonciation mystique": "Do we exist to the extent we speak to him or we are spoken of by him?" (200; my translation). It is this confusion which in mystical writings comes to the surface, as he explains in the last part of this essay (209ff.).

14. Certeau, *Certeau Reader*, 215; *Faiblesse de croire*, 268; Certeau and Domenach, *Christianisme éclaté*, 80–81.

15. Certeau, *Certeau Reader*, 226; *Faiblesse de croire*, 288; Certeau and Domenach, *Christianisme éclaté*, 87.

16. "Indeed, the call which is the principle of this relation cannot be known outside of the response which it receives. It has no expression of its own. We have access to Jesus only through texts which, in talking of him, narrate what he awakened and hence describe only their own status as writings of belief or of those who have turned round to respond. Jesus can only be identified in his concrete responses. We have only variants of the relation between the call and the decision, and never a statement which would lend the response an exemplary

and authentic formulation by assigning to the call a site which might be proper to it. No text, whether 'primary' or 'apostolic,' represents anything other than a 'modification' (a writing [*une écriture*]) made possible by a call which cannot objectively be uttered in its own terms and which is recognized only gradually through successive conversations" (Certeau, *Certeau Reader*, 227; *Faiblesse de croire*, 288; Certeau and Domenach, *Christianisme éclaté*, 87–88).

17. Certeau, *Certeau Reader*, 227; *Faiblesse de croire*, 288; Certeau and Domenach, *Christianisme éclaté*, 88.

18. See the paragraph "Travail d'un 'excès'" in the original version of the essay (Certeau, *Faiblesse de croire*, 283–93). See also Certeau, *Certeau Reader*, 226–27; *Faiblesse de croire*, 288: "An excess which in history is named Jesus calls forth a decision which is inscribed as renewing in objective situations. The call to 'follow' and the possibility of 'change' entertain a formal relation which finds its truth in no single concrete expression."

19. Certeau, *Certeau Reader*, 235; *Faiblesse de croire*, 301; Certeau and Domenach, *Christianisme éclaté*, 94–95.

20. See the 1971 essay entitled "La rupture instauratrice," in Certeau, *Faiblesse de croire*, 183–226. See also Bastenier, "Le croire et le cru."

21. Certeau, *Certeau Reader*, 221; *Faiblesse de croire*, 279.

22. Though, in this context, Certeau sometimes speaks of destruction. Mentioning the "Christian specificity" as a "break in operative rationalities," he speaks of "ruin[ing] the discourse from within." But in that case too, the destruction is not meant to build something new but "à lui faire avouer ainsi l'ineffabilité du sujet se disant." *Certeau Reader*, 221–22; *Faiblesse de croire*, 279.

23. Certeau, *Certeau Reader*, 222; *Faiblesse de croire*, 279: "l'ineffabilité du sujet se disant."

24. See my essay "Jochanam ben Sakkaï Revisited: Reflections on Michel de Certeau's reading of Freud's *Moses and Monotheism.*"

25. "The caesura is at work everywhere, from the birth which upsets a whole genealogy to the death which disjoins the covenant between an elect people and the one God, from the world which rings false through to the miracle which resolves. In line with the signifying practice which organizes the text, everything splits, the homogeneity of traditions, the coherence of belongings, the unity of a people or of a public of listeners, the relation of authorities to their authoritative sources, etc." (Certeau, *Certeau Reader*, 235; *Faiblesse de croire*, 302; Certeau and Domenach, *Christianisme éclaté*, 95).

26. "The relation which this break marks out in the site (that of the Covenant) where it is produced is called faith," in: Certeau, *Certeau Reader*, 236; *Faiblesse de croire*, 302; Certeau and Domenach, *Christianisme éclaté*, 95.

27. Certeau, *Certeau Reader*, 236; *Faiblesse de croire*, 302; Certeau and Domenach, *Christianisme éclaté*, 95–96.

28. Certeau, *Certeau Reader*, 236; *Faiblesse de croire*, 303; Certeau and Domenach, *Christianisme éclaté*, 97.

29. Certeau, *Certeau Reader*, 237; *Faiblesse de croire*, 304; Certeau and Domenach, *Christianisme éclaté*, 98.

30. Certeau, *Certeau Reader*, 226; *Faiblesse de croire*, 286; Certeau and Domenach, *Christianisme éclaté*, 87.

31. "The problem of Christianity is therefore displaced towards practices, but these could be anybody's, anonymous, stripped of distinctive rules or marks" (Certeau, *Certeau Reader*, 224; *Faiblesse de croire*, 283).

32. "In a first instance, civil society replaced the Church in the role of defining tasks and positions, leaving the Church only a marginal possibility of correcting or going beyond the delimitations of domains. Today, the ecclesial site from which a coherent strategy around border lines might be decided is, in turn, dissolving, which leaves every Christian with the risk of defining them for himself" (Certeau, *Certeau Reader*, 226; *Faiblesse de croire*, 287; Certeau and Domenach, *Christianisme éclaté*, 86).

33. Certeau, *Certeau Reader*, 214; *Faiblesse de croire*, 267.

34. Certeau, *Certeau Reader*, 226; *Faiblesse de croire*, 287; Certeau and Domenach, *Christianisme éclaté*, 86–87.

35. Certeau, *Certeau Reader*, 237; *Faiblesse de croire*, 305; Certeau and Domenach, *Christianisme éclaté*, 99.

36. A footnote is added as well, citing references in the mystical tradition to the image of a "drop of water in the sea": "See: Saint Bernard, *De diligendo Deo*, § 28; Harpius, *Theologica Mystica*, II, 3, chap. 33; Surin, *Guide spirituel*, VII, 8; Fénelon, *Instructions sur la morale et la perfection chrétienne*, in *Oeuvres*, t. 6, p. 116" (Certeau, *Certeau Reader*, 243; *Faiblesse de croire*, 305).

37. Certeau, *Certeau Reader*, 237; *Faiblesse de croire*, 305.

38. Certeau, *Certeau Reader*, 237; *Faiblesse de croire*, 305.

39. *Episteme* can be defined as a "non unified, multiple and complex field" of various discourses constituting the "discursive universe of a historical time." See for instance chapter 2 in McHoul and Grace, *Foucault Primer*, 45–46. See also Revel, *Vocabulaire de Foucault*, 25–26.

40. Foucault, *Dits et écrits*, 300–301; Revel, *Vocabulaire de Foucault*, 26–27.

41. In a way, Certeau is more interested in the changing dispositive *as such*. As if he considered change itself as a dispositive, arising from the change from Middle Ages/Renaissance to Modernity. See, for instance, Certeau, "L'énonciation mystique," 184.

42. So Foucault's final words in *The Order of Things*: "then one can certainly wager that man would be erased, like a face drawn in sand at the edge of the sea" (386).

43. Certeau quotes this sentence from Foucault, *The Archeology of Knowledge* (19) in his essay "The Laugh of Michel Foucault" (Certeau, *Heterologies*, 193).

44. Foucault, *Archeology of Knowledge*, 19; Certeau, *Heterologies*, 193.

45. Certeau, *Heterologies*, 194. He quotes Foucault, *History of Sexuality*. Vol. 2, 9.

46. See, for instance, the "signature" at the end of "Signature Event Context" in: Derrida, *Margins of Philosophy*, 330. The fact that, at the bottom of his essay, Derrida actually puts three signatures—his name, his initials, and his handwritten signature—indicates that even in the original act of signing, repetition—and, consequently, difference and inauthenticity—is structurally involved.

47. For an explanation of Lacanian theory as a theory of the subject, see the first chapter in De Kesel, *Eros and Ethics*. See also: Fink, *Lacanian Subject*; Bailly, *Lacan*.

48. See, for instance, Certeau, *Histoire et psychanalyse*. For an essay on Lacan's version of psychoanalytical theory, see especially the last chapter: "Lacan, une éthique de la parole" (168–98).

49. Lévi Strauss, *Structural Anthropology*, especially Chapter X: "The Effectiveness of Symbols."

50. Freud, *Pre Analytic Publications*, 48–49; Lacan, *Écrits*, 548, 685, 689, 799.

51. "An unfulfillable longing for a *self*": this implies that there is no *real* self. This is why Lacan defines the ultimate goal of desire not as a "self" or a "subject," but as an "object," *object small a*, which is *real* but, therefore, beyond the reach of the subject's desire.

52. Certeau, *Certeau Reader*, 235; *Faiblesse de croire*, 301; Certeau and Domenach, *Christianisme éclaté*, 94–95.

53. Certeau, *Certeau Reader*, 215; *Faiblesse de croire*, 268; Certeau and Domenach, *Christianisme éclaté*, 80–81. For Lacan, too, the "subject of the enunciation" (which is his concept), is located in the lack of the symbolic order. See the first chapter in De Kesel, *Eros and Ethics*.

54. Certeau, *Certeau Reader*, 215; *Faiblesse de croire*, 268; Certeau and Domenach, *Christianisme éclaté*, 80–81.

55. Certeau, *Certeau Reader*, 215; *Faiblesse de croire*, 267–68; Certeau and Domenach, *Christianisme éclaté*, 80.

56. Certeau, *Prise de parole*; *Capture of Speech*.

57. Certeau, *Certeau Reader*, 215; *Faiblesse de croire*, 268; Certeau and Domenach, *Christianisme éclaté*, 80–81.

58. About "saying yes" to the *rupture instauratrice*, see Certeau, *Fable mystique*, 239–40; *Mystic Fable*, 174–75. See also Derrida's comment in "A Number of Yes," in: Derrida, *Psyche*, 231–40.

59. Teresa of Avila, *Interior Castle*.

60. Certeau, *Certeau Reader*, 235; *Faiblesse de croire*, 301; Certeau and Domenach, *Christianisme éclaté*, 94–95.

61. Remember the title of the essay: "From the Body to Writing, a Christian Transit"; *Certeau Reader*, 214.

62. Certeau, *Certeau Reader*, 237; *Faiblesse de croire*, 304.

63. Certeau, *Certeau Reader*, 237; *Faiblesse de croire*, 305; Certeau and Domenach, *Christianisme éclaté*, 99.

64. Chapter 1, p. 24; quote from Fénelon, Œuvres, 156–57; my translation.

65. For a penetrating evocation of the dark side of the pur amour, see Vidal, "Du pur amour."

Chapter 9. Down with Religion, Long Live Mysticism

1. See, for instance, Frans Jespers, "Investigating Western Popular Spirituality," in Hense and Maas, Towards a Theory of Spirituality, 97–111.

2. Augustine, City of God; Hobbes, On the Citizen.

3. Farr and Williams, General Will.

4. See chapter 2, pp. 47–50.

5. In the Middle Ages, "spiritualis is defined as synonym for immaterialis, incorporalis and incorporeus; the opposite of animalis, carnalis, materialis, corporeus, naturalis, civilis, saecularis, and mundanus": Tinsley, French Expressions, 69. Spiritualitas was a common name for "the clergy," those who belonged to the sphere of the "spiritual," which was the opposite of the one of the "earthly."

6. "The noun [Spirituality] only became established in reference to "the spiritual life" in seventeenth-century France—and not always in a positive sense": Sheldrake, Brief History of Spirituality, 3. See also Tinsley, French Expressions, 226–43.

7. Bérulle, Selective Writings.

8. Sales, Œuvres.

9. Sales and Chantal, Letters of Spiritual Direction.

10. Marie of the Incarnation, Selected Writings.

11. Guyon, Selected Writings.

12. Fénelon, Selected Writings.

13. For the possibly "spiritual" (more precisely "Ignatian") inspiration behind Descartes's Discourse on Method, see for instance, Thomson, "Ignace de Loyola et Descartes."

14. For the expression "l'homme spirituel" or "femme spirituelle," see Tinsley, French Expressions, 229.

15. Hence the variety of "theories of subjectivity" in seventeenth-century spirituality literature. The Italian scholar Bergamo summarizes this literature as "the anatomy of the soul" (Bergamo, L'anatomie de l'âme).

16. Descartes, Passions of the Soul. For the contrast between the "anatomy of the soul" to be found in Descartes's writings and the one to be read in the mystical writings of his time, see for instance Bergamo, L'anatomie de l'âme, 23 ff. The "science of the saints" is at the same time a science of the modern subject; see Mino Bergamo's book of that title (Bergamo, La science des saints).

17. Balibar, "Citizen Subject," 39–44; "Citoyen sujet," 44–50.

18. Thus, Jacques-Bénigne Bossuet in his Politics Drawn from the Very Words of the Holy Scripture (written in 1679 and published in 1709): "All men

are born subjects: and the paternal empire, which accustoms them to obey, accustoms them at the same time to have only one leader" (Bossuet, *Politics*, 47).

19. Balibar, "Citizen Subject"; "*Citoyen sujet*," 35–66.

20. "However, [in the course of the seventeenth century,] both *spiritualité* and *mystique* suffer an almost immediate semantic setback from their association with quietism and other forms of false or merely suspected spirituality." Tinsley, *French Expressions*, 243. On 235, Tinsley cites strikingly Soeur Eustochie: "illusions and artifices which began with spiritualities so subtle that they evaporate the mind . . . but which ended in the greatest folly or ultimate corruption." Quoted also in Bremond, *Histoire littéraire du sentiment religieux*. Vol. XI, 134; my translation. For a general view on the "anti-mystical" tendencies in the seventeenth century, see Cognet, *Crépuscules*, 34–50; Certeau, *Histoire spirituelle*, 277–81.

21. Of course, "hypothetically," because believing this would not be in conformity with the Christian doctrine at all. See above, chapter 2 and 3.

22. On the voluntarist base of Madame Guyon's *pur amour*, see for instance Cognet, *Crépuscules*, 78.

23. De Kesel, "In, Not Of the World."

24. Hobbes, *On the Citizen*, 120.

25. Remember the famous *Memorial* that Pascal wrote down in his decisive mystical night: "The year of grace 1654, Monday, 23 November, day of St. Clement, Pope and Martyr. . . . From about half-past ten in the evening until about half-past twelve, FIRE. God of Abraham, God of Isaac, God of Jacob, not of the philosophers nor of the Wise. Assurance, joy, assurance, feeling, joy, peace. . . . Just Father, the world has not known thee but I have known thee. Joy, joy, joy, tears of joy" (Pascal, *Pensées*, 265–66).

26. Weil, *Gravity and Grace*, 15.

27. Dujardin, *Simone Weil*, 107–52.

28. Chenavier, *Simone Weil*, 10.

29. Valabek, *Titus Brandsma*; Alzin, *Petit moine dangereux*.

30. Weil, *Gravity and Grace*, 164–69.

31. Chevanier, *Simone Weil*, 19–20; See also Gustave Thibon's "Introduction" in Weil, *Gravity and Grace*, xviii.

32. This is why modernity, in a way, often "obliges" religion to become conservative; standing in the abyss of freedom, it is inclined to choose the certainties of before—often interpreted as "tradition." By doing so, however, modern religion (free as it is) in fact changes that tradition from a hybrid, multi-interpretable frame of reference into a one-dimensional doctrinal certainty. It, so to say, projects the paradigm of modernity (i.e., the Cartesian certainty) onto its tradition.

33. Bremond, *Histoire littéraire du sentiment religieux*. Vol. II, 168–82; Tremblay, *Comme en plein jour*; Pierre, *Le père Joseph*.

Chapter 10. Selflessly Powerful

1. In his *Tractatus Logico-Philosophicus*, Wittgenstein clearly demarcates the sayable as that which falls within the boundaries of his positivist paradigm. In the closing (statement 6.522), he then writes: "There are, indeed, things that cannot be put into words. They *make themselves manifest*. They are what is mystical" (89; italics by Wittgenstein).

2. See Acts 17, 34.

3. *The Celestial Hierarchy* 141A; Pseudo-Dionysius, *Complete Works*, 150; translation modified.

4. Pseudo-Dionysius, *Complete Works*, 47–131.

5. *The Celestial Hierarchy* 164D–165A; Pseudo-Dionysius, *Complete Works*, 153–54; translation modified.

6. *The Celestial Hierarchy* 124A; Pseudo-Dionysius, *Complete Works*, 147.

7. Think of Eusebius Pamphilius's well-known eulogy of Emperor Constantine: "[T]he Word of God. From whom and by whom our divinely favored emperor, receiving, as it were a transcript of the Divine sovereignty, directs, in imitation of God himself, the administration of this world's affairs. This only begotten Word of God reigns, from ages which had no beginning, to infinite and endless ages, the partner of his Father's kingdom. And [our emperor] ever beloved by him, who derives the source of imperial authority from above, and is strong in the power of his sacred title, has controlled the empire of the world for a long period of years." *Oration in Praise of the Emperor Constantine*, last sentence of chapter 1 and first sentence of chapter 2; Eusebius Pamphilius, *Church History*, 583.

8. "And surely monarchy far transcends every other constitution and form of government: for that democratic equality of power, which is its opposite, may rather be described as anarchy and disorder. Hence there is one God, and not two, or three, or more: for to assert a plurality of gods is plainly to deny the being of God at all. There is one Sovereign; and his Word and royal Law is one: a Law not expressed in syllables and words, not written or engraved on tablets, and therefore subject to the ravages of time; but the living and self-subsisting Word, who himself is God, and who administers his Father's kingdom on behalf of all who are after him and subject to his power." Eusebius Pamphilius, *Church History*, 584.

9. Agamben, *The Kingdom and the Glory*.

10. See, among others, Mondzain, *Image, icône, économie*: 25–31.

11. The term *oikonomia* obtained this Christian conceptual meaning at the same time as the rise of Trinitarian thought around the turn of the second century, basically in the writings of Hippolytus and in Tertullian (Agamben, *The Kingdom and the Glory*, 35–39).

12. Agamben specifically refers to a detail from a fresco in the church Saint Paul's Outside the Walls in Rome, where the throne of Christ shows all the signs of his crucifixion but remains empty itself (Agamben, *The Kingdom and the Glory*, xiii). This detail is reproduced on the cover of the English edition of his book.

13. Agamben, *The Kingdom and the Glory*, 56.

14. Agamben, *State of Exception*.

15. Agamben takes this statement from Foucault, when he writes that, "a society's 'treshold of biological modernity' is situated at the point at which the species and the individual as a simple living body become what is at stake in a society's political strategies" (Agamben, *The Omnibus "Homo sacer,"* 6). Before modernity, power defined itself according to the paradigm of sovereignty: "Power . . . was essentially a right of seizure: of things, time, bodies, and ultimately life itself; it culminated in the privilege to seize hold of life in order to suppress it" (Foucault, *History of Sexuality*. Vol. 1, 136).

16. Agamben, *The Omnibus "Homo sacer,"* 10.

17. Agamben refers to one of the most important studies on this topic: Bennet, "Sacer esto."

18. Agamben, *Homo sacer*, 12; Agamben's italics.

19. Agamben, *Homo sacer*, 71–74.

20. On what Agamben calls "un' esclusione inclusiva," see, for instance, Agamben, *Homo sacer*, 12.

21. Agamben, *Homo sacer*, 4, 6.

22. Until the third century, the Roman emperor profiled himself as a *princeps* (*inter pares*) and did all he could not to look like a *rex* (king) or a monarch according to the Eastern model (as was the case with the Persians, sworn enemies of the Empire). By the end of the third century, the emperor increasingly profiled himself as *dominus et deus*, a "Lord and God." He resided in palaces, was surrounded by an enormous court, could no longer be approached directly, demanded prostration from whoever addressed him, et cetera. In short, the *Principate* turned into a *Dominate*. See, among others, Praet, *God der goden*, 137.

23. Lefort, *Democracy and Political Theory*.

24. Claude Lefort's basic intuition is also shared by political scholars such as Ernesto Laclau and Chantal Mouffe. See, among others, Mouffe and Laclau, *Hegemony and Socialist Strategy*; Mouffe, *Over het politieke*.

Chapter 11. Selflessness and Science

1. Lallemant, *Spiritual Doctrine*, 97. The *Doctrine spirituelle* by the Jesuit Lallemant (1588–1635) is a posthumously published collection of maxims and instructions dating back to the 1620s and '30s. They were recorded by his student Jean Rigoleuc.

2. See his *Traité des passions de l'âme* (1649), translated as *The Passions of the Soul*. Descartes's treatise is developed in response to his correspondence with Princess Elisabeth of Bohemia; Elisabeth of Bohemia and Descartes, *Correspondence*.

3. See, for instance, what Jean-Maurice Monnoyer writes about this in his introduction to Descartes's *Les passions de l'âme*; 64–75. In Descartes's treatise, see article 43, 180–81. Descartes had already discussed his ideas about this *glande* in his *Traité de l'homme*. Descartes, *Œuvres philosophiques*, 441–49.

4. Nadler, "Occasionalism and General Will"; "Occasionalism and Mind-Body."

5. La Mettrie, *Machine Man*, 1–39.

6. Holbach, *System of Nature*, 40; *Système de la nature*, 104.

7. Holbach, *System of Nature*, 46, original emphasis retained; *Système de la nature*, 118.

8. Cited in Coleman, *Virtues of Abandon*, 92.

9. Coleman, *Virtues of Abandon*, 94.

10. Coleman, *Virtues of Abandon*, 97.

11. *Thérèse philosophe* (English and French edition); Trousson, *Romans libertins*, 557–658; Darnton, *Forbidden Best-Sellers*, 249–99. For a discussion, see Richardot, "Thérèse philosophe"; Darnton, *Forbidden Best-Sellers*, 89–114.

12. *Thérèse philosophe* (English), 4; *Thérèse philosophe* (French), 34; Trousson, *Romans libertins*, 575.

13. Trousson, *Romans libertins*, 559.

14. Lotterie 2007: 17 ff. For a comprehensive recent study, see Choudhury, *Wanton Jesuit*; Lamotte, *L'affaire Girard-Cadière*, 92–98.

15. *Thérèse philosophe* (English), 4; *Thérèse philosophe* (French), 34–35.

16. Réage, *Histoire d'O*; *Story of O*. The film *Fifty Shades of Grey* is based on the eponymous novel by E. L. James. For an academic discussion on the latter, see for instance Illouz, *Hard-Core Romance*.

17. De Kesel, "The Brain."

18. Freud, *Pre-Analytic Publications*, 283–397.

19. Hence, Lacan situating the subconscious *"entre chair et cuir"* (between skin and flesh); Lacan, *Séminaire. VII*, 64; *Seminar. VII*, 51. For the term *psychical apparatus*, see Freud, *Pre-Analytic Publications*, 320 ff (and further throughout *Project for a Scientific Psychology*).

20. Freud, *Pre-Analytic Publications*, 305; 318; 326.

21. Cited in Wolfe, "Brain Theory," 179.

22. Northoff, *Neuropsychoanalysis*; Solms, "Justifying Psychoanalysis"; "Neuropsychoanalytical Approach"; Solms and Turnbull, *The Brain and the Inner World*; De Kesel, "The Brain."

23. Freud, *Pre-Analytic Publications*, 291.

24. For this reason, French psychoanalytical theorist Jacques Lacan speaks about a *"logique du fantasme,"* which is also the title of a (yet to be published)

seminar he conducted in 1966–67 (http://staferla.free.fr/S14/S14%20LOGIQUE.
pdf).

25. Freud first developed this notion in *Jenseits des Lustprizips* (*Beyond the
Pleasure Principle*), an essay that is as famous as it is contested.

26. Following the definition of *signifier* as concealed definition of the
subject that Lacan first formulated in his lecture of 6 December 1961 (in his
Seminar on Identification, 1961–1962; unpublished; http://staferla.free.fr/S9/S9.htm).

27. Lacan, *Séminaire* XXIII, 13.

28. For an extensive analysis of the concept of *jouissance*, see De Kesel,
Eros and Ethics, 121–61.

29. Thébert, *Petite mort*.

30. John of the Cross, *Collected Works*, 110–11.

Bibliography

Agamben, Giorgio. *Homo sacer: Sovereign Power and Bare Life.* Translated by Daniel Heller-Roazen. Stanford: Stanford University Press, 1998.

———. *The Kingdom and the Glory: For a Theological Genealogy of Economy and Government ("Homo sacer" II,2).* Translated by Lorenzo Chiesa and Matteo Mandarini. Stanford: Stanford University Press, 2011.

———. *The Omnibus "Homo sacer."* Translated by Daniel Heller-Roazen. Stanford: Stanford University Press, 2017.

———. *State of Exception.* Translated by Kevin Attell. Chicago: University of Chicago Press, 2005.

Alzin, Josse. *Ce petit moine dangereux: Le Père Titus Brandsma, recteur d'université, martyr de Dachau.* Paris: Bonne Presse, 1954.

Assmann, Jan. *The Price of Monotheism.* Translated by Robert Savage. Stanford: Stanford University Press, 2009.

Astell, Ann W., and Catherine Rose Cavadini. "The Song of Songs." In *The Wiley-Blackwell Companion to Christian Mysticism,* edited by Julia A. Lamm, 25–40. Chichester, UK: Blackwell, 2013.

Augustine. *The City of God.* Translated by Marcus Dods and with an introduction by Thomas Merton. New York: Modern Library, 2000.

———. *The Confessions of Saint Augustine.* Edited by Hal M. Helms and with a foreword by Mark Henninger. Brewster, MA: Paraclete Press, 2010.

Bailly, Lionel. *Lacan: A Beginner's Guide.* Oxford: Oneworld Publications, 2009.

Balibar, Étienne. "Citizen Subject." In *Who Comes After the Subject?,* edited by Eduardo Cadava, Peter Connor, and Jean-Luc Nancy, 33–57. New York: Routledge, 1991.

———. *"Citoyen sujet" et autres essais d'anthropologie philosophique.* Paris: Presses Universitaires de France, 2011.

Ball, Hugo, *Flight out of Time: A Dada Diary.* Translated by Ann Raimes and edited by John Elderfield. Berkeley: University of California Press, 1996.

Barth, Karl. *Church Dogmatics*. Vol. 1, *The Doctrine of the Word of God*. Pt. 2. Translated by G. T. Thomson and Harold Knight and edited by G. W. Bromiley and T. F. Torrance. London: T&T Clark, 2004.

Baslez, Marie-Françoise. *Comment notre monde est devenu chrétien*. Tours: Éditions CLD, 2008.

Bastenier, Alfred. "Le croire et le cru: Les appartenances religieuses au sein du christianisme européen revisitées à partir des travaux de Michel de Certeau." *Social Compass* 54, no. 1 (2007): 13–32.

Bellori, Giovan Pietro. *The Lives of the Modern Painters, Sculptors, and Architects*. Translated by Alice Sedgwick Wohl, with notes by Hellmut Wohl and an introduction by Tomaso Montanari. Cambridge: Cambridge University Press, 2005.

Bennet, Harold. "Sacer esto." *Transactions and Proceedings of the American Philological Association* 61 (1930): 5–18.

Bergamo, Mino. *L'anatomie de l'âme: De François de Sales à Fénelon*. Translated by Marc Bonneval. Grenoble: Jérôme Millon, 1994.

———. *La science des saints: Le discours mystique au XVIIe siècle en France*. Preface by Jacques Le Brun. Grenoble: Jérôme Millon, 1992.

Bérulle, Pierre. *Bèrulle and the French School: Selective Writings*. Edited by William M. Thomson and translated by Lowell M. Glendon, with a preface by Susan A. Muto. New York: Paulist Press, 1989.

Blanchot, Maurice. *The Book to Come*. Translated by Charlotte Mandell. Stanford: Stanford University Press, 2002.

———. *L'espace littéraire*. Paris: Gallimard, 1955.

———. *Le livre à venir*. Paris: Gallimard, 1959.

———. *The Space of Literature*. Translated, with an introduction by Ann Smock. Lincoln: University of Nebraska Press, 1982.

Bossuet, Jacques-Bénigne. *Politics Drawn from the Very Words of the Holy Scripture*. Translated and edited by Patrick Riley. Cambridge: Cambridge University Press, 1990.

Boyer, Jean-Baptiste de, Marquis d'Argens. *Thérèse philosophe ou Mémoires pour servir à l'histoire du Père Dirrag et de Mademoiselle Eradice*. Edited by François Moureau. Saint-Étienne: Publications de l'Université de Saint-Étienne, 2000.

Boyer, Jean-Baptiste. *Thérèse philosophe*. Translated by Brett Tonaille. N.p.: Tartopwol Books, 2011.

Bremond, Henri. *Histoire littéraire du sentiment religieux en France*. Vol. II, *L'invasion mystique*. Paris: Bloud et Gay, 1923.

———. *Histoire littéraire du sentiment religieux en France*. Vol. XI, *Le procès des mystiques*. Paris: Bloud et Gay, 1933.

Carrard, Philippe. "History as a Kind of Writing: Michel de Certeau and the Poetics of Historiography." *South Atlantic Quarterly* 100, no. 2 (2001): 465–82.

Cassin, Barbara, ed. *Vocabulaire européen des philosophies: Dictionnaire des intraduis-ibles*. Paris: Le Robert/Seuil, 2004.

Caussade, Jean-Pierre de. *Bossuet, maître d'oraison: Instructions spirituelles en forme de dialogues sur les divers états d'oraison suivant la doctrine de M. Bossuet*. Edited by Henri Bremond. Paris: Boud et Gay, 1931.

Certeau, Michel de. *"The Capture of Speech" and Other Political Writings*. Edited and with an introduction by Luce Giard, translated by Tom Conley. Minneapolis/London: University of Minnesota Press, 1998.

———. *The Certeau Reader*. Edited by Graham Ward. Oxford/Malden, MA: Blackwell, 2000.

———. *L'écriture de l'histoire*. Paris: Gallimard, 1975.

———. *"L'énonciation mystique."* *Recherches de science religieuse* 64, no. 2 (1976): 183–215.

———. *La fable mystique*. Vol. 1, XVIe–XVIIe siècle. Paris: Gallimard, 1982.

———. *La faiblesse de croire*. Edited by Luce Giard. Paris: Seuil, 1987.

———. *Heterologies: Discourse on the Other*. Translated by Brian Massumi, with a foreword by Wlad Godzich. Minneapolis/London: University of Minnesota Press, 1986.

———. *Histoire et psychanalyse entre science et fiction*. Edited by Luce Giard. Paris: Gallimard, 1987.

———. *Le lieu de l'autre: Histoire religieuse et mystique*. Paris: Gallimard/Seuil, 2005.

———. *The Mystic Fable*. Vol. 1, *The Sixteenth and Seventeenth Centuries*. Translated by Michael B. Smith. Chicago: University of Chicago Press, 1992.

———. *"La prise de parole" et autres écrits politiques*. Edited by Luce Giard. Paris: Seul, 1994.

Certeau, Michel de, et al. *Histoire spirituelle de la France: Spiritualité du catholi-cisme en France et dans les pays de langue française des origines à 1914*. Paris: Beauchesne, 1964.

Certeau, Michel de, and Jean-Marie Domenach. *Le christianisme éclaté*. Paris: Seuil, 1974.

Chenavier, Robert. *Simone Weil: Attention to the Real*. Translated by Bernard E. Doering. Notre Dame: University of Notre Dame Press, 2012.

Cherel, Albert. *Fénelon, ou la religion du pur amour*. Paris: Denoël et Steele, 1934.

Choudhury, Mita. *The Wanton Jesuit and the Wayward Saint: A Tale of Sex, Reli-gion, and Politics in Eighteenth Century France*. University Park: Pennsylvania State University Press, 2015.

Chrétien, Jean-Louis. *The Arch of Speech*. Translated by Andrew Brown. New York: Routledge, 2004.

Cognet, Louis. *Crépuscule des Mystiques: Bossuet–Fénelon*. Edited by Jean-Robert Armogathe. Paris: Desclée, 1991.

Coleman, Charly. *The Virtues of Abandon: An Anti-Individualist History of the French Enlightenment*. Stanford: Stanford University Press, 2014.

Cottingham, John, Robert Stoothoff, and Dugald Murdoch, eds. *The Philosophical Writings of Descartes*. Cambridge: Cambridge University Press, 1984.

Coxon, A. H. *The Fragments of Parmenides*. Edited with new translations by Richard McKirahan, with a preface by Malcolm Schofield. Las Vegas: Parmenides, 2009.

Craymer, Suzanne L. "Margery Kempe's Imitation of Mary Magdalene and the 'Digby Plays.'" *Mystic Quarterly* 19, no. 4 (1993): 173–81.

Darnton, Robert. *The Forbidden Best-Sellers of Pre-Revolutionary France*. New York/London: W. W. Norton, 1996.

De Kesel, Marc. *Auschwitz mon amour*. Amsterdam: Boom, 2012.

———. "The Brain: A Nostalgic Dream. Some Notes on Neuroscience and the Problem of Modern Knowledge." In *Neuroscience and Critique: Exploring the Limits of the Neurological Turn*, edited by Jan De Vos and Ed Pluth, 11–21. London/New York: Routledge, 2016.

———. *Eros and Ethics: Reading Jacques Lacan, Seminar VII*. Albany: State University of New York Press, 2009.

———. *Goden breken: Essays over monotheïsme*. Amsterdam: Boom, 2010.

———. "In, Not Of the World: A Brief Note on the Christian Background of Modern Freedom." *Theoforum* 45 (2014): 233–43.

———. "Johanan ben Zakkai Revisited: Reflections on Michel de Certeau's reading of Freud's *Moses and Monotheism*." In *Spiritual Spaces: History and Mysticism in Michel de Certeau*, edited by Inigo Bocken et al., 125–46. Leuven: Peeters, 2013.

De Libera, Alain. *L'invention du sujet moderne. Cours du Collège de France 2013–2014*. Paris: Vrin, 2015.

Derrida, Jacques. *Margins of Philosophy*. Translated with additional notes by Alan Bass. Brighton: The Harvester Press, 1982.

———. *Psyche. Inventions of the Other*. Vol. II. Edited by Peggy Kamuf and Elisabeth Rottenberg. Stanford: Stanford University Press, 2008.

Descartes, René. *Œuvres philosophiques*. Vol. 1, *1618–1637*. Edited, presented, and annotated by Ferdinand Alquié. Paris: Garnier, 1963.

———. *Les passions de l'âme*, preceded by *La pathétique cartésienne* by Jean-Maurice Monnoyer. Paris: Gallimard, 1988.

———. *The Passions of the Soul*. Translated by Stephen Voss. Cambridge, MA: Hackett, 1989.

Dosse, François. *Michel de Certeau: Le marcheur blessé*. Paris: La découverte, 2002.

Driessen, Henk. *Pijn en cultuur*. 5th ed. Amsterdam: Wereldbibliotheek, 2015.

Dujardin, Philippe. *Simone Weil: Idéologie et politique*. Grenoble: Presses Universitaires de Grenoble, 1975.

Duperray, Eve, ed. *Marie Madeleine dans la mystique, les arts et les lettres*. Paris: Beauchesne, 1997.

Eckhart [Meister]. *The Complete Works of Meister Eckhart*. Translated and edited by Maurice O'C. Walshe. Revised with a foreword by Bernard McGinn. New York: Crossroad, 2009.

———. *The Essential Sermons, Commentaries, Treatises, and Defense*. Translated by Edmund Colledge, O.S.A. and Bernard McGinn. Mahwah, NJ: Paulist Press, 1981.

———. *Werke I: Predigten*. Text and translation by Joseph Quint. Edited by Niklaus Largier. Frankfurt am Main: Deutscher Klassiker Verlag, 1993.

Ehrman, Bart D., ed. *The Apostolic Fathers* (2 Volumes). Cambridge/London: Harvard University Press, 2003.

Eisenstadt, S. N. "Multiple Modernities." *Daedalus*, 129, no. 1 (2000): 1–29.

Elisabeth of Bohemia and René Descartes. *The Correspondence between Princess Elisabeth of Bohemia and René Descartes*. Edited and translated by Lisa Shapiro. Chicago: The University of Chicago Press, 2007.

Endō, Shūsaku. *Silence*. Translated by William Johnston, with a foreword by Martin Scorsese. New York: Picador Modern Classics, 2016.

Eusebius Pamphilius. *Church History, Life of Constantine, Oration in Praise of Constantine*. Edited by Philip Schaff, translated by Arthur Cushman McGiffert. New York: Christian Literature, 1890.

Farr, James, and David Lay Williams. *The General Will: The Evolution of a Concept*. New York: Cambridge University Press, 2015.

Fénelon, François de. *Christian Perfection*. Edited and prefaced by Charles F. Winston, translated by Mildred Whitney Stillman. New York/London: Harper and Brothers, 1947. https://fullgospel.us/2019/02/06/christian-perfection/.

———. *Correspondance*. Vol. II: *Lettres anterieures à l'épiscopat*. Edited by Jean Orcibal. Paris: Édition Klincksieck, 1972.

———. *Œuvres I*. Edited by Jacques Le Brun. Paris: Gallimard (Bibliothèque de la Pléiade), 1983.

———. *Œuvres II*. Edited by Jacques Le Brun. Paris: Gallimard (Bibliothèque de la Pléiade), 1997.

———. *Œuvres de Fénelon Archevêque-duc de Cambrai*. New, revised, and corrected edition. Vol. V. Paris: Tenré et Boiste, 1822.

———. *Selected Writings*. Edited, translated, and introduced by Chad Helms. New York/Mahwah, NJ: Paulist, 2006.

———. *Telemachus, son of Ulysses*. Edited and translated by Patrick Riley. Cambridge: Cambridge University Press, 1994.

Fénelon, François de, and Madame Guyon. *Spiritual Progress* or *Instructions in the Divine Life of the Soul*. Edited by James W. Metcalf. New York: M. W. Dodd, 1853.

Fink, Bruce. *The Lacanian Subject: Between Language and Jouissance*. Princeton: Princeton University Press, 1995.

Foucault, Michel. *The Archeology of Knowledge*. Translated by E. M. Sheridan Smith. New York: Routledge, 1989.

———. *Dits et écrits*. Vol. 3: *1976–1979*. Edited under the direction of Daniel Defert and François Ewald. Paris: Gallimard, 1994.

———. *The History of Sexuality*. Vol. I: *An Introduction*. Translated by Robert Hurley. New York: Pantheon Books, 1978.

———. *The History of Sexuality*. Vol. 2: *The Use of Pleasure*. Translated by Robert Hurley. New York: Vintage Books, 1990.

———. *The Order of Things: An Archeology of the Human Sciences*. New York: Pantheon Books, 1971.

Freud, Sigmund. *Beyond the Pleasure Principle*. Introduction by Gregory Zilboorg. In *Standard Edition of the Complete Works of Sigmund Freud*, edited by James Strachey, in collaboration with Anna Freud. Vol. 18: *Beyond the Pleasure Principle, Group Psychology, and other works 1920–1922*. New York/London: W. W. Norton, 1961.

———. *Pre-Analytic Publications and Unpublished Drafts, 1886–1899*. In *Standard Edition of the Complete Works of Sigmund Freud*, edited by James Strachey, in collaboration with Anna Freud. Vol. 1. London: The Hogarth Press, 1966.

Gaddis, Michael. *There Is No Crime for Those Who Have Christ: Religious Violence in the Christian Roman Empire*. Berkeley/Los Angeles: University of California Press, 2005.

Gillespie, Michael Allen. *The Theological Origins of Modernity*. Chicago/London: The University of Chicago Press, 2008.

Gold, Barbara K. "Simone Weil: Receiving the Iliad." In *Women Classical Scholars: Unsealing the Fountain from the Renaissance to Jacqueline de Romilly*, edited by Rosie Wyles and Edith Hall, 359–76. Oxford: Oxford University Press, 2016.

Gorday, Peter. *François Fénelon: A Biography—The Apostle of Pure Love*. Brewster, MA: Paraclete Press, 2012.

Gregory of Nyssa. *The Life of Moses*. Translation, introduction, and notes by Abraham J. Malherbe and Everett Ferguson, preface by John Meyendorff. New York/Mahwah, NJ: Paulist Press, 1978.

Guyon [Madame = Jeanne-Marie Bouvier de la Motte Guyon]. *Œuvres mystiques*. Edited by P. Max Huot de Longchamp, with introductions by Dominique Tronc. Paris: Honoré Champion, 2008.

———. *Selected Writings*. Translated, edited, and introduced by Dianne Guenin-Lelle and Ronney Mourad. New York/Mahwah, NJ: Paulist Press, 2012.

———. *Les Torrents* et *Commentaire au Cantique des cantiques de Salomon, 1683–1684*. Edited, presented, and annotated by Claude Morali, Grenoble: Jérôme Millon, 1992.

———. *La Vie par elle-même et autres écrits biographiques*. Vol. I. Critical edition with introduction and notes by Dominique Tronc, literary study by Andrée Villard, Paris: Honoré Champion, 2014.

Guyon [Madame], and François Fénelon. *La correspondance secrète, avec un choix de poésies spirituelles.* Edited by Benjamin Sahler, introduction by Étienne Perrot. Paris: Dervy-Livres, 1982.

Harrill, Albert J. "Divine Judgment against Ananias and Sapphira (Acts 5:1–11): A Stock Scene of Perjury and Death." *Journal of Biblical Literature* 130, no. 2 (2011): 351–69.

Heidegger, Martin. *The End of Philosophy.* Translated by Joan Stambaugh. Chicago: University of Chicago Press, 1973.

Hense, Elisabeth, and Frans Maas, eds. *Towards a Theory of Spirituality.* Leuven/Paris/Walpole, MA: Peeters, 2011.

Highmore, Ben. *Michel de Certeau: Analyzing Culture.* London/New York: Continuum, 2006.

Hillenaar, Henk. *Le secret de Télémaque.* Paris: Presses Universitaires de France, 1994.

Hobbes, Thomas. *On the Citizen.* Edited and translated by Richard Tuck and Michael Silverthorne. Cambridge: Cambridge University Press, 1998.

———. *Leviathan.* Revised edition by Richard Tuck. Cambridge: Cambridge University Press, 1996.

Hoenen, Maarten J. F. M. "Via Antiqua and Via Moderna in the Fifteenth Century: Doctrinal, Institutional and Church Political Factors in the *Wegestreit*." In *The Medieval Heritage of Early Modern Metaphysics and Modal Theory, 1400–1700*, edited by Russell L. Friedman and Lauge O. Nielsen, 9–36. Dordrecht: Kluwer, 2003.

Holbach [Baron d' = Paul-Henri Thiry]. *The System of Nature: Or Laws of the Moral and Physical World.* Translated by H. D. Robinson. Boston: J. P. Mendum, 1889.

———. *Système de la nature.* Vol. 1. Paris: Fayard, 1990.

Holte, Ragnar. "Logos Spermatikos: Christianity and Ancient Philosophy according to St. Justin's Apologies." *Studia Theologica—Nordic Journal of Theology* 12, no. 1 (1958): 109–68.

Illouz, Eva. *Hard-Core Romance: Fifty Shades of Grey, Best-Sellers and Society.* Chicago: The University of Chicago Press, 2014.

Jacobus da Voragine. *The Golden Legend: Readings on the Saints.* Translated by William Granger Ryan, with an introduction by Eamon Duffy. Princeton/Oxford: Princeton University Press, 2012.

James, E. L. *Fifty Shades of Grey.* New York: Vintage Books, 2012.

Jean de Saint-Samson. *Épithalame: Chant d'amour.* Modern transcription and presentation by Jean Perrin. Paris: Seuil, 1997.

———. *La pratique essentielle de l'amour.* Edited by Max Huot de Longchamp and Hein Blommestijn. Paris: Cerf, 1989.

John of the Cross. *The Collected Works of John of the Cross.* Translated by Kieran Kavanaugh, O.C.D. and Otilio Rodriguez, with revisions and introduction by Kieran Kavanaugh, O.C.D. Washington, DC: ISC Publications/Institute of Carmelite Studies, 1991.

Koyré, Alexandre. *From the Closed World to the Infinite Universe*. Baltimore: John Hopkins University Press, 1957.

Lacan, Jacques. *Écrits*, Paris: Seuil, 1966.

———. *Écrits: The First Complete Edition in English*. Translated by Bruce Fink, in collaboration with Héloïse Fink and Russel Grigg. New York/London: W. W. Norton, 2006.

———. *Le séminaire*, Book VII: *L'éthique de psychanalyse*. Edited by J.-A. Miller. Paris: Seuil, 1986.

———. *Le séminaire*. Book XXIII: *Le sinthome, 1975–1976*. Edited by J.-A. Miller. Paris: Seuil, 2005.

———. *The Seminar of Jacques Lacan*. Book VII: *The Ethics of Psychoanalysis, 1959–1960*. Translated by Dennis Porter. New York/London: W. W. Norton, 1992.

Lallemant, Louis. *The Spiritual Doctrine of Father Louis Lallemant of the Company of Jesus Preceded by Some Accounts of His Life*. Edited by Frederick William Faber. London: Burns and Lambert, 1855.

La Mettrie, Julien Offray de. *Machine Man and Other Writings*. Translated and edited by Ann Thomson. Cambridge: Cambridge University Press, 1996.

Lamotte, Stéphane. *L'affaire Girard-Cadière: Justice, satire, et religion au XVIIIe siècle*. Aix-en-Provence: Publications de l'Université de Provence, 2016.

Le Brun, Jacques. *Le pur amour: De Platon à Lacan*. Paris: Seuil, 2002.

Lefort, Claude. *Democracy and Political Theory*. Translated by David Macey. Cambridge: Polity Press, 1988.

Lévi-Strauss, Claude. *Structural Anthropology*. Translated by Claire Jacobson and Brook Grundfest Schoepf. New York: Basic Books, 1963.

Liagre Böhl, Herman de. *Miskotte: Theoloog in de branding, 1894–1976*. Amsterdam: Prometheus, 2016.

Lotterie, Florence. "Présentation." In *Thérèse philosophe ou Mémoires pour servir à l'histoire du Père Dirrag et de Mademoiselle Eradice*, presentation, notes, chronology, and bibliography by Florence Lotterie, Paris: GF Flammarion, 2007.

Mack, Gerhard. *Rémy Zaugg: A Monograph*. Luxembourg: Mudam, 2006.

Maintenon [Madame de = Françoise d'Aubigné]. *Dialogues and Addresses*. Edited and translated by John J. Conley, SJ. Chicago/London: The University of Chicago Press, 2004.

Malebranche, Nicolas. *Œuvres de Malebranche* Vol. XIV: *Traité de l'amour de Dieu, Lettres et réponses au R. P. Lamy*. Edited by André Robinet. Paris: Vrin, 1963.

———. *Œuvres II*. Edited by Geneviève Rodis-Lewis, index by Jean Letrouit. Paris: Gallimard (Bibliothèque de la Pléiade), 1992.

Marie of the Incarnation. *Selected Writings*. Edited and translated by Irene Mahony. Mahwah, NJ: Paulist Press, 1989.

Matter, E. Ann. *The Voice of My Beloved: The Song of Songs in Western Medieval Christianity*. Philadelphia: University of Pennsylvania Press, 1990.

Mauss, Marcel. *The Gift: The Form and Reason for Exchange in Archaic Societies*. With a foreword by Mary Douglas, translated by W. D. Halls. London: Routledge, 2002.

———. *Sociologie et anthropologie*. Edited by Claude Lévi-Strauss. Paris: Presses Universitaires de France/Quadrige, 1950.

McHoul, Alec, and Wendy Grace. *A Foucault Primer: Discourse, Power, and Subject*. London/New York: Routledge, 1993.

Melchior-Bonnet, Sabine. *Fénelon*. Paris: Perrin, 2008.

Miskotte, K. H. *. . . als een die dient: Volledige uitgave van het 'Gemeenteblaadje Cortegene,' 27 oktober 1923–4 april 1925*. Baarn: ten Have, 1976.

———. *Als de goden zwijgen* (VW [Collected Works] 8). Kampen: Kok, 1983.

———. *Bijbels ABC*. Utrecht: Kok, 2016.

———. *Uit de dagboeken 1917–1930* (VW [Collected Works] 4). Kampen: Kok, 1985.

———. *When the Gods Are Silent*. New York: Harper and Row, 1967.

Mondzain, Marie-José. *Image, icône, économie: les sources byzantines de l'imaginaire contemporain*. Paris: Seuil, 1996.

Montaigne, Michel de. *The Complete Essays*. Translated by M. A. Screech. London: Penguin, 1993.

Morgan, Ben. *On Becoming God: Late Medieval Mysticism and the Modern Western Self*. New York: Fordham University Press, 2012.

Morgan, Vance G. *Weaving the World: Simone Weil on Science, Mathematics, and Love*. Notre Dame: The University of Notre Dame Press, 2005.

Mouffe, Chantal. *On the Political*. London/New York: Routledge, 2005.

Mouffe, Chantal, and Ernesto Laclau. *Hegemony and Socialist Strategy*. London: Verso, 1985.

Moulakis, Anastasios. *Simone Weil and the Politics of Self-Denial*. Translated by Ruth Hein. Columbia: University of Missouri Press, 1998.

Nadler, Steven. "Occasionalism and General Will in Malebranche." *Journal of the History of Philosophy* 31 (1993): 31–47.

———. "Occasionalism and the Mind-Body Problem." In *Studies in Seventeenth-Century European Philosophy*, edited by M. A. Stewart, 75–95. Oxford: Clarendon Press, 1997.

Northoff, Georg. *Neuropsychoanalysis in Practice: Brain, Self, and Objects*. Oxford/New York: Oxford University Press, 2011.

Nygren, Anders. *Agapè and Eros*. Translated by Philip S. Watson. Philadelphia: The Westminster Press, 1953.

Pascal, Blaise. *Pensées*. Edited and translated by Roger Ariew. Indianapolis/Cambridge: Hackett, 2005.

Pessoa, Fernando. *A Little Larger than the Entire Universe: Selected Poems.* Edited and translated by Richard Zenith. London: Penguin, 2006.

Pierre, Benoist. *Le père Joseph: L'éminence grise de Richelieu.* Paris: Éditions Perrin, 2007.

Porete, Marguerite. *Le miroir des simples âmes anéanties.* Translated from ancient French by Claude Louis-Combet, presented and annotated by Emilie Zum Brunn. Grenoble: Jérome Millon, 1991.

———. *Le mirouer des simples ames anienties et qui seulement demourent en vouloir et desir d'amour.* Provisional edition by Romana Guarnieri. Roma: Edizioni di storia e litteratura, 1961.

———. *The Mirror of Simple Souls.* Translated and introduced by Ellen L. Babinsky, prefaced by Robert E. Lerner. New York/Mahwah, NJ: Paulist Press, 1993.

Praet, Danny. *De God der goden: De christianisering van het Romeinse Rijk.* Kapellen: Pelckmans, 1995.

Pseudo-Dionysius. *The Complete Works.* Translation by Colm Luibheid; foreword, notes, and translation collaboration by Paul Rorem; preface by René Roques; introductions by Jaroslav Pelikan, Jean Leclercq, and Karlfried Froehlich. New York/Mahwah, NJ: Paulist Press, 1987.

Réage, Pauline. *Histoire d'O.* Paris: Pauvert, 1954.

———. *Story of O.* Translated by Sabine d'Estrée. New York: Ballantine Books, 1979.

Renouard, Antoine-Augustin. *Lettre de Fénelon à Louis XIV.* Paris: Paul Renouard, 1825.

Revel, Judith. *Le vocabulaire de Foucault.* Paris: Ellipses, 2002.

Richardot, Anne. "Thérèse philosophe: Les charmes de l'impénétrable." *Eighteenth Century Life* 21, no. 2 (1997): 89–99.

Rowen, Herbert H., ed. *From Absolutism to Revolution 1648–1848.* New York: Macmillan, 1963.

Sachot, Maurice. *Quand le christianisme a changé le monde.* Vol. 1: *La subversion chrétienne du monde antique.* Paris: Odile Jacob, 2007.

Sales, François de. *Œuvres.* Edited by André Ravier in collaboration with Roger Devos. Paris: Gallimard (Bibliothèque de la Pléiade), 1969.

———. *Treatise on the Love of God.* Translated by Rev. Henry Benedict Mackey. New York: Cosimo, 2007.

Sales, François de, and Jeanne de Chantal. *Letters of Spiritual Direction.* Selected and introduced by Wendy M. Wright and Joseph F. Power, translated by Péronne Marie Thibert, preface by Henri J.M. Nouwen. Mahwah, NJ: Paulist Press, 1988.

Sánches, Francesco. *Daß nichts gewußt wird—Quod nihil scitur.* Lateinisch-Deutsch. Introduction and notes Kaspar Howald. Hamburg: Meiner, 2007.

———. *That Nothing Is Known.* Edited and translated by Elaine Limbrick and Douglas F. S. Thomson. Cambridge: Cambridge University Press, 2008.

Schmitt-Maass, Christoph, Stefanie Stockhorst, and Doohwan Ahn, eds. *Fénelon in the Enlightenment: Traditions, Adaptations, and Variations.* Introduction by Jacques Le Brun. Amsterdam/New York: Rodopi, 2014.

Schultess, Daniel. "S'oublier soi-même: Malebranche et la question de l'amour pur." *Revue Philosophique de Louvain* 107, no. 4 (2009): 637–46.

Shapin, Steven. *The Scientific Revolution.* Chicago: The University of Chicago Press, 1996.

Sheldrake, Philip. *A Brief History of Spirituality.* Malden, MA/Oxford: Blackwell, 2007.

Smyth, Frances P., ed. *The Age of Correggio and the Carracci: Emilian Painting of the Sixteenth and Seventeenth Centuries* (Catalogue of exhibition in Washington: National Gallery of Art; New York: Metropolitan Museum of Art; Bologna: Pinacoteca Nazionale). Cambridge: Cambridge University Press, 1986.

Solms, Mark. "Justifying Psychoanalysis." *The British Journal of Psychiatry* no. 203 (2013): 389–91.

———. "A Neuropsychoanalytical Approach to the Hard Problem of Consciousness." *Journal of Integrative Neuroscience* 13, no. 2 (2014):173–85.

Solms, Mark, and Oliver Tumbull. *The Brain and the Inner World: An Introduction to the Neuroscience of Subjective Experience.* New York: The Other Press, 2002.

Spearing, Elisabeth, ed. *Medieval Writings on Female Spirituality.* New York/London: Penguin, 2002.

Surin, Jean-Joseph. *Correspondance.* Texts presented and edited by Michel de Certeau, preface by Julien Green. Paris: Desclée De Brouwer, 1966.

———. *Guide Spirituel.* Edited and presented by Michel de Certeau s.j. Paris: Desclée De Brouwer, 1963.

Teresa of Avila. *The Interior Castle.* London: Bottom of the Hill Publishing, 2010.

Terestchenko, Michel. *Amour et désespoir: de François de Sales à Fénelon.* Paris: Seuil, 2000.

———. "La querelle du pur amour au XVIIe siècle entre Fénelon et Bossuet." *Revue de MAUSS* 2, no. 32 (2008), 173–84.

Tinsley, Lucy. *The French Expressions for Spirituality and Devotion: A Semantic Study.* Washington, DC: The Catholic University of America Press, 1953.

Thébert, Angélique. *Petite mort: Philosophie de l'orgasme,* Paris: Éditions M-Editer, 2010.

Thomson, Arthur. "Ignace de Loyola et Descartes: L'influence des exercices spirituels sur les oeuvres philosophiques de Descartes." *Archives de Philosophie* 35, no. 1 (1972): 61–85.

Tremblay, Jean-Paul-Médéric. *Comme en plein jour: Dossier sur l'Éminence grise, alias François Leclerc du Tremblay, en religion le père Joseph de France, frère mineur capucin (1577–1648).* Sainte Foi, Quebec: Édition Anne Sigier, 1995.

Trémolières, François. "Donner à lire Mme Guyon." *Dix-septième siècle* 3, no. 248 (2013): 547–54.

Trousson, Raymond, ed. *Romans libertins du XVIIIᵉ siècle*. Paris: Robert Laffont, 1993.

Valabek, Maria, ed. *Titus Brandsma: Carmilite, Educator, Journalist, Martyr*. Rome: Carmel in the World Paperbacks, 1985.

Veillard-Baron, Jean-Louis. "L'âme et l'amour selon Malebranche." *Les Études philosophiques* 4 (1996): 453–72.

Vetö, Miklos. *La métaphysique religieuse de Simone Weil*. Paris: L'Harmattan, 2014.

Vidal, Daniel. "Du pur amour: Mystique et désaffect." *Essaim: Revue de psychanalyse* 2, no. 10 (2002), 49–72.

Weil, Simone. *Attente de Dieu*. Preface by Christiane Rancé. Paris: Albin Michel, 2016.

———. *Gravity and Grace*. With an introduction and postscript by Gustave Thibon, translated by Emma Craufurd and Mario van der Ruhr. London/New York: Routledge, 2002.

———. *L'Iliade ou le poème de le force, et autres essais sur la guerre*. Paris: Rivage, 2014.

———. *Œuvres*. Edited under the direction of Florence de Lussy. Paris: Gallimard (Quarto), 1999.

———. *Œuvres complètes VI/2: Cahiers (septembre 1941–février 1942): La science de l'impossible*. Paris: Gallimard, 1997.

———. *Œuvres complètes VI/3: Cahiers (février 1942–juin 1942): La porte du transcendant*. Paris: Gallimard, 2002.

———. *Œuvres complètes VI/4: Cahiers (juillet 1942–juillet 1943): La connaissance surnaturelle (Cahiers de New York et de Londres)*. Paris: Gallimard, 2006.

———. *La pesanteur et la grâce*. Introduction by Gustave Thibon. Paris: Plon, 1948.

———. *Waiting for God*, Translated by Emma Craufurd, with an introduction by Leslie A. Fiedler. New York: Harper and Row, 1973.

Weinhart, Martina, and Max Hollein. Ich: Katalog Ausstellung in Schirn Kunsthalle Frankfurt. Köln: Verlag der Buchhandlung Walther König, 2016.

Wittgenstein, Ludwig. *Tractatus Logico-Philosophicus*. Translated by D. F. Pears and B. F. McGuinness, with an introduction by Bertrand Russel. London/New York: Routledge, 2001.

Wolfe, Charles T. "Brain Theory between Utopia and Distopia: Neuronormativity Meets the Social Brain." In *Alleys of Your Mind: Augmented Intelligence and Its Traumas*, edited by Matteo Pasquinelli, 173–84. Lüneburg: Meson Press, 2015.

Yamamoto-Wilson, John R. *Pain, Pleasure, and Perversity: Discourses of Suffering in Seventeenth-Century England*. Farnham, UK/Burlington, VT: Ashgate, 2013.

Zini, Fosca Mariani. "Peut-on être indifférent à soi-même? Difficultés stoïciennes dans le pur amour de Fénelon." In *Emotional Minds: The Passions and the Limits of Pure Inquiry in Early Modern Philosophy*, edited by Sabrina Ebbersmeyer, 257–78. Berlin: De Gruyter, 2012.

Žižek, Slavoj. *Did Somebody Say Totalitarianism? Five Interventions in the (Mis)use of a Notion.* London/New York: Verso, 2001.

Index

9 781438 494159